## FIFTEENTH EDITION

KU-521-307

# You &
# the Law
# in Spain

## DAVID SEARL

SANTANA BOOKS

## ACKNOWLEDGEMENTS

We would like to express our sincere gratitude to all those people who have taken time from their busy schedules in government offices, private practice, real estate agencies, moving companies, and on through a long list, to answer our questions and then the questions that arose from their answers.

There is always more to find out. Among these helpful people, we offer our special thanks for service beyond the call of duty to:

Maribel Aizpurúa, sector chief at the Málaga Tax Agency office, for her endless patience with complicated tax questions, and to her entire staff.

Lawyer Manuel Ubeda Castañeda of Ubeda-Retana y Asociados legal services in Fuengirola, for always being on the other end of the telephone with the right answer.

Lawyer Jorge Retana Alumbreros of Ubeda-Retana in particular for his thorough knowledge of Spanish tax legislation affecting foreigners.

Tax Consultant Sergio Llull Cejudo, also of Ubeda-Retana, for his expertise on Spanish business practices and labour legislation.

Marbella Gestor Ricardo Sanchez Bocanegra, for his many years of experience with foreigners in Spain.

Tax Consultant and Property Administrator Juan Jose Lopez Guzman, for his wide familiarity with tax problems and Community issues.

Anette Skou, Marta Rey and Luisa Machen of the Mijas Department of Foreign Residents. They are ladies who help.

Fuengirola Insurance Broker Caroline Ford, of Pitarch-Ford in Fuengirola, for her help on Spanish insurance regulations.

## IMPORTANT NOTICE

You and the Law in Spain
Published by Ediciones Santana S.L.,
Apartado 422,
29640 Fuengirola (Málaga), Spain.

First published September 1985
Second edition - March 1986
Third edition - October 1987
Fourth edition - April 1988
Fifth   edition  1 - May 1989
Sixth edition - June 1990
Seventh edition - May 1993
Eighth edition - January 1996
Ninth edition - June 1997
Tenth edition - March 1999
Eleventh edition - April 2000
Twelfth Edition - March 2001
Thirteenth Edition - May 2002
Fourteenth Edition - March 2003
Fifteenth Edition - March 2004

Design and typesetting by Graham Banks
for grahamsgraphics.com

Printed and bound in Spain by
Gráficas San Pancracio, S.L.
Pol. Ind. C/. Orotava, 17, Malaga

ISBN: 84-89954-32-1
Deposito Legal: MA-357/2004

# Contents

# Living in the Spanish Sun

This 15th edition of *You and the Law in Spain* includes all of the information of its sister book, *The Spanish Property Guide*, combining the two volumes into one. It includes the complete translation into English of Spain's Horizontal Law, which regulates Communities of Property Owners, along with commentary that informs you on what really happens in practice.

This revised and updated edition tells you what you need to know about annual Spanish taxes on property, capital gains tax on sales by residents and non-residents, and whether you are liable for Spanish income tax. It gives you the Traffic Code, and much more useful information.

They tell us now that Spain is becoming more and more like its European partners to the north. As one foreign resident remarked, "Spain is no longer an exotic country." That, at least, is the theory.

In real life, foreigners who live or own property in Spain find that this country is still, as the tourist posters used to proclaim, somewhat "different".

When a foreign resident reads the law prohibiting any vehicle from producing sounds louder than a certain number of decibels, and then he directly experiences the same screaming motor bike passing beneath his window again and again, he starts to wonder.

The law grants a tourist stay of 90 days only to any visitor to Spain, whether he is European Union or not. When the visitor talks to foreigners who have lived in Spain for 10 years, with no residence document, and with only brief absences and no problems with the law, he wonders more.

When he is advised that strict rules provide heavy penalties for people who under-declare the real value of a property transaction in order to minimise transfer taxes, and then his lawyer tells him he can put less than half the real purchase price on the contract, he is totally baffled. We can help.

Spanish laws and practices have both changed greatly since the first edition of *You and The Law in Spain* was published in September 1985. Fifteen successive editions have kept readers up to date since then.

This revised and updated 2004 edition of *You and the Law in Spain*, is designed to serve the tens of thousands of Britons, Northern Europeans and Americans who take up residence or buy a holiday home in Spain every year. These foreign property purchasers have among them bought billions of euros worth of Spanish real estate in recent years.

According to official estimates 1.5 million foreigners own property in Spain. More than half a million foreigners hold residence and work permits, meaning that Spain is their real home.

The Spanish property market, led by British buyers with strong pounds, has been booming for almost ten years. On the Costa del Sol alone, foreign buyers are purchasing at more than a million euros a day.

All these full- and part-time residents are confronted with an unfamiliar legal system and a language they don't usually speak. They have unusual new problems to solve and are offered opportunities of which they are often unaware.

In general, Spanish authorities hope that you will like the country, bring some money into it, and live happily ever after here. They are perfectly aware that foreign residents in Spain are cashing their pension cheques in Spanish banks every month, producing prosperity for all. They do not wish to discourage this.

While this book cannot explain all the ins and outs of the Spanish legal system to you, we hope that its guidance will make your adjustment to your new country a little easier and more comfortable.

# What's new in this edition

## EU CITIZEN RESIDENCE CARDS

A revised Foreigner's Law which makes some EU citizens in Spain exempt from the need to obtain a residence card caused an outbreak of enthusiastic over-reaction as people jumped to the mistaken conclusion that EU persons no longer needed to stand in line for residence cards.

It simply isn't true. The new Foreigner's Law exempts only those EU citizens who work in Spain and pay into the Spanish Social Security system and those retired persons who receive pensions from the Spanish State. All others, including retired EU pensioners, still need a residence card.

The law may not have been completely thought out by the Spanish legislature and even Spanish police authorities recommend that exempt persons obtain a residence card in any case. There are many procedures for which a foreigner needs to document his status. A resident bank account is different from a non-resident account, a non-resident mortgage is treated differently from a resident's mortgage, and capital gains tax is charged differently, for example.

The EU citizen can obtain a certificate of his residency from the foreigner's department of his police station but the certificate is good for only six months. The next time he needs it, he will have to wait in line again, and so on. On balance it seems easier to get the card.

On the positive side, the new law makes it easier for EU persons to apply for residence. They need only present their passports, photocopy, four photos and the filled-up form. The need for proof of income, medical insurance, and other documents has been done away with.

## TRAFFIC CODE REQUIRES REFLECTIVE VESTS

The revised 2004 traffic code requires all vehicles to carry a reflective vest that drivers must wear when they get out of a stopped or damaged vehicle at night or in conditions of poor visibility. The requirement goes into effect in July of 2004.

Many will remember the problems with obtaining the red triangles when they were first made obligatory. There just weren't enough of them. The reflective vests, however, are readily available at many shops. They come in various colours at prices under 10 euros.

The new traffic code cracks down on drunken driving with stiffer penalties and for the first time empowers police to retain a driver's licence when they estimate that he is not in condition to operate his vehicle safely.

## ANDALUSIAN INHERITANCE TAX BREAK

The Andalusia region has made individual inheritors up to €125,000 exempt from tax as long as the total estate does not exceed €500,000. Both testator and inheritors must be immediate family and Andalusian residents

## VALENCIA LAND LAW PROTESTS

Protests continue to mount over the Valencia region's "land-grab law" under which hundreds of property owners, both foreign and Spanish, face seizure of their land for new urbanisations, with only minimal compensation. A petition with 10,000 signatures was presented to the European Parliament, which has promised to send investigators.

# 1    Moving to Spain

Spain's revised foreigner's law, which went into effect on March 1, 2003, has made it easier for European Union citizens to apply for residence and has even made EU citizens who are working in Spain exempt from the need to renew their permits.

## EUROPEAN UNION CITIZENS

EU citizens coming to reside in Spain now need to present only their application form, four photographs and their passport with photocopy in order to apply for a residence card. (See Chapter Two, Resident or Tourist)

They no longer need to demonstrate proof of income or that they have medical insurance.

**Pensioners:** Even under terms of the new Foreigner's Law, a European Union pensioner still needs a residence card. However, they are no longer required to show proof of income There is one important step they should take, however, before leaving home.

**Form E-121:** EU pensioners should obtain Form E-121 from

11

their own country, which enables them to transfer their rights to national health care to the Spanish Social Security medical system. The form shows that the pensioner has been into his home country's national health and so he is entitled to the same rights in Spain. These "E" for "European" forms are readily available in all EU countries. You must obtain the form at home before you come to Spain.

EU citizens who are of retirement age and receive private pensions or pensions from a non-EU country can also settle in Spain, but they will not be entitled to Spanish health care. They will have to take out a private medical insurance. Under the former law this was obligatory, but the new law has removed the requirement.

**Non-Pensioners:** EU citizens under retirement age and who do not receive a state pension may apply for residence. Under the new law, they no longer need to demonstrate proof of income or that they hold a private medical insurance.

**EU Workers:** An EU citizen intending to work or start a business in Spain, can simply arrive in the country and begin his paperwork immediately.

EU citizens looking for work in Spain can apply for employment at Spain's national employment service under exactly the same conditions as Spaniards. When they get a job, they can obtain their work and residence card on application. They will be required to pay into the Spanish Social Security system in return for medical care and an eventual pension.

Those intending to start a business will face a labyrinth of permits and licences, just as Spaniards themselves do, but it can all be overcome. (See section on Working and Starting a Business for details.)

**Consulates Have Information:** Ask the Spanish consulate for a copy of the "C" leaflet, which explains many details about moving to Spain. The leaflet number varies from country to country but it is Leaflet C16 in the UK. This leaflet explains about importing your household goods, and gives information about driving licences, for example. It also lists requirements for obtaining the *visado de residencia*, the residence visa, which is necessary for non-EU citizens intending to reside in Spain. (See Below).

Some consulates have a great deal of information available besides that contained in leaflet C16. If you are interested in specific data on a certain region, for example, be sure to ask if they have any relevant pamphlets.

The Spanish government, like all governments, produces many publications to inform visitors and investors. Not all consulates have all these publications, of course, but they can often order them for you. Don't be afraid to ask for any information you are particularly interested in.

You may also be surprised at the information available from your own government. They publish pamphlets on doing business in Spain, explaining import and export restrictions and currency controls, for example. They probably have data about what is produced and what is needed and current information about how money flows between Spain and your country.

Ask at your Foreign ministry or Commerce ministry about any subject that particularly interests you, whether it be teaching or onion farming. There is probably a government publication bearing on it.

## NON-EUROPEAN UNION CITIZENS

First, go to the Spanish consulate in your home country. If you are from a non-EU country, you will need to obtain the *visado de residencia*, a visa you must present when you apply for a residence permit after you have arrived in Spain.

The visa can only be obtained from the Spanish Consulate in your home country before you leave for Spain.

There are, in fact, seven different types of visa, depending on whether you are a retired pensioner, an investor, an executive of a multinational company, or carrying out a cultural or sporting activity. Make sure you request the right one for your circumstances.

Second, go to your bank and make sure they understand exactly how your money is to be sent to you. Make absolutely sure they know a corresponding bank in the area of Spain where you will live. Transfers of money can take weeks when not properly handled.

There are bank branches which simply do not understand international transactions. There are others that do not have corresponding banks in your home country.

You will need to establish that the bank you choose in Spain has a working relationship with your bank at home and can readily receive funds from them.

Transfers have been known to get stuck in a main office in Madrid and not reach their destination until weeks, even months later, after heated telephone calls and faxes.

Once you have a bank account in Spain, you can deposit your foreign cheques, or make direct transfers, and then write euro cheques for payments on your new property, or your rent, making money matters much easier.

Holding a Spanish bank account will work in your favour when you apply for your visa at the consulate in your country. It is not, however, strictly necessary.

For non-EU persons, this application for the visa is your first legal step towards acquiring residency in Spain. It gives the Spanish authorities a chance to examine your financial situation before they decide whether you will make a useful resident. Once you have the visa, you are practically assured of obtaining the residence permit.

Information sheets issued by Spanish consulates in various countries will show how much income you need in order to get this visa.

The Spanish consulate in Washington, DC, requires US citizens to show an income of at least $10,000 a year per person if they wish to retire in Spain. An American wishing to start a business or invest in Spain has to demonstrate capital of about €18,000.

If you have this income, you are all right. If you haven't, do not assume that you will be denied the visa. Many other details also come into the picture. You may have capital which is not at the moment producing income, for example, or your income may not start until some future date.

The consular officials will judge each case on its merits. But they do want to be sure that you have sufficient means to support yourself in Spain. If you intend to start a business, for example, you will need to show that you are bringing into Spain enough money to do so, unless you are from an EU country.

***Visado de Residencia:*** When you are ready to apply for the visa, you will need to present a valid passport and evidence supporting your source of income. You may also be asked to show that you have made some arrangements for remitting this income to Spain.

You will also need a *certificado penal*, a paper showing you have no prison record, issued by your local police. The Spanish consulate in your country can tell you exactly how to obtain it in your area.

You then fill out the visa application form in duplicate. If you are a couple, each of you must sign the form. Make it clear that you intend to take up residency, as this affects your right to import your furniture into Spain free of duty (see section below on "Importing Your Possessions").

You will be asked to provide a reference in Spain and one in your home country. If you have bought or rented property in Spain, your seller would make an excellent reference. Or your new bank manager or lawyer in Spain. You will need two passport photos.

You must enter Spain and have your passport stamped within 60 days of the time the visa is issued to you. So it is best to gather all your information and the necessary documents in advance, but leave the final application until a month or so before your intended departure date.

The visa sometimes is issued quickly, but it's best to ask.

NOTE: If you are a non-EU citizen already established in Spain but still on tourist status, it is possible to apply for exemption from the visa requirement so that you do not have to return to your home country. You will need a good reason for this, such as illness, in order to obtain the exemption.

With the visa in hand, you can then apply for duty-free import of your furniture. Your removal company should be able to handle all the paperwork involved. Again, see the section on "Importing Your Possessions".

## IMPORTING YOUR POSSESSIONS

European Union citizens may skip this section, as duties on importation of household goods have disappeared with free circulation of goods within the EU. If they are moving to Spain, and bringing all their possessions, their moving company will know how to handle the forms required. (For details on importing their cars, EU citizens should see the chapter "You and Your Car").

**New Resident Free of Duty:** When you come to Spain from outside the EU to take up residence, the Spanish government grants you the privilege of importing your household effects and personal possessions free of customs duty. This privilege is a one-time grant and is only available to those who take out an official residence permit.

You do not have to purchase property in order to justify this privilege, but you will have to show a residence permit, and you will have to make a prior deposit, which will be returned to you within a year.

For those who wish to import furniture for a second residence or holiday home, there is a second form of importation. For this *vivienda secundaria* exemption, you need not become a resident. You must make a deposit, however, just as the resident does. The non-resident must wait two years, however, for the return of his money.

In both cases, the deposit will be about 50 per cent of the estimated value of the goods.

The conditions are that you have not been a resident in Spain during the two years prior to the importation of the goods; that your goods enter the country within three months of your own arrival in Spain; that the goods are used, being at least six months old, and that you undertake not to sell them for two years.

Under this provision you can import, among other things, furniture, books, works of art, personal effects and collections, musical instruments, food and liquor, washing machines, electric or gas cookers, refrigerators, vacuum cleaners, floor polishers, radios and television sets.

The Spanish authorities remind you that the electric current in Spain is 220 volts and 50 cycles. This difference is especially important for Americans and Canadians, who will find their stereo sound equipment needs various adaptors to function properly and that their television sets will not function at all because the European system is different from the North American television system.

All the appropriate information is presented in Spanish leaflet C16, which you should request from the Spanish consulate in your home country at the beginning of your application to come to Spain to take up residency. See section "Before You Leave". (This is leaflet C21 for Americans and its number varies from country to country.)

At the consulate or through your removal company, you fill out a form requesting the Head of the Customs Office, *La Direccion General de Aduanas*, to allow your goods to enter Spain free of duty. You will need a complete list, in duplicate, of all your possessions. The list must be in Spanish. The consulate will legalise your application and list by stamping them, for a small fee.

You can obtain the forms by writing to the nearest consulate or you can collect them in person. Your removal company should include most of this paperwork in its services. Be sure to ask them.

The selection of a removal company is extremely important. Some companies are familiar with the paperwork, have experienced agents at the borders and customs depots, and know how to keep your property from winding up in Barcelona in the customs shed for three months, which quite often happens when all the papers are not in order. Make enquiries among people who have moved to Spain until you find a company with satisfied clients.

There are a lot of things that can go wrong with international removals, so take your time in finding the right company. You must also present a photocopy of the first five pages of your passport, correctly legalised by the Spanish consulate, to your removal agents. They need to show this at the customs office at the Spanish border when they enter with your goods.

17

Make sure that your removal company guarantees delivery to your door in Spain. There have been cases where goods were held up in customs and a different removal company which brought them from the Barcelona depot later collected more money for the distance travelled within Spain.

## One-Year Time Limit To Recover Deposit

From the time your goods enter Spain, you have one year in order to produce a residence permit to the customs authorities and request the return of your deposit.

Be warned. If you wait more than 12 months from the time your furniture enters Spain, you will not be able to claim the return of your deposit. Some unwary foreigners have allowed the time limit to lapse and lost their deposits.

You might think that the professional customs agent employed by the removal company or by you personally to handle the deposit guaranty would inform you when this time limit was near, but you would be wrong in many cases. You yourself must be alert and must see your customs agent to make sure the procedures are correctly carried out, on time.

When you have your residence card in hand, you need to obtain a certificate from your local Town Hall that the furniture is still in your possession. They will send a policeman or an inspector to visit you. He will check the list against the furniture itself and sign the certificate. With this document and your residence permit-along with the receipt given you showing that this is your first application for a Spanish residence permit-you can claim the release of your deposit.

The deposit will have been made into a Spanish bank, which in turn will issue a certificate that is presented to the customs office. The certificate guarantees that the funds have been deposited in the Spanish bank for the purposes of the customs guarantee. When the customs office releases the deposit, you present that paper to the bank, which releases the funds back to you.

This deposit system also applies when a foreign non-resident purchases or rents property in Spain and wishes to import goods to furnish this property, even though the foreigner will not reside

18

there full-time. You can do this, duty-free, by following the same procedure outlined above. This time, however, you have a time limit of two years.

At the end of the two years, you obtain the document from the Town Hall certifying that the goods are still in your possession, and the customs office will authorise the release of your deposit. This is called a *vivienda secundaria* plan, for a second home.

One condition for obtaining this exemption is that you must not let the property to others. It must be for your own personal and exclusive use.

**Bride's Trousseau Exempt:** A foreign woman who marries either a Spaniard or a foreigner officially resident in Spain may bring into Spain free of duty her wedding gifts and trousseau. This is not a genuine regulation, but a courtesy granted by the Customs Office upon special application. It is only granted in cases where reciprocal treatment is given to a Spanish woman who marries a citizen of another country.

## IMPORTING YOUR PET

What about your dog or cat? Yes, of course, you can take your faithful pet to Spain with you, but it's a bit complicated.

You need a health certificate for your pet issued by a veterinary authorised by the appropriate ministry in your country. This certificate must be issued not more than 15 days before you enter Spain with the pet.

In addition you will need a certificate of vaccination against rabies, also issued by an authorised veterinarian. Animals less than two months old do not require this. Animals between two and three months of age must have been vaccinated not less than one month before they are imported. Animals of three months or older must have been vaccinated not less than one month and not more than 12 months before being imported. If the animal has no anti rabies certificate, it may be quarantined for 20 days.

Finally you will need a certificate declaring that the area in which the animal was normally kept is free from animal diseases. This certificate usually comes from your agriculture ministry.

19

All these certificates must be stamped and legalised by the Spanish consulate, for which they charge a small fee.

Once you have arrived in Spain, you will want to have your pet fitted with a new microchip which gives your address in Spain. UK pet owners can now take their dogs back with them when they return home. They must start the procedures in Spain at least a month before their trip, however, in order to obtain the required certificates.

## CARS, CARAVANS AND BOATS

For information on importing cars, caravans and boats, see the section on "You and Your Car".

## GLOSSARY

**Agente de Aduana** – Licensed customs agent

**Dirección General de Aduanas** – General Customs Directorate

**Certificado Penal** – Certificate of prison record

**Visado de Residencia** – Special visa obtained from Spanish Consulate for persons taking up residency.

**Vivienda Secundaria** – Second home, holiday home

# 2     Resident or tourist?

If you live more or less full time in Spain, you should hold an official residence permit. The law specifies that a person who has been present in Spain for six months must either leave the country or apply for a residence permit.

The disadvantages of being an official resident are largely imaginary, and it is becoming more and more difficult to remain on tourist status when you are really a resident.

Furthermore, some real tax savings are available for residents who sell property or who bequeath Spanish property on their deaths. (See final section below on Resident Tax Savings).

Let's take a look at both possibilities.

## YOU AS A TOURIST

First of all, what is a tourist? When you visit Spain for a short holiday, you are a tourist. If you have a holiday home or a second home in Spain where you spend months at a time, you are still a tourist of sorts, as your principal residence is in another country.

If your principal residence is in Spain and you spend most of your time here, you can still technically be on tourist status if you do not take out a residence permit. But the Spanish authorities are growing stricter about allowing people to remain on "tourist status" when they really live full-time in Spain.

The concrete definition is this. A tourist is a person who spends less than six months in Spain in one calendar year.

The "tourist" stay in Spain for EU and non-EU citizens alike is limited to 90 days. To stay another 90 days, you are required to obtain a *permanencia,* which is an extension that is stamped in your passport. (See below)

Anyone who stays more than six months must apply for a residence permit.

Some foreigners who are really resident in Spain continue to remain on tourist status by crossing the frontier from Spain into France or Portugal or Morocco, where they have their passports stamped. They then return to Spain to begin a new 90-day period of "tourism".

There are people who have gone on for years in this way. For those who live near borders and who want to keep their official presence in Spain as undocumented as possible, this has been an acceptable practice, even if not quite cricket.

However, Spanish authorities have become stricter and people who have crossed a particular border every three months for years with no complications, now find their passports being carefully examined. Some have been stopped and ordered to obtain a residence permit. Others have been refused entry.

***Permanencia:*** It is also possible to get further 90-day extensions, called *permanencias.* However, you are entitled to only one *permanencia* in a calendar year, so even with this extension, you have a total of six months.

When you hear old Spain hands say things like: "Don't worry about it. They have given me nine *permanencias* in a row and never made any problems about it," be aware that this was only out of the authorities' laxity or the goodness of their hearts. It is no longer true.

The word *permanencia* means a temporary stay, not a permanent one, as you might think when comparing it to the

English word. In fact, the verb *permanecer* in Spanish means "to stay" or "to remain", not "to be permanent".

You apply for this *permanencia*, which is stamped in your passport, by going to the Foreign department of your local police station, or *comisaria*. You need your passport, a couple of photos, and some evidence of your ability to finance your continued stay in Spain. There is no specific cash requirement, though authorities suggest an income of €600 a month as an acceptable minimum. A copy of your Spanish bank statement or evidence that you receive a pension from abroad would be acceptable.

One *comisaría* requires that you have €1,800 in a Spanish bank to grant the 90-day extension. Ask locally, as practice varies. With these papers in hand, the *permanencia* is routinely granted, and you can stay another 90 days as a tourist.

## Benefits of Tourist Status

With Spain's full entry into the European Union, most advantages of remaining on tourist status have disappeared.

Formerly, only a non-resident could hold bank accounts in freely convertible pesetas or other currencies. With the introduction of the euro, currency exchange restrictions no longer exist, for Spaniards or residents.

Formerly, only a non-resident could own an automobile on tax-free tourist plates. Now, as European Union citizens, no EU person can do this, as he is not a "tourist" in the EU. Non-EU citizens, however, continue to enjoy the right to the tourist registration, without paying Spanish taxes.

So there aren't really many advantages to remaining on tourist status when you really are a resident.

People sometimes think that a person on tourist status does not become liable for Spanish income tax and that he will not need a Spanish driving licence. It is simply not true.

A person who lives in Spain more than 183 days in one calendar year, whether or not he holds a residence permit, becomes legally liable to pay Spanish income tax.

European Union citizens can continue to use their EU national driving licence after they take out a Spanish residence permit, so even that is not a problem. However, they must have their licence stamped by the Spanish traffic department. (See chapter On the Road in Spain).

## YOU AS A RESIDENT

On balance, if you really reside in Spain, it seems wiser to take out a formal residence permit. If you are an EU citizen, we should not call it a "permit". It is a residence card.

If you intend to earn money in Spain, you will need a work permit. Many residents do not have work permits, their papers being stamped "not valid for working in Spain".

It is illegal to work in Spain without a work permit, or an EU registration card - *tarjeta comunitaria* - if you are a working EU citizen. The normal residence permit is renewed once every five years. Renewal is usually a simple matter. The EU card is issued for one year, and five years on renewal.

### Tax Advantages for Residents

Foreigners often think that taking out an official residence permit in Spain will cost them money and expose them to Spanish taxes which non-residents can avoid.

The truth is often the reverse. The resident property owner has a number of tax advantages over the non-resident.

1.  If you are a resident and more than 65 years of age, and you have lived in your home for three years, you will not be subject to Spanish capital gains tax when you sell it, no matter how great your profit.

2.  If you are a resident, your maximum capital gains tax is 15 per cent, and it can be even less, whereas the non-resident pays 35 per cent.

3.  If you are a resident and you sell your property, you are not subject to having 5 per cent of the total purchase price withheld and deposited with Spain's tax agency as a guarantee against your tax liabilities.

4.  If you are a resident and you bequeath your home to a spouse or child who is also a resident, you can probably avoid Spanish inheritance tax on 95 per cent of the

valuation. The conditions are that you have owned and lived in your home for a minimum of three years. The inheritor must be a resident and must undertake not to sell the property for 10 years, while continuing to be a resident. Top limit on the 95 per cent reduction is €120,000. Over that, you must pay.

5. Spanish property owner's imputed income tax does not apply to the owner's principal residence. A resident of Spain also has an exemption on the first €108,000 of valuation for Spanish capital assets tax, "wealth tax". The non-resident pays from the first euro of valuation. If a husband and wife jointly own a property worth €120,000 and they are non-resident, they will pay a non-resident property owner's income tax of €600 each year plus €240 of Spanish wealth tax, a total of €840 per year. The resident is exempt from these taxes. For wealth tax, the exemption is €108,000 each for husband and wife. (see section on Taxes for more details)

6. If you really live most of the year in Spain, you are violating the law if you do not obtain a residence card. The law says that your tourist stay, even as a European Union citizen, is limited to 180 days per year. You can be fined €300 if you over stay this limit.

## HOW TO APPLY FOR A RESIDENCE PERMIT

**Residence card easier for EU Citizens:** Spain's revised Foreigner's Law, which went into effect March 1, 2003, has made it easier for EU citizens to apply for a residence card and even exempted some of them for the need to renew their card. Early enthusiasm for the new law started people saying that no EU citizen needs a residence card, but it simply isn't true. The only persons exempt are those who are living and working in Spain and paying into the Spanish Social Security system. EU pensioners still need a card.

The residence law is Royal Decree 178/2003 of 14/02/2003. It applies to EU member states and to Norway, Iceland, Liechtenstein and Switzerland, as members of the European Economic Area.

Two groups of people are exempt. These are workers who presently pay Spanish Social Security and those retired workers entitled to a Spanish State pension who have lived in Spain more than three years and have worked in the 12 months before retirement. All others need a card.

In any case, it seems that even those who are exempt will do better to renew their present cards. If you want a resident mortgage at the bank instead of a non-resident mortgage or if you want to exchange your UK driving licence for a Spanish one, the card will be easy proof of your status.

**Non-EU Citizen:** Now you will need that *visado de residencia* which you obtained from the Spanish Consulate in your home country before you came to Spain to settle. Obtaining the visa gave the Spanish authorities a chance to check you out, along with your financial means, even before you arrived.

In addition, you will need:

1. Proof of financial means. European citizens can be accepted to live in Spain without working on minimum financial means but non-EU persons will be required to show higher incomes. No specific figure is set but you ought to have more than €700 per month coming in or you will never get the visa.

2. *Certificado de Antecedentes Penales* (Certificate of Criminal Record). This certificate shows that you have no criminal record. You will need this in order to obtain the visa. You can request this from your local police authorities. Ask the consulate in your home country for proper form.

3. Medical certificate. Necessary for obtaining the visa.

4.  Consular inscription. This a letter from your own nation's Consulate in Spain showing that you are registered with them.

5.  Medical Insurance. Your private medical coverage must be contracted with a company which has an office in Spain.

6.  Passport and photocopy.

7.  Marriage certificate and official translation.

8.  Three passport-size photos.

9.  Payment of fee in differing amounts, depending on your country of origin. The fee is not high.

10. Statement from your Spanish bank showing that your income is arriving from abroad and being deposited in Spain.

11. Title deeds to Spanish property or a rental contract, with photocopy.

12. Birth certificates of children under 18 if they are included in the residence application. Translations.

13. The filled-up form requesting the residence permit

BE ADVISED: To pay the small administrative fee for Form 750, you must first obtain the form, then take it to the bank and pay the fee. All European Union citizens pay the same six euros. Other nationalities pay at differing amounts. The bank returns to you the form stamped as paid. If you can obtain the form from your police station beforehand and pay it in advance, you will save yourself waiting time. If you can't, ask for the form as soon as you arrive, take it to the bank, and then join the queue.

Try to find out in advance just what you will have to present. We try to keep this book up to date, but some offices may want four photos instead of three, for example. Well-organised offices will actually give you a list when you make your first enquiry.

If you are not an EU citizen and are requesting the unified

work permit/residence permit, you will have a number of other documents to present, relating to your employer in Spain, or the money you are bringing in to start a business, if that is the case. See the section on "Working and Starting A Business" for more details.

## NIE IS TAX IDENTIFICATION NUMBER

Your residence permit will include your *Número de Identificación de Extranjero* (NIE), which identifies you to the Spanish tax authorities. The number is necessary for practically any transaction in Spain, such as paying your taxes. Even a non-resident who has any relation with the Spanish tax system, either by owning property or by drawing interest from a bank, also needs this NIE.

All this sounds complicated but if you speak just a little Spanish and want to have some direct contact with official procedures in your new country, you can handle your request for a *residencia* yourself. Assembling the necessary documents and dealing with the different people and offices involved is an education in Spanish ways of doing things.

You can also use the services of a *gestoría* to lead you through the process. The *gestor* is licensed by the government as an official middleman between you and the State, and provides, for a reasonable fee, many useful services. It is his business to know which little window to go to at what time, and a good one can save you much time and trouble. This Spanish institution is more fully described in the section on "You and Your Legal Advisers".

## EVEN NON-RESIDENT
## E.U. CITIZENS CAN VOTE

Finally, if you are an EU citizen, you will be able to vote in Spain's municipal elections even if you are non-resident. Not only can you vote, you can be elected to office. If this prospect appeals to you, be sure to present yourself at your town hall immediately to be registered in the *padrón*, the list of municipal inhabitants, which is the basis of the voter list. Obtain a *certificado de empadronamiento* proving that you have registered. (See section on Voting in You and the Spanish Authorities)

Some months before the elections you must check to make sure that you appear on the voting list, or you will not be permitted to cast your ballot. Perhaps the Popular Party, who are the Conservatives, or the Socialist Party will ask you to stand for office as well.

## GLOSSARY

**Autorizacion de Residencia** – residence permit

**Certificado de Antecedentes Penales** – certificate of prison record

**Certificado de Empadronamiento** – certificate of registration in municipality.

**Formulario** – Form

**Gestoria** – professional administrative agency

**Numero de Identificacion de Extranjero (NIE)** – tax identification number

**Padron** – registry of inhabitants in municipality

**Permanencia** – 90-day extension of tourist visit

# 3   Buying Property

**Y**ou're right. You should have bought a holiday home or a retirement residence in Spain two years ago. Depending on the area, you would have seen an average 30 per cent rise in the value of your property, and even more in some areas.

Do not despair. Experts predict that prices of Spanish property will continue to rise for the immediate future, and that they certainly will not drop. This means that you are still in time to make a sensible purchase that will bring you pleasure and keep your investment safe.

You have a wide choice of sunshine property available to you now. New construction of high quality is booming all over Spain and particularly in the Mediterranean areas as well as in the major cities of Madrid and Barcelona. Mortgage rates, at under 6 per cent, are at record lows and are not expected to rise soon. Spanish property sellers are also giving prospective purchasers good terms and more professional service.

Property experts all agree that the introduction of the Euro can only benefit the purchase of holiday homes as buyers see that even today's prices in Spain compare favourably with housing costs in the rest of Europe. The unsettled stock market continues to make real estate look like a good investment.

---

**FACT:** *The Economist reports that house prices in the last 20 years have risen faster in Spain than anywhere else in the world.*

---

But the foreign buyer needs to take care. Too many purchasers seem to leave their common sense at the airport when they enter Spain.

You need sound legal advice from a Spanish professional who may be a lawyer, a registered estate agent, a specialised *gestor,* or an *administrador de fincas,* any of whom is qualified to act in your interests and make sure you are protected and well-advised in the transaction. It's foolish to depend entirely on the seller of the property to make sure you are treated fairly.

## REAL ESTATE AGENTS

Let's start at the beginning. Your first contact when you decide to buy property in Spain will almost certainly be the estate agent.

In many countries, an estate agent is a registered professional who can be held financially responsible if he intermediates in a sale and the terms later turn out to be falsely based.

In Spain there is no law regulating real estate agents. Anyone at all may act as intermediary in property sales. This means it is difficult to hold an estate agent responsible when a purchase goes wrong. Citizens of Scandinavian countries, or the UK, for example, where consumers are more carefully protected, even from their own mistakes, should be warier in Spain.

There are, however, two professional associations that require examinations and set standards for their members. One of these offers the title of *Agente de la Propiedad Inmobiliaria,* or API for short. The other is the GIPE, the *Gestor Intermediario de Promociones y Edificaciones.* You will do well to deal with an estate agent who holds one of these titles.

Even so, if your Spanish estate agent causes you to suffer loss, either through negligence or honest error, you will have a hard time obtaining any recompense. Ask your agent if he carries Professional Indemnity Insurance, and, if so, how much. You may again be surprised to find that most estate agents have either no insurance at all or a minimum amount required by the official Spanish agent's association.

Also ask your agent if he operates a Bonded Client's Account, into which any deposits will be placed, and which is untouchable except for the stated purpose of the deposit. Here is what can happen if you pay your deposit directly to the seller.

A British couple found a villa they liked on the Costa del Sol. They agreed a price of €180,000, and they transferred a deposit of €18,000, 10 per cent of the price, to reserve the villa from its German owners.

The British couple used a Spanish lawyer plus the advice of a British property agent working in Spain and they felt all was well. The couple sold their home in the UK, shipped their furniture to Spain, wound up their business, and came to Spain for the closing of the sale, when they would pay the rest of the price and sign the deed.

Just before the date with the Notary, their lawyer received a message from the German sellers, saying they could not make it that day and that they would be in touch later. This set off alarm bells with everybody involved. It turned out that the owners had in fact sold the property a month earlier for €210,000 to another buyer, had kept the €18,000 deposited with them, and had left Spain for parts unknown.

Of course the unfortunate British buyers have a clear case against the German sellers for breach of contract, with the right to recover their deposit, plus damages and loss, but how are they going to find them? In fact, they have the right to a sum twice the amount of the deposit if the seller backs out of the deal.

In many European countries, the buyers would also have a case against the estate agent and perhaps the lawyer as well for negligence in performing their services. In Spain they also have a case but where standards are less strict and where the lawyer and estate agent declare that they simply followed accepted practice and were just as dismayed as their clients, a Spanish court might well accept their arguments.

So, be sure to take care that any deposit you make goes into that escrow account, a blocked account, where neither party can get at it until the sale is closed.

In a few cases, unscrupulous estate agents have taken advantage of distressed or innocent sellers, telling them that they can obtain only a very low price for their property. This might be a widow, who has returned to her home country and wants to sell her Spanish property because she needs the money. The agent tells her he can get only €90,000 for the property.

She had the idea it must be worth €120,000 or more in today's brisk market, but she lets herself be convinced. The agent also convinces her to sign an agreement which authorises him to keep anything he can get over that price. The agent then sells the property for €125,000, just as he knew he could, making himself a "commission" of €35,000.

The buyer makes out the cheque to the estate agent, who puts €35,000 in his own account and €90,000 to the owner. All legal and in order. He never tells the seller what he sold it for, and since the buyer and seller never come into contact, the truth is never discovered. Even if it was, the agent has done nothing illegal. After all, the seller signed the agreement, didn't she? This sort of sharp operating becomes a great temptation for agents where owners are often absentee and ignorant.

Even the final figure of the purchase price on the sales contract may be the under-declared amount of €90,000. Since the agent is acting with a power of attorney to sign the contract for the absentee seller, nothing could be done about it after the fact, in any case.

These cases and others like them make a powerful argument for using a Spanish lawyer when you buy property. I will say it again and again. You should use a Spanish lawyer when you buy property in Spain. You should use a lawyer in your own country when you buy property. Why should it be different in Spain?

Having stated this warning, we find that most Spanish estate agents, or foreigners selling property in Spain, are both registered and honest. They only want to make a fair commission by selling good properties which will make their buyers and sellers both happy. Be careful anyway.

## COMMISSIONS IN COASTAL AREAS

Most Europeans will be surprised to find that estate agents dealing with Spanish holiday property take commissions starting at five per cent and going up to 10 per cent. These high commissions, say the agents, are justified because they have to deal with many unusual factors in a market where a buyer comes from one country and the seller from another and the transaction takes place in Spain, a third country. They also cite high marketing expenses from international advertising.

Let's just say that, when you are in the final stages of negotiating your purchase price, even the amount of the estate agent's commission might come on the table for a little reduction. Keep in mind that the API, for example, recommends three per cent commission for its agents in most areas of Spain.

Spain has all sorts of estate agents, ranging from the small office in the High Street, who has been in the town for many years and knows everybody personally, to the most modern international real estate offices, filled with computers.

Some of the major agencies can contact their offices in Frankfurt or London by Internet, and screen you five views of their offerings right there on the computer. In addition, there are many "Euro agents" of all nationalities who quite legally operate in Spain, although their credentials may not be as well established.

One of these agents should be able to find the property you are looking for. Very few agents in Spain are exclusive, so you might even find two agents showing you the same property.

The estate agent is working for the seller, so his presentation of the property will be the most favourable one, and you should check the facts carefully through your own representative. A reputable estate agent will be very happy to have you verify any of his information through your own lawyer, for example.

## YOUR SPANISH LAWYER

Quite a number of the Spanish lawyers who practice in areas where foreigners settle speak excellent English, among other languages, and are accustomed to dealing with foreign residents in Spain and their special problems, including property transactions.

How to find a good Spanish lawyer? Good question. Here is perhaps the only area in which you can ask advice from people you know. Ask around until you find some satisfied clients.

Consulates maintain lists of lawyers who speak the language of their nationality. The British and American consulates, for example, can provide you with the names of lawyers in your area who speak English. They are not recommending these lawyers as the best available but only because they speak your language.

How much will it cost? Figure the lawyer will charge you around one per cent of the value of the transaction, unless there are some unusual complications. Settle this with him before you start.

## WHAT TO WATCH OUT FOR

Both the European Union and the Spanish government have investigated fraud reports in holiday property, revealing the presence of illegal urbanisations where unwary buyers end up having problems of unpaid taxes, unregistered title deeds, and difficulty in obtaining municipal services or building permission. Spaniards have also been defrauded and problems with house purchase make up a principal area of complaint for the Spanish consumer associations.

To make sure your urbanisation is legal and registered, ask to see the *plan parcial* approved by your *Ayuntamiento,* or town hall. The *plan parcial* is not a partial plan, as it sounds, but the plan of *parcelas*, or building plots, which must be approved. This assures you that your urbanisation is legal and registered. If it isn't, you may have problems later with your community of owners, with municipal services such as light and water, and obtaining from the contractor all the elements promised in your sale.

If it is on the beach, make sure the development is approved by the *Jefatura de Costas* as well as the town hall. Spain's 1988 *Ley de Costas,* or Law of Coasts, empowers the authorities to

37

restrict building and to control height and density within 100 metres of the high-water mark.

## NEW PROPERTIES

In the case of a new property, you want to make sure that the property has been declared to Hacienda for IBI, as you can incur more fines for not registering it. Make sure that your developer has made a *declaración de obra nueva,* a declaration of new building, and has paid the small tax associated with this, as well. Make sure that your *escritura* mentions the house you have purchased as well as the plot of land on which it stands. Sometimes the deed only refers to the land.

This makes you the owner of anything standing on the land, of course, but you may find yourself subject to taxes and fines relating to an undeclared building. Even worse, you may have bought an illegally constructed house that can never be registered because of zoning regulations. Check this at your Town Halls *Urbanismo* department.

Sometimes, the purchase of an undeclared building can even work in your favour, but you will need expert advice to make sure you stay within the law. Once you are sure that the building can in fact be registered, you make a contract to purchase only the land from the seller. That's all he has title to, anyway.

The price for the land alone is much lower than the price for the land and house together, for a considerable saving on the property transfer tax of 6 per cent. You purchase the house separately by a private contract.

Then the new buyer makes the *declaración de obra nueva,* just as if he himself has built the house. Building permits and other papers are necessary for this, but it can all be arranged, and the buyer will pay only one half of one per cent, compared to the transfer tax of 6 per cent. It has been done but sound legal advice should be taken because the plan will not work in all areas and situations.

## TOWN URBAN PLAN

It is also important to have a look at the Town Planning maps of the area around you. A newly prosperous Spain is improving the road system all around the country. What if one of those highways is planned for the bottom of your garden? You can find out from the town's urban plan. This plan is called the *Plan General de Ordenación Urbana,* the PGOU for short. If you yourself cannot read plans, and few of us can, have your lawyer do it.

## BEFORE SIGNING ANYTHING

Before you sign anything in Spain, even a small reservation deposit agreement, there are some pieces of paper you should see. These include:

1.  The seller's own title, known as the *escritura publica,* and a report from the Property Registry called a *nota simple.*

2.  The paid-up receipt for his annual property tax, the IBI.

3.  The Catastral Certificate giving the exact boundaries and square metres of area.

4.  Paid-up receipts for the annual fees of the Community of Property Owners, the Statutes of the Community, and the minutes of the last AGM.

5.  Paid-up receipts for all utility bills.

## *ESCRITURA PUBLICA*

The *Escritura Publica* is the registered title deed of the property. It is inscribed in the *Registro de la Propiedad,* the Property Registry, and it is the only ironclad guarantee of title in Spain. If your seller cannot produce an *escritura publica*, something is wrong. In this title deed you will find a description of the property, the details of the owner. If any mortgages or court embargoes exist against the property, they will be registered here as marginal notes. You want to see the seller's title deed, if only to make sure that he really is the owner of the property being sold to you.

39

Your lawyer can obtain a *nota simple* from the Registry, containing the pertinent details and notes of any mortgages against the property. As of 2002, you can obtain a *nota simple* very rapidly on the Internet if you are entered in the Registry program. However, it would be best if you could see a copy of the complete deed.

Strange things can happen with deeds. In one recent case, a widow was selling her property in Spain. However, living in another country, it had never occurred to her to declare the death of her husband in Spain, and his name was still entered on the title deed as half owner of the property. This was done in perfect innocence, because she simply considered herself the full owner of the property when her husband died.

By Spanish law a property held jointly in two names cannot be sold without the signatures of both parties. Because no one had seen the full *escritura* before the scheduled closing and final payment, the fact did not come to light until both parties were ready to sign at the Spanish Notary.

The signing had to be postponed for months until the widow could declare her husband's death, which had happened 10 years before, prove that she was the heir, formally accept the inheritance, re-register the property in her own name, and finally sign to sell it.

One fortunate consequence of her error was that she did not have to pay any Spanish inheritance tax, because the demand for the tax lapses after five years. Some people do this deliberately, but her lack of action was inadvertent.

All this inheritance settlement could have taken place early in the negotiations if the title deed had been available for examination. You will do well to insist on seeing the complete *escritura*. It's a good idea to know that the seller is really the owner of the property, after all.

**IBI RECEIPT**

One very important paper you must see before purchasing any second-hand Spanish property is the *Impuesto sobre Bienes Inmuebles* (IBI), the municipal real estate tax. When purchasing from the second or third owner, you must always ask to see the latest paid-up receipt for the IBI before you sign any contract with the seller. If he doesn't have it, you may find yourself liable for back taxes and penalties. Here again your lawyer or property consultant will have valuable advice. A new property bought from a developer will not have an IBI receipt yet and it will be your responsibility to register the property for this tax.

The IBI receipt will show the property's catastral reference number and also your *valor catastral,* the official assessed value of the property. This is a very important figure because various taxes are based on it. (See section on Taxes). The assessed value is almost always considerably less than the real market value, but it has been steadily raised over the last few years.

Your annual real estate tax is charged by the municipality. It can be as low as €120 if you own a small cottage in one of the typical villages, or as much as €2,000 a year if you own a new luxury villa on acres of land near Marbella.

A surcharge of 20 per cent will be placed on the bill if it is not paid on time. You can arrange to have this bill paid directly through your bank, in order to avoid forgetting it. You fill out the forms authorising the bank to pay it, and the tax people will send the bill directly to the bank. In many municipalities those who pay their IBI tax early get discounts of 10 per cent, and a standing order at the bank will ensure that this is done.

So when buying an older property, whether apartment or villa, you want to see the last IBI receipt. If not available, something is amiss. Really, you want to see the IBI receipts for the last five years, not just the current one, because you can be liable for five years of back tax.

The current IBI receipt must be presented to the Notary at the signing of the contract, because it contains the catastral reference number, but you as the buyer want to see it well before that.

## REFERENCIA CATASTRAL

Every property sale must include a mention of the *Referencia Catastral.* As noted above, this reference number appears on your IBI receipt.

The Catastro is a second system of property registration,

concentrating on the exact location, physical description and boundaries of property, unlike the Property Registry, which focuses on ownership and title. The Catastro is also concerned with the valuation of property and is the source of the famous *valor catastral,* the assessed value of property for tax purposes.

These two systems, strangely enough, have never even communicated with each other, and we find that the catastral description of a property sometimes differs greatly from the one in the Property Registry.

As a first step in trying to bring the physical reality into line with statements people sometimes make in contracts, the Spanish authorities have begun to require that all property transactions now include at least a mention of the Catastro reference number in addition to the *escritura.*

It is a very good idea for the buyer to request the actual certification from the Catastro with a full description of the property. If it matches the data given in your contract, you are all right. If there are large differences, perhaps something is wrong.

The certification itself comes in two parts, one being a description in words of the property and the other being a graphic representation, either a plan or an aerial photo. Get both of them. It costs only a few euros, although it can take up to two months for the Catastro to deliver the certificates, so you had better start early.

It is astonishing how often the boundaries and square metres of a property can differ so much. This is because people through the years have simply accepted the vague descriptions made in the title deed, and do not check any further. Be warned that, when you ask the seller or the estate agent for this catastral certificate, they will pooh-pooh the idea, saying it is not legally necessary yet, although it will be in the future. Do not pay much attention to them. Insist on getting it, so you can be sure of your real boundaries and the real size of the property.

The Notary is also empowered to call attention to the fact that discrepancies exist between the Catastro and Property Registry descriptions. The buyer and seller can go ahead with their transaction, but they have been advised of the discrepancy.

## COMMUNITY FEES, STATUTES
## AND MINUTES OF THE AGM

If you are buying a flat, a townhouse, or a villa on an urbanisation, ask also to see the latest paid-up receipt for community fees. These are the fees charged by your *Comunidad de Propietarios,* the Community of Property Owners, which is the Spanish term for "condominium", meaning the legal body that controls all the elements held in common. In a building this would be the lift, gardens and pool for example.

In an urbanisation, the Community as a whole jointly owns the roads, gardens, pool, lighting system and other elements as well. Each owner is assigned a quota, or percentage of the expenses, which he must pay, by law. See the section on Communities for full details. Just remember that you become a member of the Community, with legal rights and obligations, just by purchasing your property. Only those who buy a country property or a house on a normal street in a town will not have to deal with Community problems.

The receipt for Community fees assures you that the fees are paid and gives you a good idea of your monthly charges in the future.

Read the Statutes, the regulations, of the community, too, as they will be binding on you once you have signed the purchase contract. If the basic Statutes that rule the Community prohibit the keeping of pets in the building or on the estate, you will have real problems if you want to keep your dogs, for example. Get a copy of these Statutes in a language you can read, even if the Spanish regulations are the only valid ones.

Then you want to see the Minutes Book, the official record, of the last Annual General Meeting of the Community. Decisions are taken by majority vote of the owners at each year's AGM, and these actions are recorded in the Minutes Book, which is an official document. If you find that the principal point at last year's meeting was how to solve the Community's chronic water shortage, then you will know you are going to have problems in your new house. Talk to the President of the Community if this is possible. A well-run Community can add thousands of euros to a property's value, and a Community with problems is a source of endless aggravation.

## UTILITIES BILLS

You want to see the owner´s paid-up receipts for such utilities as electricity, water, rubbish collection, and even telephone. This assures you that the bills are paid and also gives you an idea of what it will cost to run the place.

If you should get stuck with unpaid utilities bills by the previous owner, be aware that these are personal bills from private companies. They do not attach to the property, only to the person who signed the electric or water company contract.

The company will insist that they will cut off the service if the bills are not paid. Let them cut it off. For a reasonable fee, you simply go into the company office and sign a new contract, starting fresh without the previous owner's bills. This fee is exactly the same as the charge for changing the electricity contract into your own name in any case.

Once you and your lawyer or adviser are satisfied with these checks into the situation of the property, and you and the seller have arrived at a price, you can factor into your calculations the amount of taxes and fees that will be paid on the transaction.

## TRANSFER COSTS RAISED IN ANDALUSIA

What are the taxes and fees going to cost you? They will probably be less than 10 per cent of the purchase price if the breaks are with you, but can go as high as 15 per cent if certain taxes turn out to be higher than usual in your individual case.

You have two taxes and two fees to pay. The bad news for 2004 is that, in Andalusia, the transfer tax for private re-sales was raised last year from 6 per cent, the national standard, to 7 per cent. In addition, Andalusia has doubled the documents fee, from one-half of one per cent to one per cent.

**Notary:** You pay the *Notario* a fee fixed by an official scale. The fee varies according to the amount of land, the size of the dwelling and its price, but let's say between €350 and €600.

**Property Registry:** Then there is a fee for the inscription of the property in your name in the official *Registro de la Propiedad.* This will be a similar amount.

**Transfer Tax:** The transfer tax, called *Impuesto de Transmisiones Patrimoniales* in Spanish, is 6 per cent (7 per cent in Andalusia) of the value declared in the contract for private sales. If you purchase new property from a developer, this tax will be IVA (value added tax), at 7 per cent because the sale is a business operation, not a private deal between two individuals. In addition to this, you pay a documents fee, or stamp duty, of one half of one per cent (one per cent in Andalusia) so buying a new property will draw tax of 7.5 or 8 per cent.

***Plus Valía:*** The other tax on property sales is the *arbitrio sobre el incremento del valor de los terrenos,* the municipal tax on the increase in the value of the land since its last sale. This is usually called the *plus valía* for short, and it can vary widely.

In the case of an apartment or a townhouse in a new urbanisation, where little land is involved and where there has been no real increase in value because such a short time has passed since it was developed, the tax can be very low. It will be much higher if you buy a house with several thousand square metres of land, which has not changed hands for 20 years and which has been recently re-zoned from rural to urban land, thus jumping greatly in value.

This tax is based on the official value of the land, which is always lower than the market value, and it varies from 10 per cent up to 40 per cent of the annual increase, depending on the length of time between sales and the town where it is located. The land is officially re-valued periodically for this purpose.

Do not confuse this *plus valía* tax with the non-resident's 35 per cent capital gains tax on profits from the sale. (See Tax section).

You can find out exactly how much your *plus valía* will be simply by going into the municipal tax office in your town and asking. They keep the records there for each property and will be glad to tell you the assessed value, so you can find out in advance. Or have your lawyer or property consultant do it.

**Warning to Buyers:** Since January 1, 1999, the *plus valía* tax can be charged directly against the property itself, meaning that an unscrupulous seller might promise to pay it, then "forget" to pay it, leaving the new owner stuck with the tax, or losing his property

## WHO PAYS WHAT?

In deciding who pays what, the buyer and seller are free to contract whatever terms they choose. There is no Spanish law that requires that one of the parties must pay any particular tax.

Traditionally, the seller has paid the notary's fees and the *plus valía* tax, as he is the one making the profit on the increase in the land's value, while the buyer pays the *impuesto de transmisiones* and the registry fee, as he is the one who is interested in making sure the property is truly registered to his name. Spanish consumer regulations state that this should be the normal division of costs.

It is a frequent practice, however, for the contract to state that the buyer will pay *todos los gastos,* all the expenses arising. There is nothing illegal about this. Remember that the two parties are free to make any contract they choose.

This practice, which may seem unfair to the buyer, has come about because tax bills, especially the *plus valía,* have often gone unpaid, especially by non-resident sellers. By the time the new purchaser realised this, the seller was gone and the buyer stuck with the taxes anyway, as they were billed to the owner of the property if the seller did not pay. Charging the new owner with all the taxes is at least straightforward and avoids complications.

Nevertheless, you can use this point in negotiating your final price. If the contract you are offered states that you as the purchaser must pay all taxes and fees, you could suggest that the seller take something off the price.

## HOW MUCH TO DECLARE?

Formerly it was the practice to declare a ridiculously low amount for the value of the house, in order to minimise the transfer tax, but now Spanish lawyers advise sellers and buyers to declare the approximate market value, normally the real value of the sale. Spanish tax inspectors will make their own assessment if they feel the declaration is too low.

Spain's Tax Agency maintains its own tables of values on property, and they are empowered to set a higher value on a sale if they judge the declaration to be under market value. More than one property purchaser has been disconcerted to discover that he has to pay extra taxes when he gets a new tax bill six months after the sale.

If they discover that the transfer has been under-declared by more than €12,000 and 20 per cent, they can apply heavy penalties to both the buyer and seller under the terms of Spain's 1989 *Ley de Tasas* - the law of public fees - which was enacted to prevent precisely this dodge.

When in doubt, you can ask the tax office what value they will accept on any particular property. Inquire at the *oficina liquidadora,* the payment office, at your nearest Tax Agency office, and they will tell you exactly what value they assign to your purchase. They base their valuation on a careful study of various factors, such as location, size, quality, age, and others. Or just do as more and more people are doing today, and declare the actual amount of the sale.

**Buyer Beware:** When you go to resell your property, you will be charged Spanish capital gains tax on any profit you make. If you are a resident, you pay as part of your income tax with a maximum of 15 per cent. If you are non-resident, you face the 35 per cent capital gains tax on the profits you have made. If you declare a low value now, you will be liable for tax on a much bigger profit when you sell later. It is in your own best interests, as the buyer, to declare the full amount of the sale. (See section on taxes for more details.)

**THE CONTRACT**

Let's suppose that you have found a property that suits you, that all of the pre-purchase checks have satisfied you, and you have negotiated the price down to what you can pay. Terms of the sales contract will be your next concern.

Because most buyers take some time to assemble the cash needed for the purchase, it is usual for the buyer and seller to make a "private contract " first, with the buyer putting down a non-returnable deposit of, say 10 per cent. This reserves the property while the buyer brings his money into Spain or perhaps obtains a Spanish mortgage.

If the seller finds another buyer willing to pay more and sells the property, the first buyer can claim twice the amount of the deposit back. If the buyer fails to complete the sale, he loses his deposit.

Remember never to pay the deposit directly to the seller. Make sure that it goes into an escrow account, a blocked account, called a Bonded Client Account, from which it will not be released until the sale is final. Insist on this.

The seller, through the estate agent, will certainly have a prepared private contract all ready for you to sign. The contract they offer may suit you perfectly, but it is quite likely that it will contain some clauses more favourable to the seller than to you, the buyer. This is when you want your lawyer to read the contract and make suggestions.

It is a very good idea to have the contract made in Spanish, with a translation into English or German or your native language, so you can be absolutely sure about what you are signing.

Although most property sales between individuals follow this system of private contract and deposit, followed by closing and final payment, there is nothing binding about it. If you like the property and have the price ready, you can proceed directly to the Notary, pay over the full price, and get your title deed.

This private contract, although it sets out all the details of the agreement, such as payment terms and who pays what share of the taxes, is not the final document for the sale.

## ESCRITURA DE COMPRAVENTA

The final document is the *escritura de compraventa* and it must be signed by you and the seller in the presence of a Spanish *Notario* in order to make it legally binding. You can make a *poder* - a power of attorney - allowing another person to sign for

48

you if you cannot be present. (See section below for more on Power of Attorney).

The *Notario,* or Notary, is an official of the State who makes sure that contracts are legal. He keeps the original document in his files in case any question arises later. The *Notario* is a public official, not a private lawyer. His duty is to certify that the contract has been signed, the money paid, and that the purchaser and seller have been advised of their tax obligations.

He does not verify or guarantee the accuracy of the statements made in the contract. He only certifies that the parties have signed it properly. Too many people think that the *Notario* assures them that all statements made in the contract are true. This is not so. The Notary can, however, give useful advice to both parties.

## POWER OF ATTORNEY

A *poder general* or general power of attorney is frequently used in Spain. The power comes in a standard form, which lists all of the actions that can be carried out by the holder. These include buying and selling property, handling bank accounts, spending and receiving money, taking out a mortgage or other loan, and just about anything that the person himself can do with his assets.

The form contains a clause declaring that all of these actions shall be taken for the benefit of the granter of the power. This means that, if you decide to take the money and run, the granter has a case against you for defrauding him, if he can find you.

There are also other forms of power of attorney, limited to carrying out certain specific actions in the name of the granter, such as signing a contract for the sale of a specified property at a given price, during a given time period, after which the power lapses.

But the general power of attorney is the one most used, simply because situations change and unforeseen complexities arise in any transaction. This can mean that the holder of the power is unable to act because the power does not mention a specific circumstance that has arisen, such as signing at the bank to obtain the money transfer from abroad.

The wide powers of the general power of attorney avoid these problems. In an international property market, we often find that a seller or a buyer cannot be physically present at the moment of signing a purchase deed at the Spanish Notary, so he gives his lawyer or some other trusted person a general power of attorney to sign for him.

Once the deed is accomplished, the granter then revokes the power of attorney, again at the Notary, and all goes on as before.

You make the *poder general* at the Spanish Notary. Although it is always a good idea to consult a lawyer before taking any important legal step, it is not necessary. The Notary has the power of attorney forms, probably in his computer, which will print copies for you while the Notary himself retains the original power of attorney.

A reminder: you need copies authorised by the Notary in order to use the power of attorney at a bank or in a property sale. The simple copies you can also obtain are for information only.

The only documents necessary are the national identity document or the passport of the maker of the power. He will need the name and identity document or passport details of the holder. The entire operation should not cost much more than €60.

The recipient of the power of attorney does not need to appear at the Notary. The document requires his signature, but he can do this at his own convenience. So the maker of the power can simply post it to the recipient.

Contracts can be simple or complicated

Contracts can be quite simple if you are paying one lump sum and the property is to be delivered at once, but if you are paying over time there will be a number of further provisions in your contract, relating to the timing and amount of the payments.

The seller might insist on a clause stating that the buyer loses all sums paid out if he fails to keep up the payments, as well as having to vacate the property immediately.

If a buyer who cannot keep up the payments takes his case to court, he will find that the court will almost certainly allow him to receive some of his money back in exchange for vacating the property, which he loses.

What he gets back depends on how many payments the buyer has already made. If he has already paid more than half of the full price, the court will not allow the seller to keep it all.

The penalty clause for failure to keep up with the payments is negotiable and the buyer really needs a Spanish lawyer to make sure this kind of complicated contract is fair to him.

## FREE OF ALL CHARGES AND LIENS

Another extremely important item in your contract is the clause stating the property is sold free of all charges, liens and mortgages. Fine, you say, but how do you really know this is true?

This is where your lawyer comes in. He can make a check at the property registry, the *Registro de la Propiedad,* where any such mortgages or liens must be registered against the *escritura.* The *Registro de la Propiedad* is an extremely important office for the property purchaser.

Any mortgage on the property must be registered there, and the true owner of the property is listed. For a small fee, the *registro* will give you a *nota simple* for any property. This is a summary of the property's entry into the registry books, which would include a reference to any mortgages pending on the property.

Such a check-up can avoid problems. One horrible case occurred when a British owner returned to Spain to find that his new house had been seized by court order and auctioned off to pay an outstanding mortgage left by the seller. The locks had been changed and the house, for which he had paid, was no longer his.

His only remedy was to sue the fraudulent seller for breach of contract and fraud. That is, if he could find him.

He could also have solved the problem if he had been aware that his property was under threat. If he himself had been present in Spain to receive legal notice of the coming seizure and auction, he could have arranged with the court to pay the mortgage, which attaches to the property itself, not to the previous owner.

Paying the mortgage would have been an unpleasant experience but much cheaper than losing the entire property.

Notices of such legal actions appear by law in the *Boletín Oficial*, the official legal gazette, and often in the local newspapers as well. If the new owner cannot be located by the court, these published notices constitute sufficient legal notice to make the seizure of the property correct in law. Overworked Spanish courts have been severely criticised for failure to make sufficient attempt to locate the absentee owners, but the practice continues.

Your lawyer will also check to make sure that no back taxes are owed on the property and that its original registration is in order. Back taxes must be checked with Hacienda or the Town Hall. They are just about the only debts not listed at the Property Registry.

## CONTRACT MUST DESCRIBE
## THE PROPERTY ACCURATELY

The contract must accurately describe the property being sold. This is one area where the catastral certificate is important. Too many buyers have discovered too late that their boundaries are not what they thought they were, and the hedgerow at the bottom of their garden, an obvious division, is not the legal line after all but belongs to their neighbour. This sort of error does not necessarily imply bad faith on the part of the seller. He may have happily accepted the boundaries and square metres set out in his title deed, and never checked them.

Remember that we mentioned the *Registro de la Propiedad* is concerned mainly with ownership of property, while the *Catastro* is concerned mainly with the physical measurements and characteristics. The Property Registry is quite often wrong, so get the catastral certificate and be sure.

If you really have problems with boundaries, you should have an official surveyor, a *topógrafo*, come and survey the plot. On a transaction of €200,000, the €500 or so that he charges is very little.

Even those buying apartments will do well to measure their square metres of enclosed space and terraces, to make sure they

52

match the description offered. It is astonishing how often the flat actually has fewer square metres than stated. If you discover this, it may make a bargaining point for getting the price down.

Buyers of rural land will certainly need a property surveyor to measure the land and identify its boundaries. In these cases, even the Catastral department may not have the correct data. The titles to many rural properties state only that the *finca* borders on the north with Juan Garcia's farm, and that is simply not good enough.

## CONTRACT MUST IDENTIFY BUYER AND SELLER

The contract must also fully identify the seller and buyer. Remember that the seller is the owner of the property, not the estate agent handling the deal. It is not a good idea to make your cheque out to an agency. You should know exactly who the seller is and make your cheque directly to him.

If the seller insists on anonymity, meaning a bearer cheque, make sure that no money changes hands until you are actually at the Spanish Notary, where you will sign the final contract.

Make your cheques out only to the name of the seller. In the case of reserve deposits before the sale is completed, and where you may never have met the absentee seller, insist that your cheque be deposited in an escrow account, a Bonded Client Account. Then the money can be paid out only to the seller and only when the specified time limit has elapsed.

## BUYING OFF-PLAN

If you are buying your property "off-plan", which means you see only the plans and you start paying before construction has even started, you want to make sure your contract states that your payments go into an escrow account to which the developer has no access until the flat is finished and delivered to you. Most of today's reputable developers offer this plan. The bank guarantees the sums you have paid if anything goes wrong.

This system has a small extra cost but it means that you are safe if the builder has problems. It also avoids the chance of outright fraud, where a developer simply takes the money and disappears.

## FINAL TITLE AND REGISTRATION

The *escritura de compraventa* contract does not fully assure your title until it is registered with the Spanish Property Registry, thus making it an *escritura publica,* a public document. It is, in fact, the same document, now registered and with the stamps of the *Registro de la Propiedad* on it.

The registered document is then returned to the Notary, where it is kept safely on file. If you, or any official body, needs a copy of it, you request it from the Notary, who produces an authorised copy. The copy is what you take home. You yourself will never have the original of your *escritura publica.*

In fact, you no longer sign the contract itself. In these modern times of easy and foolproof copying, the parties to the contract sign a blank sheet of paper, and the Notary keeps these samples in his files for later authentication when necessary. So, nobody can copy your signature from a copy of your title deed because it isn't there.

Slow as the administrative bureaucracy may be, your deed should be registered within a few months. Usually your lawyer or whoever is handling the matter will ask you for a deposit of money in advance to cover the estimated taxes and fees, and will either bill you for the remainder or refund to you the overpayment when the deed is registered. This is normal and acceptable practice.

If the matter drags on for more than a few months, you had better look into what is happening. There was a case where one property consultant used his clients' deposits for a year or so before presenting the deeds to the registry office.

The deeds were registered in due course and his clients, all of them living abroad, assumed that 18 months was the normal time it took to get a deed registered. This is simply not true. Depending on the area and work-load of the Registro involved, it should take no more than two to three months to get your deed registered.

The danger of a delay such as this is that someone else could have the property registered before you. In cases where the same piece of property has been fraudulently sold two or three times, the purchaser who first has it registered will be the owner, regardless of the dates of the other sales.

To speed up the registration, when the title deed is signed you can have a special notification sent by fax directly from the Notary's office to the *Registro de la Propiedad*. This notification will ensure that no one else can register the property during the time it takes for your title deed to be registered.

## METHOD OF PAYMENT

Give some thought to your method of payment. One point to consider is whether you are buying from a resident or a non-resident.

In the old days before the European Union, property buyers had to pay Spaniards or residents in pesetas, and had to prove importation of foreign currency if they later wanted to export the money from Spain. With the lifting of exchange controls, this is no longer necessary, although a report must be made to the bank.

You can pay for your Spanish property in euros, through a bank cheque, from your Spanish bank, along with a bank certificate that you have imported foreign currency for this purpose. You can also pay by a cheque in foreign currency. You can also pay by direct transfer from your foreign bank to the seller's foreign bank, so that no money enters Spain.

## CERTIFICATE OF NON-RESIDENCE

If you wish to keep the money transfer completely undocumented inside Spain, you can do this, but you must then obtain a certificate of non-residence from the Spanish authorities. Be warned that this can take up to two months to obtain, and the Notary will not authorise the completion of the sale without it. If you file your bank certificate and use a normal cheque, this certificate is not necessary.

## FIVE PER CENT TAX DEPOSIT

If you buy from a non-resident, you must deposit five per cent of the total purchase price with Hacienda in the seller's name, as a guarantee on his taxes. A few sellers, who have owned their Spanish property for a long time, will be exempt from this deposit.

You pay the seller only 95 per cent of the price, and pay the other five per cent directly to Hacienda, presenting Form 211 to justify your payment. The Notary will want to see your copy of Form 211, showing that you have made the payment and filed the form with the Tax Agency.

This amount serves as a guarantee against the non-resident seller's Spanish capital gains tax liability and for his payment of the annual Spanish wealth tax and non-resident property owner's imputed income tax.

Non-resident owners of Spanish property are required to declare two per cent of the official rated value, the *valor catastral,* of their property as if it were income. They then must pay real income tax on this imaginary income. The non-resident pays at a flat rate of 25 per cent. (See section on Taxes for more details).

If Hacienda discovers that the non-resident seller has failed to keep up his yearly imputed income tax payments, they can retain this amount from the deposit of 5 per cent.

**Capital gains tax**: The deposit is mainly designed, however, to cover the non-resident's liability for Spain's capital gains tax of 35 per cent on his profit. As of December 31, 1996, Spain ended the exemption from capital gains for those who owned their property more than 10 years.

This was replaced by an inflation correction factor that reduces the capital gains tax but can never eliminate it completely, so most non-resident sellers will be liable for some Spanish capital gains tax. (See Tax section for full details on how this works).

## PROPERTY PURCHASE CHECK-LIST

1. Advice from a Spanish lawyer or property consultant.

2. The seller's *escritura publica,* or title deed, as registered in the *Registro de la Propiedad.*

3. A *nota simple* from the Property Registry, showing that no mortgages are registered against the property.

4. *Referencia Catastral.* The number itself appears on the IBI receipt, but you want the full certification document, the *Certificado Catastral,* that describes the property in detail.

5. A check on the legality and *plan parcial* if you buy in an urbanisation, and assurance of a building permit if you buy a plot.

6. A paid-up receipt for the IBI, *Impuesto sobre Bienes Inmuebles,* or the *declaración de obra nueva.*

7. Receipt for paid-up community charges and a copy of the Statutes if you buy in a condominium.

8. Copies of owner's receipts for electricity, water, rubbish collection and even the telephone.

9. A contract, in Spanish, and a translation into your own language, with terms you understand.

10. A decision about your form of payment, whether in euros or other currency, and be sure to insist on declaring the full amount.

11. An *escritura de compraventa* signed before a *notario.*

12. Payment of fees and taxes, and the five per cent deposit to Hacienda if you buy from a non-resident, using Form 211.

13. An idea of how and when you will get your final *escritura pública,* which makes you the real owner.

## BUYING WITHOUT AN *ESCRITURA*

Surprisingly often, the seller does not have an *escritura pública*, in most cases for perfectly legitimate reasons or at least for reasons which will not affect you the purchaser.

One reason for owning property on a private contract only, without a public title deed, is that the property cannot be seized by the court in order to pay a debt of the owner. Only registered property can be attached by a court.

Another reason is simply to avoid the payment of the transfer taxes and fees, which can total 10 per cent or even more of the value. Or perhaps the owner wants to conceal assets, either from a creditor or the tax man, or an ex-wife, for example. When the Property Register is checked, there is nothing listed under that name.

On the Spanish Costas, where there was a freewheeling property market for some years, many properties changed hands so quickly as buyers sought quick profits that they simply did not register them. They just waited for the next buyer to carry out all the formalities, thus avoiding transfer taxes.

It is possible that a house you fancy has had two or three owners in the last five or six years and that not one of them ever got his final *escritura pública*. It might be that the house does not legally exist, as it has never been declared to the tax authorities in a *declaración de obra nueva*. The only legal document for the property simply refers to the plot of land and does not even mention the house.

Or you might buy a tract of land in the *campo,* the owners of which are seven brothers whose family has owned the land for a hundred years but never had a written document.

There are perfectly legal ways of solving all these problems.

You can have the piece of land made over to you by the original seller, three owners back. You yourself can make the *declaración de obra nueva,* even though you did not build the house.

But be careful. If you want to establish the title through a series of private contracts, you may find that you are liable for quite a lot of back taxes, perhaps two or three *plus valías* which have never been paid by the previous owners. This tax may be charged to the present owner of the property.

58

## 205 PROCEDURE

One completely legal and frequently used solution for property that has no registered title at all is called a 205 procedure, after the number of the regulation which controls it. In this process, you obtain from the Property Registry what is called a "negative certification". This means that the Registry has searched its files and finds no registered owner for the property. Here again you will find the *certificado catastral* useful, because it will have an accurate physical description.

You then request that the property be registered in your name because you have bought it from whoever is the seller, who in turn justifies his title by whatever document or evidence he presents. This transaction must be published and posted publicly in case anyone wishes to protest. If no protest is made against your claim, at the end of about a year's time you will get a solid title.

If you are going to buy under these conditions, be sure to hold back a percentage of the price until the property is registered in your name. No matter how simple the procedure appears when you start, there is always the possibility of some unknown person coming forward with a claim to the title. There is an element of risk.

## *EXPEDIENTE DE DOMINIO*

This process, roughly translated as an ownership proceeding, requires more time and expense than the 205 procedure, because it involves more investigation and court action. The *expediente de dominio* can also be used to establish title when the property is in fact registered, but in the name of a person who no longer claims it either because he has sold it to someone on a private contract, who has never registered the sale, or perhaps because the original owner has died. This will take about two years.

The claim must be published in the official bulletin and evidence taken in court. Finally, the court will rule on the title and it will be solid. There is always the chance of some nephew who should have inherited the property making a claim of his own against the present purchaser, and the court will decide where the best claim lies.

In any of these procedures to establish title and register the property, be warned that you will be unable to obtain any mortgage funding, and you cannot borrow against the property for two years after its registration.

In any of these cases, you need sound legal advice. Ask around among older residents for an *abogado* or an *administrador de fincas* or a *gestor* whom they trust.

## FINANCING YOUR SPANISH PROPERTY

There are a number of ways in which you can finance your Spanish property, just as you probably did when you first purchased a house in your own country. Mortgages of 20 and 30 years, along with mortgages of 100 per cent of the value of the property, are now available in Spain. For a non-resident buyer, however, the mortgage is usually limited to around 70 per cent of the valuation of the property.

### Financing by the developer

Let's look first at financing which may be offered you by the developer of the project where you purchase. There are dozens of different schemes here and you should be wary.

The contract must stipulate the down payment, enumerate the following payments and state when such payments end. It will be clear from the total of these payments just how much the developer's financing will cost you in comparison to paying cash. If the difference is acceptable, you have a deal.

Make sure you know what happens if you miss a payment. There should be some provision that is not too harmful to you, allowing you to make a certain number of late payments for only a small penalty.

Another essential provision will allow you to pay off the remainder of the contract in a lump sum at any time you choose, without having to pay the total remaining interest. You might at a future date come into money, enabling you to make such a payment. Or you may wish to pay off your terms with the developer in order to resell the property.

Developers often offer excellent terms to purchasers who begin their payments before the building is finished. This can be favourable to the buyer, but he must be sure that the developer is reliable and solvent, and can bring the project to completion.

The developer must offer a bank guarantee that assures the buyer the return of his invested money if the project stalls or fails. An important point is that this bank guarantee must not cost the buyer anything. If the developer offers this guarantee, details must be clearly spelled out, either in the contract or in a separate document.

Finally, Spanish consumer legislation passed in 1996 requires that all contracts spell out terms clearly. Do not be afraid to ask plenty of questions. And use a Spanish lawyer.

## Bank Loans and Mortgages

With the introduction of the euro and the lifting of almost all exchange controls, both residents and non-residents may now obtain loans and mortgages against their Spanish property in any currency from any bank in the world - if they can find a bank willing to lend against property in another country. Even very long-term endowment mortgages are beginning to appear, offered by Spanish branches of UK lending institutions.

The good news is the inflation and interest rates are at an all-time low in Spain. Spanish bank mortgages are now being offered at rates of less than five per cent, the lowest in Europe. Signs for early 2004 are that rates should continue low. The euribor, the base lending rate for the euro, showed no signs of being raised by the Central European Bank.

Those people purchasing a second home in Spain may find they can obtain a mortgage in their home country for the purchase of property in Spain. This could represent an ideal solution, but UK residents in particular must be careful about losing MIRA tax relief on their UK tax when they mortgage to purchase property outside the UK. They will have to pay UK tax on their loan repayments to the Spanish bank should they mortgage in Spain because the Spanish lending bank will not mortgage in Spain because the Spanish lending bank will not pay these taxes.

## Subsidised Housing

In Spain, as in most countries, the government subsidises some types of housing. Ordinarily, this housing is destined for the poor and is offered to them on favourable terms.

Such housing is known in Spain as V.P.O., or *Vivienda de Protección Oficial*. You may think that this housing is not meant to help well-to-do foreigners purchase vacation homes, and you would be right. But there are several classes of V.P.O. projects. One class, operated by the Spanish government, is available only to the poor, who must make a declaration of poverty in order to obtain it.

The other class, more frequently seen, is based on the provision of cheap government financing to the project developer, and these apartments are available to foreigners, although controls are becoming stricter. Purchasers now must be residents and they cannot have incomes of more than about €1,500 a month.

Remember, when purchasing V.P.O. flats, the offer will stipulate that you make a very small down payment, but if you can make a larger payment of €20,000 or so, and thus totally clear the constructor's own financial contribution to the project, this will be very advantageous. The balance, payable over 15 years or more on favourable terms, will then repay only the cheap government loan and not contribute further to the constructor's profit.

There are, of course, controls on the resale of such flats, which block speculators profiting at the expense of the government.

## INSURING YOUR HOME

As in any country, it is sound practice to carry homeowner's insurance protecting you against damage to the building itself, damage or theft of its contents, and against claims from others who may suffer injury or damage resulting from your ownership.

This is especially important when you are absent from your Spanish property for long periods, but be alert to clauses in your contract that render your insurance invalid if you are away from the property for more than a stated period of time. Often, by paying an extra premium, you can be covered even though you are absent much of the time.

Both Spanish and international insurers offer various policies at various prices. Make enquiries among older residents to find a company that has given good service.

As in most countries, you fill out a form in which you put a value you wish to insure on your house and its contents. Remember that, should you choose to insure your property for only half its real value, the insurance company, which makes its own evaluation, will pay you only half the value of any individual items that are stolen or damaged. People sometimes think they can insure half and then get full value when only two or three items are stolen or damaged, but this is not so.

The company will also ask you to report on whether your property will be unoccupied for lengthy periods, how old the building is, how many doors and windows there are, whether they are guarded by iron-barred *rejas,* if there is a burglar alarm system, and so on. If you do not respond truthfully to these questions, there can be grounds for a later denial of any claim you make. Your premiums will vary according to your situation.

Be sure to read the fine print in your policy. Often, insurance against theft of the contents of your property will not pay unless entrance has been forced and there is evidence for this. If a "guest" at one of your parties makes off with your wife's jewels, you will not be paid. If there is no copy of the contract available in your language, have someone translate for you.

What will insurance cost you? Policies and conditions vary, but you can estimate that about one euro per year per thousand euros of value will cover the building itself against damage by natural causes or fire or explosions, if the building is located in a town. An older house in the country, far from fire-fighting services, would cost more to insure.

Insurance of your furniture and household effects will be somewhere around €2.50 per thousand euros of value if you live in an apartment; up to €3.50 per thousand if you live in a detached villa. This covers fire and theft.

If one of your steps collapses and the postman breaks his leg, or you leave the bathtub water running until your downstairs neighbour's apartment is flooded, they can claim compensation from you as the owner. You can cover yourself for claims up to €50,000 for less than €20 a year

Most Spanish companies offer a comprehensive policy covering the building, the contents and third party claims. One company quoted a figure of €1,200 per year for comprehensive coverage of a villa and contents valued at €240,000. An apartment or townhouse would be less costly.

## OFF-SHORE COMPANIES

You might be offered property already owned by an offshore company registered in one of the many "tax havens" around the world.

This means that the property is not registered in the name of the owner but in the name of a company located in Gibraltar or Panama or the Caiman Islands. The owner of the company owns the property.

These "tax havens" earn their name because they are legal jurisdictions where taxes on locally registered companies are nil or very small, and secrecy is assured from the owner's own tax jurisdiction.

The advantages are clear. When you sell your Spanish property, it is only the company that is transferred. The same company continues to own the same Spanish property, so no Spanish transfer taxes are charged. Only the offshore company has a new owner. The same applies for inheritance tax when the company is bequeathed to an inheritor. The offshore location charges no tax on this.

The disadvantages are that Spain, keenly aware of the tax loss, has placed a flat tax of three per cent per year on any property held by an offshore company. They have a list of tax havens. European Union authorities are also preparing to place restrictions on these companies, so it is becoming a doubtful proposition.

As a buyer, you have a choice between purchasing the off-shore company itself or buying as an individual and paying the transfer taxes. See section on Taxes for advantages and disadvantages of off-shore companies.

## BANK REPOSSESSIONS
## AND PUBLIC AUCTIONS

After the 1990 crash of the Spanish property boom, the sunshine coasts were littered with real bargains. Some of these bargains were on sale by people who could not keep up the payments on their property, some of them were offered at cut-rate prices by developers who were stuck with stock they couldn't sell, and some of them were villas and apartments that had been repossessed by banks.

Bank foreclosure of mortgages is one of the few Spanish legal procedures that works quickly and effectively. A few of the properties were even those seized by courts and sold at auction to satisfy a debt against the owner.

The consensus of opinion in the property world is that most of these bargain properties have been sold and the few remaining are so undesirable that nobody wants them at any price. This is mainly true, but there are still some bargains available if you look for them.

One of the easiest ways to make a stab at buying a cut-price property is simply to walk into the offices of bank managers in an area where you would like to live. Go into the bank and say that you would like to speak with the manager about a business matter. He will probably speak English and he will probably receive you after a short wait. Say to him you are interested in buying a repossessed property. *Reposesión*. Ask him if he has any on his books.

You may be as astonished as I was when he points to a stack of *escrituras* on his desk and says, "How about one of these?" If the bank is a bit more modern, he may punch up a list on his computer terminal and inquire about the price range that interests you. So, you look at the list and pick a villa or an apartment that seems promising. You view it, like it, and buy it from the bank for maybe half what it would fetch on the market. It can be that easy. Or you might find that banks in your area do not have anything that interests you.

So why aren't these properties already sold, you ask. Good question. The answer seems to be that banks simply don't know how to sell real estate. A few of them have established their own departments for selling their repossessed properties, but most of them just sit in the files until the court gets around to auctioning them off at official proceedings.

If you really feel like getting into the system, you could even try the court-ordered auctions of property being sold to satisfy debts. These auctions, called *subastas,* can offer some incredible buys to those who get into the inside on how they work. Properties have been sold at one-tenth their real value, for example.

In northern European countries this simply cannot take place, but under the Spanish system the court is obliged to take the highest offer, no matter how low, after the property has been offered several times.

You are right if you think that this system attracts abuses. In many courts there are professional *subasteros* who work together, sometimes in collusion with corrupt court officials, to offer low bids. Later, these professionals split the take among themselves. They often assign the properties to third parties, who are not real buyers, but who also get their share of the profits once the property is sold on again.

## TIMESHARE LAW

A comprehensive Spanish law regulates important legal aspects of timeshare itself and provides consumer protection that brings the country into line with European timeshare regulations.

Putting a crimp into the high-pressure selling techniques of the timeshare touts around bus stations and tourist spots, the law provides a 10-day cooling-off period during which no deposit may be taken and the buyer can withdraw from the contract he has signed without any penalty.

Furthermore, the law requires that the timeshare operator provide full information and a contract in the buyer's own language. If any element of the purchase does not meet the brochure or written description or match the contract terms, the buyer has a further three months to rescind the contract unilaterally with no penalty.

The law also provides that any loan that the buyer may have taken out to purchase the timeshare will also be cancelled. This has put an end to the situation in which buyers found they were still liable to pay back to the bank tempting low-interest loans they had accepted from the time-share company.

The law also provides that all contracts will be subject to Spanish law. That is, even if the buyer's contract states that its terms are subject to the laws of some distant offshore jurisdiction, where the timeshare company's headquarters is located, this provision is not valid and the contract will be subject to interpretation in Spanish courts.

This has been a thorny point in many timeshare contracts because the buyers found it difficult to dispute any point when the court was thousands of miles away.

Even the service companies that maintain the resorts have, until now, often been registered in offshore tax havens. This made it difficult for timeshare buyers to bring action against the companies when they failed to keep the resorts in good condition.

Under terms of Spain's new law, the service companies must have a permanent establishment registered inside Spain, where they can be held legally responsible.

Furthermore, the new law makes the resort owner finally responsible for proper maintenance of the resort, and action can be taken against the resort owner if the service company fails to perform.

On the other hand, the resort operator can repossess an owner's holiday weeks if the owner fails to pay one year's maintenance charges. The operator must give 30 days certified notice before he can do this, and, unless this right is specifically renounced in your contract, he must pay back the owner the value of his remaining weeks in the scheme.

That is, a timeshare plan may run from a minimum of three years to a maximum of 50 years. If an owner has used his weeks for 25 years in a 50-year plan and then defaults, the operator must pay him back half of his original price, as well as assuming the debt owed by the owner to the service company.

However, it is also possible for the timeshare contract to contain a penalty clause that will let the company keep the entire amount originally paid. Watch out for this clause in your timeshare contract.

The law also provides that timeshare contracts can be registered in Spain's Property Registry as a special right, although the law is also very careful to note that timeshare is not a property right as such, that it is a service contract not a property sale.

The full name of the law in fact is The Law Regulating the Rights of Rotational Enjoyment of Real Estate for Touristic Use, and it forbids any mention of property rights in timeshare publicity.

Unfortunately, the law does not mean that all timeshare sales are now regulated and controlled to protect the consumer. Timeshare companies have already come up with new schemes relating to "vacation plans" and "point systems" to move their products out of the area controlled by the law.

## EXPROPRIATION OF PROPERTY

For most people, any improvement of the road system or flyovers and bypasses to increase safety is good news.

It may not be such good news if your property borders a projected highway or is affected by a new bypass, because the authorities - represented by a public works department such as the *Ministerio de Obras Públicas y Transportes* or MOPT - can expropriate your property and put you off it.

They must pay you, of course. The doctrine of *justiprecio* applies, meaning they must pay you a fair price. You may have to fight them to get it, however, and there are legal avenues open to you to protect your rights in the matter.

First, the authorities must officially inform you that expropriation proceedings are about to begin against you. They will send you an official letter inviting you to attend the *acta previa a la ocupación*. This is a hearing, usually held in your town hall, at which you may present any protest you have about the extent of your property being expropriated.

Money is not discussed at this first hearing, only the amount of land being taken. You should take skilled legal counsel with you when you go to this hearing.

If the authorities are only interested in a few square metres of your vast finca, then you have no real problem. If, however, they want to put the road through the kitchen and reception area of your popular restaurant, or if the amount of land they take will leave you with too few square metres to be buildable, then there must be some negotiating.

In such a case, some lawyers advise that you attempt to make the authorities expropriate your entire property and not just part of it. This obviously is because the property, once divided, becomes all but worthless and such a situation is manifestly unfair to the person involved.

In these negotiations, the authorities are usually reasonable and fair, but they will be even more fair and reasonable when confronted by skilled counsel.

Your chances of resisting expropriation altogether are very poor indeed. The entire concept of expropriation or Eminent Domain exists because sometimes the public good takes precedence over private ownership. They are going to build the highway and your chance of moving the route away from your private property is very small.

Once the amount of land being expropriated is agreed, the authorities take the situation under analysis and then communicate their offer of payment to each owner. If the offer is acceptable, you inform them and the deal is done.

If, however, as is more frequent, you are not satisfied with their offer, you negotiate again. The doctrine of *justiprecio* is not just a word and it can be enforced. You will need to prepare a case for a higher price on your property, including sales prices of land around you, improvements you have made, and so on. You will need expert advice for this.

If you are unable to come to an agreement with the authorities by negotiation, you have recourse to the *Jurado de Expropiaciones,* which is a special court set up for this purpose only. The presiding members of this tribunal are not only judges; real estate experts are also included, and decisions it has rendered have ensured that fair market value is paid to many owners.

Beyond that, you can appeal this tribunal's ruling to the normal courts all the way up to the Supreme Court.

To sum up, in any expropriation proceedings, you have little chance of resisting entirely the order. But you do have two opportunities to protest both the amount of land being taken and the payment offered. Skilled counsel can make sure your interests are protected.

## GLOSSARY

**Abogado** – Lawyer, solicitor

**Administrador de Fincas** – Licensed professional property administrator

**API - Agente de la Propiedad Inmobiliaria** – Real estate agent, member of long-established association.

**Arbitrio sobre el incremento del valor de los terrenos** – Municipal tax on property sales, see *Plus Valía*.

**Boletin Oficial** – Official State gazette, where laws are published

**Catastro** – Land Office, concerned with measurements and physical description

**Certificado Catastral** – Catastral certificate describing land and buildings

**Comunidad de Propietarios** – Community of Property Owners

**Declaración de Obra Nueva** – Declaration of new construction

**Escritura de Compraventa** – Sales contract

**Escritura Publica** – Registered title deed

**Expediente de Dominio** – Ownership Proceeding, to establish title

**Finca** – Any plot of land or property

**Gestor** – Licensed administrative expert in Spanish procedures

**GIPE** – *Gestor y Intermediario de Propiedades y Edificios,* title awarded by association of estate agents and property administrators.

**Hipoteca** – Mortgage

**Impuesto sobre Bienes Inmuebles (IBI)** – Annual real estate tax

**Impuesto de Transmisiones Patrimoniales (ITP)** – Property transfer tax

**Jurado de Expropiaciones** – Special tribunal for expropriations

**Justiprecio** – Doctrine of fair price by the State in forcible purchase

**Ley de Costas** – Shores Act, protecting coastline

**Ley de Tasas** – Law of public fees

**Ministerio de Obras Publicas y Transportes (MOPT)** – Ministry of Public Works and Transport

**Nota Simple** – Certificate of registration from Property Registry

**Oficina Liquidadora** – Tax office that assigns values on sales

**Plan General de Ordenación Urbana (PGOU)** – Town development plan

**Plan Parcial** – Plan of building plots on urbanisation

**Plus Valia** – Municipal tax on property sale

**Poder** – Power of attorney

**Registro de la Propiedad** – Property Registry

**Reja** – Iron grillwork protecting windows and doors

**Reposesión** – Repossessed property

**Subasta** – Auction

**Subasteros** – Professional auction buyers

**Topografo** – Property surveyor

**Urbanismo** – Town planning department

**Valor Catastral** – Assessed value of property for tax purposes

# 4    Selling property

Now is a good time to sell your Spanish property. Prices are rising steadily and demand from northern Europeans is brisk.

Sellers should be aware, however, that they are subject to Spanish capital gains tax on the profits from their sale, whether they are resident or non-resident.

Furthermore, a sale of Spanish property attracts transfer costs that can total as much as 20 per cent of the price, in addition to that capital gains tax.

In some areas, real estate agents charge commissions of 10 per cent, although the Spanish estate agents' association recommends 3 per cent. Add to this the taxes and costs that total about 10 per cent and you are looking at some very high transfer costs.

Non-residents pay capital gains tax at a flat rate of 35 per cent on their profit from the sale. The Spanish Tax Agency requires that someone buying property from a non-resident withhold 5 per cent of the price and pay it directly to the tax agency. Residents pay a maximum of 15 per cent, with the tax calculated as part of their income tax. They are not subject to the withholding of 5 per cent.

You may be exempt from capital gains in the following three cases:

You originally bought your property before 1987.

You are 65 years old, a resident, and you have lived in your home for a minimum of three years.

You are resident and you use the full purchase price to buy another principal residence in Spain.

For full details on taxes involved in selling property, see the following section "Taxes on Property."

## PROPERTY SELLER'S CHECK LIST

### 1. Your real estate agent

First, read the section on Real Estate Agent in the previous chapter, Buying Property.

One rule often cited by those who have sold their homes in Spain is: Don't try to do it yourself. Get an estate agent, or several, and let them handle the showing of the place and dealing with prospects. Otherwise you can go crazy. There may be exceptions to this rule, but most sellers are in agreement.

Very seldom do Spanish estate agents demand the exclusive right to market your property, so you will probably list your sale with several agents in your area. Each agent will have his own form of agreement with you, in which his commission is stated if he brings the client who eventually buys your property. This agreement will contain the commission charged. Some agents charge as high as 10 per cent. Five per cent is more frequent. You make your own deal on this.

An agent can help you get your price right. He will know the market in your area. You can then decide if you want to put a higher price and wait longer to sell, or a lower price in order to attract an immediate buyer. Be warned that an agent will not work very hard to market your property if he thinks it is overpriced and unlikely to sell.

A good estate agent will see you through the entire process of finding a buyer, negotiating the price, making the contract, securing the payment, signing before the notary, paying the necessary taxes, and all the other details that arise.

The usual sequence is:

1. Seller and buyer agree all the details of the purchase on what is called a "private contract", at which time the buyer makes a substantial deposit, usually 10 per cent.

2. This deposit takes your property off the market and holds it while the buyer assembles the full amount of the purchase price, either from his own resources or by obtaining a mortgage. If the buyer does not complete the sale, he loses his deposit. If you, the seller, accept a higher offer in the meantime, you have to return double the amount of the deposit. Be warned. It is astonishing how often an apparently serious purchaser is unable to come up with the cash. Don't count your chickens before they have hatched. Be warned also that many buyers will try to make stage payments and get possession. If they do not complete the payments, you will have plenty of trouble getting them out and recovering your property. (See section below on Lawyers).

3. When the two parties are ready to complete the sale, they go to the Spanish Notario and sign the sales contract at his office. The contract can also be signed by proxy. This often happens with an absentee seller. He gives his lawyer a power of attorney, called a poder in Spanish. This poder empowers the attorney to sign in the name of his client. A seller who does not wish to return to Spain can even make this proxy at the Spanish consulate in his own country. (See Power of Attorney section in Buying Property chapter).

75

4.  This sales contract is stamped by the Notary and it should be immediately taken to the Property Registry office, where it is converted into the famous *escritura* - the title deed. The contract is called an *escritura de compraventa*, a purchase contract, and the title deed is called an *escritura publica*, because it is a registered document of public record. They are exactly the same document, before and after its registration. The original deed is then kept at the notary's office. You yourself never have it. You have only an official copy.

    It is only this public deed that makes the buyer the new owner, with a title proof against all comers. Discuss the entire procedure step by step with your agent, so you know what is going on at each stage.

The steps listed above are the most usual form of property transactions, but there are many possible variations. If your buyer has the cash ready and you have your title deed clear, there is no reason why you cannot go directly to the Notary and complete the sale immediately.

Don't forget that you want a proper bill - *factura* - from your estate agent, listing the amount of the commission and adding 16 per cent IVA to this sum. Make this clear at the beginning of the transaction. The entire amount is deductible from your profit as a legitimate expense when you go to calculate your capital gains tax.

## 2. Your Spanish lawyer

Conventional wisdom says the buyer always needs a lawyer but the seller may not. We say the seller, in the complex world of international property transfer, really ought to have a lawyer, too. Your estate agent may be perfectly competent, but complications can arise outside his area of expertise. It is always good to have two people working for you as well so you can compare and contrast their opinions.

For example, some "buyers" will make you an offer of renting with option to buy but their sole intention is getting a cheap rental. They pay you a low rent, and then they stop paying the rent altogether, and then they leave. They had no intention ever of buying the place. And it isn't worth the expense for you to try to collect the last three or four months of rent that they didn't pay, even if you could find them. Furthermore, your property has been off the market for six months or a year.

So, when the term of option to buy is mentioned, you or your lawyer or your estate agent should be aware that it ought to mean that the buyer pays you €10,000 or €15,000 for this option, which will be deducted from the total price when they purchase. If they let the time limit of the option expire, which might be two or three months, they forfeit what they have paid for it.

The majority of property transfers are quite clear-cut and no problems arise. Some are more complicated and a few are very complicated. So, lawyer's fees vary widely. You can take one per cent of the purchase price as a guideline for a standard property transfer. Get this clear with your lawyer before you even start. Ask him how much he will charge you. Your legal fees are also deductible from your profits as a necessary expense in realising your capital gain. Again, you need a bill with Spanish IVA charged at 16 per cent.

## 3. The sales contract

Your lawyer will also explain to you some things not expressed specifically in the contract.

For example, your contract may state that your buyer pays €50,000 now and takes possession of the property, paying another €30,000 after three months and another €30,000 after an additional three months to complete a total price of €110,000. If he fails to meet any payment, he forfeits the amount already paid and the property returns to you. He promises to vacate immediately. You don't like the idea of the stage payments, but you feel safe because of this clause in your contract.

Your lawyer will warn you that this clause is not strictly enforceable and matters will not turn out so easily if the buyer fails to complete payment. If the buyer can't pay and refuses to leave, you will have to go to court to resolve your contract and get your property back. It will not happen automatically.

The court will probably rule that you indeed get your property back, but that you can't keep all of the money the buyer has already paid you. After the court makes its own calculation of how long the buyer has been in the house, plus inconvenience to you, and a series of other factors, it will decide that you can keep, say, half of the money already paid. Then, after this procedure has dragged out for months, you can again take possession of the property and start again on the process of selling it. This is only one of the many complications that come up in property transactions.

Some other points you want to study beforehand will be the division of payment of the transfer taxes and fees. Will you follow Spanish regulations and charge the notary and the plus valía tax to the seller and the transfer tax and the registration fee to the buyer? Or will you try to make the buyer responsible for all charges in the transfer? What price will you declare, the real price or a lower figure? (See below for more details on these questions).

A good contract will help you foresee and avoid some of these complications but even the best contract cannot protect you against every eventuality. The standard contract used by your estate agent is probably as good as any, but your lawyer may have suggestions to make in your own particular case.

## 4. How much you declare

It was formerly a common practice in Spain to declare a property sale at much lower than its real price in order to save money on transfer tax and wealth tax later. Since the enactment of the Law on Public Fees, which makes an under-valuation of 20 per cent punishable by surcharges, and since the tax ministry's stricter application of all the rules, this practice has largely ceased.

If Hacienda believes that your sale is undervalued - and they have their own tables of market values - they may send you a notice that your sale has been re-assessed by them, along with a bill for how much extra tax you owe.

Today, most contracts are declared at their real value. Furthermore, as buyers become more sophisticated, they have realised that a low declaration now means that they will show a larger profit on paper when they go to sell later, making them subject to a higher Spanish capital gains tax.

If you want to know exactly how much Hacienda thinks your property is worth, you can find out by asking at your regional *oficina liquidadora*. They will give you the amount listed in their own tables. Any attempt to declare a value under that figure will probably bring you a notice to pay more.

Furthermore, if Hacienda reckons that the under-declaration exceeds 20 per cent of their calculated value of the property, they can bill you, the seller, for an unjustified capital gain, which draws tax at 35 per cent for the non-resident.

That is, if you declare the sale at €90,000 but Hacienda calculates the market value of the property at €120,000, they will charge the seller 35 per cent of €30,000, or more than €10,000. In addition, they can assume the buyer has received a gift worth €30,000 and assess gift tax on him of about €6,000.

## 5. Assemble your documents

It will help your sale to go smoothly if you have all your documents in order before you even begin to advertise. It builds confidence in the possible buyer - and his own lawyer - to see all the right papers in order when they consider purchasing.

*Escritura publica*: The most basic paper of all is your title deed, which shows that you are the registered owner of record with an incontestable title. In fact, you have probably never seen your real title deed. What you have is an authorised copy. Unlike some systems of property registration, in Spain it is not the piece of paper itself that counts but the inscription in the *Registro de la Propiedad*, the property registry office.

If you lose your deed, you can always get another copy from the Notary, where it is on file permanently. Listed on the inscription in the property registry are any liens, charges or mortgages against the property. Back taxes, however, are not listed.

Your prospective purchaser will get for himself a *nota simple* from the registry, which is an extract showing the basic information and any charges against the property, but he will want to look at your copy of the full deed in any case.

In a few cases, owners have their property only on a private contract and the house may not even be registered. If this includes you, don't panic. This can be solved in various ways, depending on the individual circumstances.

You can offer your buyer the possibility of a Regulation 205 procedure or a full-scale *expediente de dominio*, (see reference in previous chapter) in which a court will study the case, publish the proceedings, and finally issue a clear title to the property. You might even find a new buyer willing to run the same risks as you in order to avoid taxes and simply purchase the property on a new private contract.

**IBI receipt:** Your receipt for the paid-up *Impuesto sobre Bienes Inmuebles*, the Real Estate Tax, is an important item. The IBI receipt shows first that the estate tax is paid for this year. It would be a good idea to have the receipts for the last five years, to show good faith.

The IBI receipt also shows the amount of the *valor catastral,* the official assessed value of the property for tax purposes. This value is almost always less than the real market value, but they are gradually being raised. The IBI receipt also confirms that the house exists and is registered for taxes, which can be an important point when no *escritura publica* exists and the owner holds the property only by virtue of a private contract. Finally, the IBI must be presented when you sign the contract at the Notary because it also displays the number of the *referencia catastral* which, since 1997, is a required part of the documentation in property transfers.

***Referencia Catastral*:** The Catastral Reference is the file number of the property's registration in the land registry, which in Spanish is called the *catastro*, a word that exists but is rarely used in English, and which means the land registry.

Property is registered here by its measurements and boundaries and physical characteristics, while the Property Registry is concerned with ownership and mortgages.

You are right if you think that it doesn't make sense to have two separate bodies - which don't even talk to each other - dealing with land and property registration. The Spanish authorities are beginning to agree and, as a first step, they now require that the catastral reference number accompany any property transfer.

Furthermore, the Notary and the Property Registry office are now authorised to make note of the fact if there is any great difference in the physical description of the property given in the *catastro* and the legal description given in the sales contract and title deed.

This difference might include the fact that the *catastro* shows a four-bedroom villa and a swimming pool while the sales contract mentions only a plot of land at a very low price. It is yet to be seen just how effectively the Notary and the Registrar of Property will inform the tax office, but the way is now clear, so be warned.

It is a good idea for the seller to obtain the completely detailed *Certificado Catastral* and include it in his documentation. This will add to the prospective purchaser's confidence, and will make it absolutely clear what he is buying.

Land descriptions on title deeds are often quite vague, even misleading. The *catastro* is usually more accurate, because they have been updating their information for some years now, sending inspectors to check the physical reality of land and houses, and using aerial photographs as well.

It can take several months to obtain the certificate and there is a small fee.

**Income tax declaration:** If you are resident and so not subject to the retention of five per cent of the price, you will be required to present your most recent income tax declaration when you sign the contract at the Notary. The income tax declaration is as important as the residence permit in proving your tax status in Spain.

If you are a non-resident, the buyer may want to see your current Form 214, on which you declare each year for the same property owner's income tax as well as Spanish wealth tax. Non-residents must pay wealth tax because they do not have the exemption of €108,000 that residents have. Non-residents should be warned that any unpaid property owner's income tax or wealth tax can be taken by the tax man from the five per cent retention.

Consult the chapter on Taxes on Property for discussion on how to calculate your capital gains tax on the sale, and the annual taxes on property that you pay every year.

**Non-residence certificate:** This belongs to the buyer, not to the seller, but be warned that if the buyer is a non-resident and the form of payment is not through a bank cheque which identifies the buyer as the issuer along with his bank, the buyer must obtain beforehand a certificate of non-residence from the Spanish Ministry of the Interior, and it can take as long as two months for this certificate to be issued.

If payment takes place abroad by transfer from the buyer's account in London to your own account in London, this is perfectly legal, but it offers the Spanish tax man no control over the transaction for documentation purposes. So, they require this certificate.

If the buyer works through a Spanish bank, he will have a certificate of changing the foreign money into euros for property purchase, and Spain can document the transaction. If the sale takes place in pounds outside Spain, this is perfectly legal, and acceptable as long as the cheque is presented when the deal is completed at the Spanish Notary.

It is only when the buyer himself wishes to keep the details anonymous and confidential that he must present the certificate of non-residence. Spain wants to know where the money comes from, or at least that someone has made a deal without telling them.

**Taxes and fees:** We have discussed in the previous chapter on Buying Property the two taxes and two fees on property sales.

The two taxes are the ITP - the property transfer tax of 6 per cent - and the *plus valía*, a sort of artificial capital gains tax charged by the Town Hall on the increase in an official set of values for the property.

The *plus valía* varies widely, depending on the amount of time that has passed between sales, as we mentioned earlier. You can find out exactly how much it will be by asking at your Town Hall. They have a *plus valía* office that will tell you the exact amount of the tax beforehand.

The two fees are for the Notary and the Property Registry. They will be in the neighbourhood of €500 but can be higher on large transactions. You can find out exactly how much by asking in advance.

If you determine the amount of these taxes and fees on your sale price in advance, you can include them in your sales presentation kit, which will impress the buyer and his lawyer with your professional approach.

**Community charges and statutes:** If you are selling a flat or townhouse that belongs to a Community of Property Owners, you will want to include your last bill for the cuota - the community yearly charge, along with a copy of the Statutes that regulate your community. The buyer will want to know what the yearly charge is and he will want to see the Statutes of the community he is joining. It would be a good idea to have a copy of the minutes of the last Annual General Meeting as well, to prove to your prospective purchaser that your community is well run and a nice place to live.

**Utility bills:** Copies of your bills for rubbish, water, electricity and even telephone are necessary parts of your sales presentation. Any buyer will want to know how much these charges are on the property, and he will also want to be sure that they are paid up.

Once you have assembled all this paperwork, it would be a good idea to prepare a folder with photocopies of each relevant document, so that you or your lawyer or your estate agent will be prepared to answer any question that a prospective buyer might have.

## GLOSSARY

**Abogado** – Lawyer, solicitor

**Administrador de Fincas** – Licensed professional property administrator

**API - Agente de la Propiedad Inmobiliaria** – Real estate agent, member of long-established association.

**Arbitrio sobre el incremento del valor de los terrenos** – Municipal tax on property sales, see *Plus Valía*.

**Catastro** – Land Office, concerned with measurements and physical description

**Certificado Catastral** – Catastral certificate describing land and buildings

**Comunidad de Propietarios** – Community of Property Owners

**Contrato** – Contract

**Escritura de Compraventa** – Sales contract

**Escritura Publica** – Registered title deed

**Factura** – Bill

**Finca** – Any plot of land or property

**Gestor** – Licensed administrative expert in Spanish procedures

**GIPE** – *Gestor y Intermediario de Promociones y Edificaciones,* title awarded by association of estate agents and property administrators.

**Hipoteca** – Mortgage

**Impuesto sobre Bienes Inmuebles (IBI)** – Annual real estate tax

**Impuesto de Transmisiones Patrimoniales (ITP)** – Property transfer tax

**IVA (Impuesto sobre el Valor Añadido)** – Spanish value added tax, charged when developer sells new property to first buyer.

**Ley de Costas** – Shores Act, protecting coastline

**Ley de Tasas** – Law of Public Fees

**Nota Simple** – Certificate of registration from Property Registry

**Notario** – Notary

**Oficina Liquidadora** – Tax office which sets values and collects tax.

**Plan General de Ordenación Urbana (PGOU)** – Town development plan

**Plan Parcial** – Plan of building plots on urbanisation

**Plus Valia** – Municipal tax on property sale

**Poder** – Power of attorney

**Registro de la Propiedad** – Property Registry

**Tasación** – Evaluation of property

**Tasador** – Property surveyor, evaluator

**Topografo** – Property surveyor

**Urbanismo** – Town planning department

**Valor Catastral** – Assessed value of property for tax purposes

# 5    Building a Home

If you intend to build your own castle in Spain, the first item on your list should be finding a good lawyer.

This may sound backwards, but when you check out the list below of all the things that can go wrong with buying property, getting a building permit, and contracting the construction, perhaps you will agree.

The second item on your list should be a promise to yourself that you are prepared to put a lot of your own time into overseeing the project, preferably from beginning to end. Getting what you want depends on your own personal supervision.

Most building projects go up just as planned, with only minor setbacks, but it is best to be prepared and take care before you start.

So, let's suppose that you are determined to buy land and build your dream house. More foreigners than ever are doing this today because of the shortage of quality ready-made villas, and more builders and architects than ever are ready to help you realise your dream.

The rewards are great. But be prepared for plenty of exasperation and, above all, don't leap in with your eyes shut.

Too often, the aspiring house-builder thinks that all he has to do is pick one model of villa from a selection that the developer or builder shows him, and that it will appear as if by magic a few months later.

Sometimes this method works out perfectly well, but not all of us can read a plan and visualise the final result with accuracy.

Too many people tell their builder that House Type B suits them very well, pay a fat deposit, and go back to their native country. When they return six or eight months later, they find that House Type B doesn't look anything like they thought it would; that the builder hasn't placed it in the spot they had agreed on and, furthermore, they absolutely hate the yellow tiles in the bathroom.

It will take your personal supervision to get it done the way you want it. With forethought and patient attention to detail, you can indeed have your dream house. But let me repeat that first warning. You simply cannot walk away and expect to return finding that your house has been built just the way you want it.

First, however, you have to find the land. Everything mentioned in the previous chapter about buying property applies here, and there is more besides.

Building land is available already divided into plots with all services on many urbanisations. Country land is also much easier to find than before because thousands of foreigners are moving inland from the coastal areas. This means that estate agents with local knowledge are making greater efforts to have on hand the sort of country plots that these foreigners want.

Now let's suppose that you have searched through the countryside and found a piece of land you like, or that you have seen a dozen urbanisations and finally chosen a plot.

## BUILDING PERMIT

The first thing you have to know is, can you get permission from the town hall to build on it? The permit is called *licencia de obra* or *permiso de obra*. Be advised that building permits cost around four per cent of the estimated construction cost. This can vary from town to town.

## URBAN LAND

If your land is in a registered urbanisation, or housing estate, with its papers in order, you will probably have no problem. Sometimes the land comes with the building permit already arranged. This land, of course, is more expensive because it has been prepared for development. But even on a registered urbanisation, some problems can arise.

There are zoning changes from time to time, and you may find your beautiful property is in the middle of a green zone where no building can take place.

Do not take the seller's word as gospel. Your town hall's *urbanismo* department is a very important stop for you. Go yourself and take someone who speaks Spanish. Your lawyer, for example.

**PGOU:** You want to see the PGOU, the *Plan General de Ordenación Urbana,* the Town Plan. These plans generally are approved every four years. Any interim changes in them must be publicly posted and approved, with a chance for affected property owners to protest or make claims.

In many municipalities, you may find that many changes have been made in the building codes and Town Plans, sometimes being approved by the town hall but still needing the final go-ahead from the regional government, which must vet and clear the municipal plans.

In some cases, there are special building codes set up for specific zones. The PGOU analysis is not for amateurs. You need a specialist to help you you understand it.

If your land is located in an existing and approved urbanisation, the permit will probably be forthcoming, but you must still check on it. You must also be sure that the urbanisation is an approved one.

There are some developments that never received official approval and where building is stopped today because they never met the legal requirements for the services they must provide, such as roads of a certain width, or water supply. You can find out by asking to see the *proyecto de urbanización* and the *plan parcial,* or the plan of parcels, building plots, at the town hall.

Be sure to check also the building regulations for plots and areas around your chosen spot. One of the worst, and most frequent, horror stories on the fast-growing coasts of Spain is the nightmare of the cut-off view. That is, you return to your pleasant villa on a hillside overlooking the Mediterranean to discover that a four-storey apartment building now blocks your view, and your new neighbours look right into your bedroom window. Make sure that you know what type of building permits will be issued around you before you buy.

---

### BUILDING COSTS

These costs are very approximate. So many variations come into building costs that it is extremely difficult to calculate an average price that means anything. Nevertheless, the table should give you some idea of what to expect.

**Basic Construction:** figure 500-600 euros a square metre.

**Good Construction:** 600-700 euros a square metre

**Quality Construction:** 900 euros a square metre and up, way up.

Basic Construction means walls of the large solid building blocks with no cavities and the use of basic flooring and finishing materials.

Good Construction at the top end of the price will include cavity walls and some higher quality finishing materials. No air-conditioning or central heating, however, and no marble.

Quality Construction: The sky is the limit here. Remember that the area of location is also an influence. Labour costs are higher in Marbella than in the interior, for example.

---

In the brisk building climate today, this check-up may be more complicated than it sounds.

In some municipalities the urban planning authorities even make special deals with developers, whereby land is re-zoned to permit greater building in exchange for part of the builder's profits going into the Town's coffers. This is neither illegal nor corrupt, as the profits help all residents of the town, but it can harm the interests of those who already have purchased.

These special arrangements are called *convenios,* meaning simply "agreements". A wave of protest has arisen in Marbella, for example, where the Town Plan (passed by the town hall but still not finally approved by the Andalusian Regional Government) provides for enormous amounts of new building, enough to triple the population.

Current residents charge that some present building permits have been granted for land zoned for parks and schools, and that such rapid new building will lower the quality of life in the town.

Be sure to talk with your new neighbours before you sign any contracts.


## COUNTRY LAND - *RUSTICO*

If your land is in the deep country, you will need to check on other factors at the town hall, such as whether you need to buy, say, 10,000 square metres of land, or 30,000 square metres of land, in order to build.

Most country land is zoned as *Rustico,* which means land not programmed for development. It might be farmland or pasture or forest.

If building is permitted at all on this type of land, it will be restricted. Regulations vary around Spain, but a frequent requirement is that a minimum building plot must be 10,000 square metres if the land has a source of water, and 30,000 square metres if it is zoned as "dry".

Do not believe a seller who tells you that you can build on 6,000 square metres illegally and later have the house registered, paying only a small fine. This has been true in the past, but most municipalities are now cracking down on such practices especially under the new Andalusian Land Law (see page 94). They can order the house demolished.

You can find this out at the local town hall. The *Urbanismo,* or development, department can tell you exactly what will be permitted or prohibited within any area of the municipality.

Visit the town hall yourself, taking someone who speaks Spanish, or send your lawyer, to make absolutely sure that a permit will be forthcoming.

The land might also have a *camino real* or a *servidumbre de paso,* an old pathway that crosses the land. It is a right of way and you can't cut it by building. People can pass over your land and it might even be transformed into a road some day.

Or an irrigation ditch might exist, which again is a legal right of way you cannot block, nor can you deny access to it for those who use it. Country land may have water problems, too. Where does the water come from? Can it be cut off? If you intend to drill your own well, you will need a special permission for this.

Have an expert check the town planning maps to see if any new highways are planned for the zone. It can come as a nasty surprise two years later when you see the bulldozers starting work next door, or you are called to a hearing where expropriation proceedings will start to take the bottom of your garden.

Once you have determined that a building permit will be forthcoming and that no special encumbrances exist on the land, you can start to find out just what land you are buying.

## LAND MEASUREMENT

The seller must have an *escritura,* a title deed, for the land, just as for a flat or land with an existing house. As we mentioned in the preceding chapter, sometimes there is no registered title for the land, only a private document. See the preceding chapter for various ways of getting the land officially registered.

But, in the more usual case where official title exists, this *escritura pública* will describe the land, but sometimes the description isn't exact enough to suit you.

Descriptions in the Property Registry often use vague terms like the bare statement that the land borders on the east with the land of Pepe Garcia. Well, Pepe Garcia has a big farm. Just what part of it constitutes the border? It could be where the fence is or where the ditch is or where the path is.

Then you need an official survey. Remember that the Property Registry is concerned with ownership, not with exact description.

A surveyor is called a *topografo,* and he will measure your plot exactly. You can have this done independently but you should also check the catastral registry.

## CHECK THE *CATASTRO*

Here again, just as with buying a house, you want to check with the *Catastro* as well as the Property Registry. The Catastral Office lists the boundaries and measurements and physical characteristics of the land. You want to be sure that this description squares with the description in the *escritura.*

If not, you may be able to get the catastral reference to square with the reality of the land, and this in turn with the title deed.

The *Catastro* will have a map, a plan of the land, so that you can see that the boundary with Pepe Garcia's farm runs along the fence. Or you might see that your plot includes some triangle of what Pepe Garcia thinks belongs to him. Especially in old country properties, there is often some confusion.

You want to have exact, officially recognised boundaries, and the number of square metres the same on the survey and the *escritura.* They probably will not agree, but you can correct this when you purchase, so that your own title and the physical description are in agreement. This clarity will be greatly to your benefit should you later wish to sell your land and house.

Ask for the official surveyor at the town hall. The survey will form part of your *escritura* when you buy the land. If your land is on an approved urbanisation, there will likely be an up-to-date survey already existing. The survey and the *plan parcial* will also show your access and where your water and electricity come from.

Once you have determined that you can indeed build and you know the exact borders of your land, you had better find out if the seller is in fact the owner of the land.

Are you buying from the developers of the urbanisation, or from an individual? If the land is in the *campo,* does Juan really own it? He may share it with his two brothers, one of whom does not want to sell. Or there may be a mortgage on it. The same rules apply as for any property purchase. Check the *Registro de la Propiedad.*

Finally, you sign the *escritura de compraventa* at the *notario,* and you are ready to proceed with building. When you checked restrictions at the town hall, you should also have discovered what building code problems you may have. Do you have to leave three metres between your boundary and any building? Can you put a wall closer to the road than one metre? Is two storeys the absolute limit? If you are in an established urbanisation, does the association of property owners require you to submit your building plans for approval?

## ARCHITECT AND LEGAL CHARGES

**Architect Fee:**  8 to 9 per cent.  (Official College sets 6 per cent, Try to negotiate.
**Building Engineer (*Aparejador*):**  1.5 per cent.  (he supervises building construction).
**Building Licence:**  4 to 5 per cent (varies by towns)
Topographic Land Survey:  0.66 per cent
**Safety Study:**  0.8 per cent
**Geological Report:**  0.94 per cent
**First Occupation Licence:**  0.5 per cent
**Declaration of New Construction:**  0.5 per cent (paid when you register House for real estate tax).
**TOTAL:**  16 to 19 per cent

We repeat that checking the building code sounds simple but in practice it is often complicated.  Many municipalities have old building codes in place, with new ones written and approved by the town council, but not yet ratified by their regional governments, which must give final approval.

This means that even official *permisos de obra*, or building permits, are sometimes granted on the basis of shaky legality.

## VALENCIA, ANDALUSIA LAWS MAY COMPLICATE MATTERS

Recent land laws enacted in the Valencian Community and in Andalusia may complicate your land purchase.  You must be alert.

94

In Valencia, the LRAU has country property owners outraged. The initials stand for the *Ley Reguladora de Actividades Urbanisticas,* becoming known as the "land-grab law." The law provides that Town Halls may designate private developers as Urbanising Agents, with the power to force private owners to sell parts of their land at low prices and to pay high charges for infrastructure.

The law is clearly open to abuse and even the UK Ambassador has taken part in questioning the Valencia government about the protection of citizen's basic rights.

If you buy in an established urbanisation, you should be all right. If you buy country land or property, make sure you check on any possible urbanisation plans in the area.

In Andalusia, the revised *Ley del Suelo,* the Land Law, has some similar provisions, but authorities affirm that more protections are in place to guarantee the rights of private owners. The revised law also cracks down on the practice of illegal construction on *suelo rustico,* or country land. Its principal first effect has been to virtually halt the sale of country plots, of any size.

## ARCHITECT IS NECESSARY

Now you need an architect. You have your rough sketches but you need someone who can turn them into real blueprints. In fact, you will need architect's drawings in order to get your building permit in any case.

The only way to find a good architect is to ask around. If you prefer to use a foreign architect for your design, you may do so. Since Spain's entry into Europe, EU architects can now practise and sign plans for approval by the official *Colegio de Arquitectos.*

Architects' fees, at least as a minimum, are standard and are set by the *Colegio.* They are about 6 per cent of the estimated cost of construction.

To this you must add another 1.5 per cent for the *aparejador* (see below), so your design and supervision will cost you about 8 per cent of your estimated construction cost. This construction cost, by the way, will be less than either your real cost or the real market value of the house when finished.

The price includes final plans that must suit you, and the six copies necessary for approval by the College of Architects and for your building permit. The six and three per cent figures are no longer obligatory, but are only suggested minimum charges, as the College no longer has the legal power to enforce the rates. Hence, you may be able to get a cheaper fee by a little negotiating.

## *MEMORIA* IS A BINDING AGREEMENT FOR BUILDING SPECIFICATIONS

The price also includes preparation of the *memoria de calidades*, or building specifications, which includes items like the size of pipes, the formula for the concrete and the type of materials to be used.

You yourself want to have a personal hand in this. You can choose here just what sort of electrical fittings and bathroom fixtures and kitchen tiles you want. This is the time to think of details about shelves and about whether you want wood window frames or aluminium, and so on.

It is important to give this a great deal of thought because the *memoria* is what you will give your builder in order to get his bid on the job. He will set his price according to the materials stated in the *memoria,* and any changes you may make later, or any additions, will cost you extra. These extras can add up to a lot of money, so the *memoria* is a very important document.

If the builder fails to install any items as set out in these building specifications, he can be held responsible.

The architect's fee includes overall supervision of the construction, but you are not likely to see your architect on the building site once he has finished the design.

The actual supervision usually falls to the *aparejador,* a professional architectural engineer who sees that the building is carried out to the specifications required. He will visit the site from time to time to check on things. He signs the documents certifying that the house is properly constructed, which you will need in order to occupy your house legally and to get your electricity connected.

Your architect will be able to recommend an *aparejador.* Often they work out of the same office.

Finally, you are ready to find a builder. It is only reasonable to get several bids on your job, remembering that the lowest bid is not always the best deal and that the highest bid does not ensure high quality. Ask around.

Your contract with the builder should include the *memoria*. It should state the total price, whether or not the site grading and preparation and final clean-up are included, the manner of payment, and give a definite completion date, with a penalty clause for late delivery. You ought to have your lawyer vet this contract.

Be advised that many building projects are not finished on time. If your contract contains a penalty clause, well and good. Often, however, the only guarantee is that you can get your money back if the project is not delivered on time.

In real life, you don't want your money back. The apartment or house is already worth 10 or 20 per cent more than you paid for it a year ago, when construction started, so you would suffer this loss.

In this case, you simply wait.

## PAYMENT SCHEDULES VARY

Payment terms are not standard, but a typical schedule might be:

1. A deposit of 20 per cent when the contract is signed.

2. Another 20 per cent when the walls and roof are completed. (At this point, it is customary to have the *bandera* party, when a flag is placed on the roof, and the owner invites the workers and his own friends to a fiesta at the site.)

3. Another 20 per cent when the door and window frames are installed and the inside is more or less complete.

4. Another 20 per cent when the house is painted and ready to inhabit, with plumbing and electricity installed and functioning.

5. A payment of 10 per cent when all the outside work included in the contract is finished, such as patios, walls, swimming pool.

6. The final payment of 10 per cent should be held back for six months to a year, if you can get the builder to agree to this, to cover any defects in construction which don't show up until the rains start, for example. There is always something.

## CONSTRUCTION LAW - *LOE*

Spain's building law of 2000 makes builders legally responsible for 10 years for any damage resulting from the foundations, load-bearing walls and other structural elements. The builder is responsible for three years for damages caused by construction material defects, and for one year for the state of finishing elements. The law is called the LOE, the *Ley de Ordenación de Edificación.*

## *DECLARACIÓN DE OBRA NUEVA*

Before you can register your new house for real estate taxes, you must first make a *declaración de la obra nueva,* a declaration of new work, in order to have the structure appear on your *escritura.* So far, your deed mentions only the piece of land, not the house you have just built.

The declaration of new construction will cost you one half of one per cent of the declared value of the construction. Again, if the Tax Agency does not agree with your declared value, they can raise it.

Your lawyer or property consultant will show you how to register the new house. If you do not register *(dar de alta)* with the tax people, you can be fined, so take care of it as soon as possible. Two per cent of the value of your house is also calculated as income when you go to file for your Spanish income tax.

When you go to make your declaration of new work and register the house, you will need the *certificado final de obra* issued by the architect, the *licencia de obra ,* the building permit issued by the town hall, and the *licencia de primera ocupación,* the permit to inhabit the dwelling, from the town hall.

Then you will be the completely legal and registered owner

of your dream house and you can begin to pay both property owner's income tax and Spanish wealth tax on your new property.

That is, if you are a non-resident. Since 1999, the resident is exempt from property owner's imputed income tax on his principal dwelling, as well as having the exemption of 108,182 euros on his wealth tax.

## GLOSSARY

**Aparejador** – Building Engineer

**Arquitecto** – Licenced Architect

**Bandera** – Flag, here referring to "flag party" when house is roofed

**Camino Real** – Royal Road, meaning right of way across land

**Catastro** – Land Registry, distinct from Property Registry

**Escritura de Compraventa** – Conveyance Deed

**Escritura Publica** – Registered title to land

**Certificado de Final de Obra** – Construction completion certificate

**Declaración de Obra Nueva** – Declaration of new construction

**Ley de Ordenación de la Edificación** – Law of Construction

**Ley Reguladora de las Actividades Urbanisticas** – Valencian Urbanisation law providing compulsory purchase

**Ley de Suelo**– Andalusian Land Law with similar provisions

**Licencia de Obra (Permiso de Obra)** – Building Licence

**Licencia de Primera Ocupación** – Licence to occupy the dwelling

**Memoria de Calidades** – Detailed building specifications

**Plan General de Ordenación Urbana (PGOU)** – Municipal building plan

**Plan Parcial** – Plan of building plots in housing estate

**Proyecto de Urbanización** – Housing estate development plan

**Rustico** – Country land, not zoned for building

**Servidumbre de Paso** – Legal right of way

**Topografo** – Land surveyor

**Urbanismo** – Urban Development Office

# 6     **Letting and Renting**

## LETTING YOUR PROPERTY

Buying to let is nothing new in Spain. It has been going on a long time. Nevertheless, there is a genuine boom in this form of investment right now.

With today's low interest rates and high rentals, you can buy a flat on the Costa del Sol, mortgage 70 per cent of the purchase price, and sit back while your rental income pays off the mortgage.

If you are paying mortgage interest at five or six per cent effective annual rate and your rentals are bringing in a return on capital of seven or eight per cent, you are making a profit of two or three per cent.

This doesn't seem like much, but you are doing it with the bank's money, not your own, and you are paying for your property. Plus you have the use of the property for part of the year because not many holiday lets attract tenants for 12 months of the year.

You also enjoy capital appreciation as your property grows in value. Many Marbella properties have doubled in value in the past five years, for example, making them a better investment than today's sagging stock market.

## TAX REDUCTION FOR LANDLORDS

This sounds like a tough deal to beat, and the Spanish tax man has further sweetened the package by introducing a reduction of 50 per cent in rental income for tax purposes. This unfortunately applies only to official residents of Spain, and is designed to stimulate the rental market.

Resident landlords can also deduct just about every expense imaginable from their rental income, meaning that most landlords will pay little or nothing in income tax.

Residents benefit from this Spanish income tax reduction, but non-residents declare their rental income on a special form 210, which is not affected by the measure. (See p. 109)

While you are raking in the money, though, you must remember that you will have certain obligations to your tenants. Being a landlord in Spain is not without its problems, especially in regard to rental extensions up to five years.

## LETTING LAW

Spain's current Law of Urban Lettings, the *Ley de Arrendamientos Urbanos,* went into effect on January 1, 1995, but many letters and renters, especially foreigners, are still unaware of its provisions.

The law brought some good news for those Spanish property owners who are still stuck with sitting tenants under the pre-1985 law, and it also brought good news for tenants who were victims of arbitrary rent rises under the law in force from 1985 to 1995.

The 1995 law ended a maze of contradictory Spanish legislation that made life difficult for tenants and landlords alike and all but ruined the rental property market in Spain.

Two of its main provisions make life easier for both landlords and tenants.

1. The current law ends the forcible extension provision of the 1964 law, which made rental contracts indefinitely renewable by the tenant. The present law allows landlords gradually to raise the old controlled and ridiculously low rents of the 1964 law to market prices today, and, eventually, to recover their own property.

2. The law also provides tenants with more security than the 1985 law stipulated, now obliging landlords to renew residential rental contracts each year for up to five years.

## THREE RENTAL SITUATIONS

We must distinguish three possible situations for rentals existing in Spain today, depending on when the original contract was made.

**1964-1985:** Under the terms of the rental laws in effect from 1964 to 1985, tenants were so protected that landlords gave up in despair and stopped building rental apartments, which led to a critical housing shortage. Almost half a million apartments in Spain are still occupied under this old law, which protected a tenant so strongly that he could pass on his rights to his children and even his grandchildren. Further, his rent could never be raised, or raised only by a small percentage related to the

103

inflation rate.

Incredibly, there are almost 500,000 apartments in Spain whose tenants pay less than €50 a month, and in Madrid there are grandchildren of the original tenants living in spacious flats in prestigious areas and paying rents of only five euros a month. Until 1985, the landlord was helpless to do anything about it, even though his real estate tax is €1,500 a year and his community fees are another €1,000. Next door, another tenant might be paying €1,200 a month for the same type of apartment, having signed his contract after 1985.

Some foreign property owners on the Spanish Mediterranean coasts fell into this trap before 1985. Thinking to make a little money on their holiday flat or eventual retirement home, they rented it out, with a contract for some specific time period.

Later they were horrified to discover that their tenants refused to vacate and had become entitled to the forcible extension of their contracts, regardless of the landlord's desire to end the letting and recover his property.

Many landlords chose to leave their apartments empty rather than risk the dangers of a sitting tenant. Landlords refused to repair the crumbling buildings that brought them no profit, and nobody would even think of constructing new rental property.

**1985-1995:** Revised rental laws passed in 1985 by the Socialist government aimed to remedy this situation in the best capitalist way, by making rental properties good business. The revised law provided that all contracts ended when they said they ended, without provision for forcible extension. The law also ended any restrictions on rent increases. Landlords immediately began to raise rents sharply and to offer short-term contracts with little protection for the tenant. Now it was the tenants who suffered, because they were unwilling to settle into a flat from which they might be evicted in one year's time, or be forced to pay sharp increases.

**1995:** The 1995 rental law now in force is designed to provide a better balance between the rights and needs of tenants and landlords and to bring at last a final solution to the generations of sitting tenants.

If you are one of the foreign property owners stuck with a sitting tenant, you are now able to recover your property, though it can take you the tenant's lifetime, plus two years. However, you will be able to raise the rent to a normal level over either five years or 10 years, depending on the tenant's income.

If the tenant earns less than €28,000 a year, his rent can be gradually raised to market levels over 10 years. If he earns more than that, his rent can be raised in five years to a market figure.

The old-law tenant still has the right to pass on the apartment to his spouse or children, and they can pass it on to their children, but only for two years. After that, the landlord will at last be able to take possession of his own property. In the meantime, of course, he will have been able to raise the rent to the price levels of today.

Landlords in this position should take legal advice from property specialists in order to make sure they are effectively exercising their rights.

There are a number of legal steps that each landlord must take before he can begin raising his rents, such as citing the tenant to declare his income. If the tenant does not respond, the landlord can then begin raising the rent to bring it to a market level within five years, the faster option.

## CONTRACT RENEWABLE UP TO FIVE YEARS

The present law provides that residential contracts, as distinct from short-term holiday lets, are subject to yearly renewals up to five years. Rental contracts are usually made for one year but the law requires that the contract is renewable for a total five-year period of tenancy.

A landlord can offer a contract of two years or three years but, if the tenant decides that he wants to stay on, this contract is renewable for a total period of five years. If the tenant himself wishes a contract of only two or three years, this is all right. The rent can be revised upward by an inflation factor each year.

At the end of the five years, the landlord can raise the rent as much as he chooses, either for his new tenant or for his existing tenant, if he decides to stay on at the new and higher rent.

## DEPOSIT

The current letting law establishes, for the first time in law, the landlord's right to a deposit as a guarantee against damages. The deposit can be held by an agency independent of both landlord and tenant. This agency will not release the deposit until both parties agree.

The deposit consists of one month's rent for a residential unit and two months' rent for commercial premises.

The deposit, called a *fianza,* can be held by the housing department of the regional government. In Andalusia, for example, it is deposited with the *Consejería de la Vivienda* of the Andalusian autonomous government, which has offices in major cities.

## EVICTION

For what reason can a landlord evict a tenant and regain his property? There can be one of several different reasons, including failure to pay the rent (courts have often ruled that these arrears must exceed six months before any action can be taken), damage done to the property, use of the property for immoral purposes, subletting without permission from the owner, causing a serious nuisance to the neighbours, and so on.

In any of these cases, a court order must be obtained against the tenant and many months could pass before you get him out.

**Necessary notification:** If you have let your property on a five-year *vivienda* contract (see above) and you wish to take possession of your property at the end of that time, remember that you must officially notify the tenant well before the end of the contract that you do not intend to renew it. If you do not do this correctly, the contract can be regarded as renewed for two years at the same rent.

## HOLIDAY RENTALS HAVE SEPARATE RULES

The new law does not affect short-term holiday rental contracts, called *arrienda de temporada*. These holiday contracts do not grant the tenant any right to automatic extension. They require that the tenant vacate the property when the contract ends.

Foreign property owners can be assured of this legal protection when they let their holiday homes for periods of several months. However, they should still take some care with vetting tenants because the legal procedures for eviction of a tenant who refuses to leave can take more than six months, even when the law is on the landlord's side.

There have been a number of recent cases in which unscrupulous tenants have signed up for holiday rentals, say for two months, and then simply remained in the apartment without paying any further rent. Four to six months later, the landlord is able to obtain an eviction order, but the tenants have lived rent-free for that period. Even though a court enters a judgement against them for the amount of the rent owed, they simply move to another town and do the same thing all over again.

## LANDLORDS, BE WARY

If you are a property owner and you wish to let your own flat or villa in Spain or go into the tourist accommodation business, you must be very careful about the terms of your contracts and the quality of your tenants.

The opportunity to pay off your property by letting it looks tempting on paper and in most cases it can work out to your entire satisfaction, but sometimes problems arise and you need to be wary.

Tenants may damage your furniture or harm your plumbing and electrical installations. Letting agents may keep your money and allow your apartment to fall into ruin while you are absent.

Or you might fall into the short-term contract trap, when your tenant tries to turn his brief holiday rental into a protected five-year residential let.

In good faith you might rent to a young Spaniard who says he has a six-month work contract in your town and needs a short-term let. Then he moves in his wife and children, who were not mentioned when he signed the contract, and brings in his own furniture,

Then he goes to court to accuse you of coercing him into signing the short-term contract when he really wanted a place

107

to live.  As he lives and works in the town, the court will probably rule in his favour, and you will have to wait five years to recover your property.

The safest way is to let only to people you know and trust. Even then it is a good idea to get the rent in advance and a deposit against possible damages as well. Electric bills always arrive late, so it is best to include an estimated charge in the rent.

If you have a telephone, you will find that having it disconnected and reconnected is an irritating exercise.  But it's worth it. You can get a lock for it, but that is never quite sufficient. Perhaps the best idea is to have the sort of phone you can unplug from the wall and remove. There have been many, many problems with telephones.

Another important fact the property owner going into long-term letting should be aware of is the right of the residential tenant to first refusal if the property is put up for sale. See **Right of first refusal** in the section on Renting in Spain below.

## LETTING AGENCIES

If you want to let your property on a casual basis and for only a few short periods each year, you will most likely let by word of mouth to people you know or to people recommended by friends.

If you want to let on a more regular basis, you will probably use an agency or holiday company.  You might find that your apartment block, or urbanisation has an office with a letting service that, for a commission, will handle all the details for you.

You might deal with one of the foreign companies that bring people to Spain for self-catering holidays. These kind of holidays are becoming more and more popular and the holiday companies are always looking for new properties to let.

Or you might choose to have a real estate agency in Spain handle your letting. Whatever you choose, try to find out if the agent or company is reputable and trustworthy. Talk to owners who have used them to see if they have been satisfied with the service.

You should also read their contracts carefully and pay special attention to clauses concerning compensation in the case of damage to your property. In the case of longer lets through an agency in Spain, make sure your letting agent is not empowered to sign extensions of contracts or make new contracts without your knowledge and consent.

## NON-RESIDENT RENTAL TAX

It is quite legal and proper for you, as either a resident or non-resident property owner in Spain, to rent out your property, but remember you should declare your rental income for Spanish income tax.

Even if your tenant pays you in British pounds before he leaves for Spain, legally this income arises in Spain because the property is in Spain. It is almost certainly true that many owners who let their property occasionally on a casual basis say nothing about it to the tax authorities and the chances of their getting caught are slim. Nevertheless, Spanish income tax is due on any income arising in Spain.

If you are a non-resident, you are liable for Spanish non-resident income tax of 25 per cent from the very first euro of rental income, declared on form 210. You may not take advantage of the new reduction of 50 per cent introduced for resident landlords in 2003.

If you are renting your property on a regular basis and dealing with short-term visitors throughout the year and providing hotel-type services, you should register your property as a tourist letting accommodation, which means inspectors will come to inspect standards.

When you let your property legally, you can put down the maintenance expenses of your property as a business expense and deduct this from your tax.

## RENTING IN SPAIN

If you decide to rent in Spain, you will find thousands of apartments and villas at prices to suit every pocket.

Some of them are very basically equipped little flats designed for self-catering holidays and often rented through agents in Britain, Holland or Germany. Others are real homes, being let by their owners in the hope of making a little money from their property until they can retire to enjoy it full time.

For those coming to Spain to live, it is a good idea to rent a place in the area where they hope to live permanently, so they can make a careful survey of local conditions before buying. Renting may also be the best plan for people whose capital is in sound investments and who do not wish to tie it up in property.

When you have found a flat or a villa that suits your needs, you will be asked to sign a rental contract.

**Foreign Contract**

If you are renting a holiday flat for a self-catering visit to Spain, you will probably find this contract in your own language, to be signed in your own country before you leave with the rental company handling the property.

This is perfectly all right. Just make sure the rental company has a sound reputation. Sometimes the accommodation promised you does not measure up to your expectations, so be alert. See below for How to Complain in Spain.

The contract forms are usually quite standard, including a list of all the equipment and furnishings, and requiring a deposit to cover any damages the tenant may cause. There is not normally any dispute about the return of this deposit if you have left the flat in good condition.

If you have seen the way some holidaymakers leave their rented flats, you would understand why the companies insist on this deposit.

**Spanish Contract**

If you are already in Spain when you rent, you will also be asked to sign a contract. It will specify the amount of the rent, the manner of payment, any deposit and the time period.

The contract will be headed, *por temporada,* which means

110

short-term. This is to distinguish it from a long-term rental, called *vivienda,* or residence, because long-term tenants have rights which short-term tenants do not.

A *temporada* contract might even be as long as one year. There is no specific time limit past which a contract becomes long-term.

However, unless otherwise specified in your short-term rental contract, the landlord may put you out at the end of the period stated, or he may offer you a new contract increasing the rent as much as he likes.

These short-term contracts are designed for holiday rentals, not as long-term or permanent residence. Such a *temporada* contract running for one year would be pushing it a little, but the idea is to show the intention of impermanence, so the tenant does not establish full rights. This does not always work as planned. Even short-term tenants can sometimes try to claim a longer contract.

The *vivienda* contract, on the other hand, is meant for those long-term lets when the tenant truly makes the apartment his home. The tenant is much more protected and Spanish law requires that a *vivienda* contract be renewable for a minimum period of five years.

This gives the tenant some stability, as he knows that he has at least this period, and he must be officially notified at least 30 days before the end of the period if the landlord does not intend to renew the contract.

**One-Year Contract**

Let's suppose you want to rent a villa in Spain for a year, or even more, and you find that a rental agency in your home country, or even in Spain, has the perfect house at the right price. They offer you a one-year contract, in German or English, with option to renew. This contract, in your own language, will not say that it is either a *temporada* or a *vivienda* contract. The agency does not think in terms of Spanish law, and they don't expect that you will, either.

This foreign-language contract is perfectly legal, although it would have to be translated into Spanish for any court proceedings, and it is a perfectly good offer and it gives you as the tenant more protection than it gives the landlord.

You can renew the contract if you want. If the landlord refuses to renew the contract and asks you to leave, you can threaten to go to court, claiming that the villa has become your retirement home. You can say that you will ask the court to have the contract extended to the full five years of the long-term let.

Usually, the landlord and the agency will be reluctant to become involved in any legal dispute in Spanish courts because they know they will probably lose their case and maybe they are not declaring all the rental income for Spanish taxes.

Even if the tenant pays the rent in marks or pounds in another country, the income derived from property in Spain is still subject to Spanish tax.

## No Contract

Some owners do not want to make any contracts, which can be perfectly allright, too. Just make sure you have clearly written receipts for the rent you pay, which will constitute an implicit contract. Such an implicit rental contract exists even if you don't have the receipts, as soon as the owner cashes your cheque, but it's better to have some piece of paper as evidence that you have paid rent.

If you are paying month to month in such a situation, the implicit contract ends at the end of each month you pay, or on the date stated on your receipt.

## Registered contract

For full security in your rental, you want your rental contract registered with the housing department. This means that you will have full legal protection in the event of any court case about your rental.

Let's face it, many rental contracts, especially with foreigners, are simply not registered and the landlords are probably not declaring the rental income for tax purposes. Your contract is still valid in court, but only the registered contract, where the landlord is completely legal in his operations, has the full protection of the law.

As we mentioned earlier in the Letting in Spain section, the landlord can ask for a deposit, usually a month´s rent, which can be deposited with an agency independent of the landlord and tenant. Though it is a common practice, it is never a good idea to pay the deposit directly into the landlord's account, as he then is in complete control over whether to release the deposit or not at the end of the let.

## RIGHT OF FIRST REFUSAL

In today's fast-moving Spanish real estate market, one of the important rights acquired by a long-term residential tenant is the right of first refusal when the property is put up for sale.

If the landlord sells the property, he is required by law to offer it first to the long-term tenant. He should do this in writing, stating the price and conditions of the sale. If the tenant does not reply or if he refuses the offer, the landlord is then free to sell the property to anyone he chooses.

If the landlord sells the property without informing the tenant in advance, the tenant even has the right to have this sale anulled and to purchase the property himself at the price declared on the sales contract.

In Spanish this right is called *tanteo y retracto*.

## COMMUNITY FEES

Long-term or *vivienda* contracts often contain provisions requiring the tenant to pay community fees, the dues charged each year by the property owners' collective for that block of flats, and even the real estate taxes, known as the IBI.

An owner is within his rights to make such a contract, but you should be wary and know what you are getting into. Such extra charges can add up. Furthermore, clauses obliging the tenant to pay the community fees and real estate taxes are considered abusive under Spanish law, and you can protest if you choose, even after you have signed the contract.

If these charges are not mentioned in your contract, they are the owner's responsibility and you can refuse any attempt by him to make you pay for them.

To sum up, in strictly legal terms the taxes and fees are for the property owner's account. However, it is not illegal for the landlord and tenant to agree in the contract that the tenant will pay them. As long as you know what you are getting into, and the amounts of these charges are clear, and you as the tenant are disposed to accept the price, then it is okay.

If, however, you feel that you have been deceived by the landlord into signing the contract, you can protest the clause and you will surely win your case.

## FORMAL NOTIFICATION

Be advised that, if you have a five-year *vivienda* contract and your landlord wishes to terminate your rental at the end of the period, he is obliged to notify you officially by a notarised letter one month before the end of the period. If he does not notify you officially, the contract can be regarded as renewed for two years and for the same rent.

In any of these situations, most Europeans will find the tenant to have more protection than is normal in many countries. That is, even though the law states that the rental period is finished, a landlord will have some trouble putting out anyone who chooses to stay. He cannot simply summon a policeman and order you out. He must get a court order for this and the procedure will take some time, even when the law is entirely on the landlord's side.

## HOW TO COMPLAIN

If you feel you have a genuine grievance against your landlord, you can complain. If you are a genuine tourist, the tourist office of the province or town where the property is located will hear your complaint. If you are a semi-permanent resident, you will do better at the O.M.I.C., the *Oficina Municipal de Información al Consumidor.* This is the consumer information office, usually directed by the regional government. Its mission is to deal with consumer problems and these include rents.

## BUSINESS PREMISES

More and more foreigners are coming to Spain to start their own businesses, which of course involves leasing, purchasing or renting a business premise. This is an area where you really need good legal advice.

## LEASING

A Spanish leasehold, which used to be called a *traspaso* but is now known as a *cesión*, gives the lessee the right to re-sell it on to a third party, although he must first offer it to the property owner. If the property owner chooses not to buy back the leasehold at the price asked, the tenant can then sell it to another person, with the landlord having the right to perhaps 10 per cent of the sale.

The new type of leasehold called *cesión* is less rigid than the old *traspaso*, and there is no exact legal format required. A property owner and a business tenant can agree on any conditions they choose, which often means that the deal is much more like a normal rental contract. These business rentals or leases are usually open-ended, with no final cut-off point as long as the tenant continues to pay the rent.

## WATCH OUT

Be particularly alert to the terms of any lease or rental contract you purchase from a presently operating business. Quite often it will be presented as a leasehold when it is simply a rental agreement which gives the tenant no rights to any of the profit from re-selling it.

When you are asked to pay a large sum of money for a "leasehold", you want to be very sure that you are buying something which you will later have the right to sell.

It is best to take legal advice before you get into a Spanish lease.

**GLOSSARY**

**Alquiler** – Rental

**Arrendamiento** – Rental, lease

**Cesión** – Lease

**Contrato de Vivienda** – Long-term residential contract

**Contrato por Temporada** – Short-term holiday contract

**Fianza** – Deposit

**Inquilino** – tenant

**Ley de Arrendamiento Urbano** – Rental law

**Propietario** – Owner, landlord

**Tanteo y Retracto** – Right of first refusal to buy property

**Traspaso** – Old form of leasehold

# 7   You and your car & On the road

## YOU AND YOUR CAR

When you move to Spain, do you sell your old car and buy a Spanish one?

Can you take your present car with you and keep it in Spain on its UK or other European registration?

If you do, what happens after you've spent some time in Spain?

Can you import the car and register it in Spain?

Can you keep your foreign-plated car in Spain to use on your holiday visits?

If you become a resident, do you have to have a car on Spanish registration?

Let's take a look at these questions one by one.

## CARS WITH FOREIGN REGISTRATION

Let's suppose that you already own a car with British or German registration. If you are a tourist in Spain, you can operate such a car for six months in a calendar year with no formalities beyond the presentation at the border of your driving licence, car registration and insurance certificate. That is, if anyone bothers to stop you at the frontier.

You can keep your foreign-registered car in Spain permanently, but you will have to garage it for six months of each year. You can only drive it on Spanish roads for six months.

With Spain's entry into the EU, the international insurance certificate, or so-called "green card", is no longer necessary, but you may find that your individual policy gives only minimum coverage when you are outside your country without it, so check to be sure.

Your driving licence from your home country will be acceptable for the first six months of your stay in Spain, though authorities recommend that you have either an international driving licence or an official translation of your licence, which you can get from the Spanish consulate in your home country.

Neither the translation nor the international licence is absolutely necessary if you are an EU citizen. For more on licences, see the next chapter.

118

If you own a vacation home in Spain that you visit at Christmas time and in the summer, you can freely operate your foreign-registered car, using your foreign driving licence, with no further problems, as long as your total visits to Spain don't pass six months in any calendar year. The six months need not be continuous. It could be three visits of two months each, for example.

Because this period lies in a calendar year, it has this peculiarity: if the visitor enters Spain after June 30, he can keep and operate his foreign-registered car for the last six months of that year, and the first six months of the following year.

The six-month period is based on the stay of the person himself in the country, rather than on the length of stay of the car. That is, a European who stays in Spain for four months without a car, then decides to return to his home country and bring his car back with him, can only operate the car in Spain for another two months. He can keep it in Spain but he can't legally drive it.

So how do they know whether or not you are driving the car? Good question. For European Union citizens, there really is no effective way to know whether the car is being driven or not. They formerly were required to have the car officially "sealed" for six months of each year, but EU citizens no longer have to do this.

If you go to the trouble of obtaining exit and entry stamps in your passport, you will have definite proof of the length of your stay.

## WARNING: SPANISH POLICE ARE CHECKING FOREIGN-PLATE CARS

We all know that many Europeans really live fulltime in Spain without obtaining a residence card, perhaps working illegally as well, and continue to operate their cars on non-Spanish plates.

The Spanish traffic police have been very lenient about these cars in the past but they are now starting to crack down. In some areas where many foreigners live, they have stopped the cars they see regularly on the road and politely asked the drivers to clarify their situation.

When the UE driver says that he comes and goes and that he is never in Spain for more than six months in one year, the police politely ask him for documentary evidence.

They understand that it is difficult to produce a passport stamp inside the UE these days, so they will accept practically any paper, such as a recently dated airline ticket or train ticket or any other evidence that the person has travelled within the last six months.

If you are coming to Spain by car, we advise you to take all the trouble necessary to obtain an exit stamp from your home country. Even if you have to go and search for a border officer, take the time and do it. This proof of your date of departure can be very handy later.

The police are also interested to observe whether the car is insured in its country of origin, or whether it is insured by one of the international companies. EU legislation requires that a car be insured in its country of registration. This means that no Spanish company can insure a vehicle registered in another country.

This is a problem because your home country's insurance companies will not insure the car without a valid inspection certificate. And you cannot obtain this because your car is in Spain. The Spanish vehicle inspection is not legally valid in your home country, although some international insurance companies will accept it.

The police also observe the last date of the vehicle inspection. If it is a UK car, and its last MOT in Britain dates from 10 years ago, this would arouse suspicion. The law says that a foreign-registered car may stay in Spain as long as it is road legal in its home country. This means that a UK car must have a current MOT. In practice the police do not usually insist on this but they can do so if they choose.

If the car has been inspected in Spain, in order to obtain the insurance, this is another piece of evidence. If the driver cannot produce any documents to prove his own absence from Spain, they have levied fines of €1,800 and more. They then require that the car be either imported into Spain and issued with Spanish registration, or immediately taken out of the country. You have been warned.

## NON-EU CITIZENS' CARS ARE SUBJECT TO SEALING

Non-EU citizens, such as Americans and Canadians, are still subject to the sealing requirement if they wish to keep their foreign-registered cars permanently in Spain.

It works like this:

If you decide to stay in Spain after your six-month period is up, and you do not wish to drive your car out of the country, you can ask the Spanish customs officials to "seal" the car for you until you wish to remove it.

To have your car sealed, or *precintado*, you notify the customs officials, a*duana*. They in turn notify the Guardia Civil, who will come, fill out the forms, and put some strips of tape across the steering wheel of the car, designed to ensure that you do not use it. The process is not expensive.

When you are ready to depart with the car, contact the customs office again and they will unseal the car.

You can then use the car six months, have it sealed until the end of the year, and use it again for the first six months of the following year. This sealing provision is useful for people who wish to keep their foreign-registered car in Spain all year round, but who only operate the car during their visits here.

Further, if you are not an EU citizen, you are required to have the car sealed if you leave it in Spain for more than two months while you yourself are absent. This sealing procedure applies only to non-EU citizens.

This is all very well, you say, for a tourist or a regular visitor, but I intend to take up full-time residence in Spain, and I want to know if I can keep my foreign-registered car with me and use it on Spanish roads.

No, you can't. An official resident of Spain must operate a car on full and normal Spanish registration. There is no way around this. After all, a Spaniard living and working in the UK would not be allowed to keep his Spanish-registered car forever, either.

## TAX-FREE IMPORTATION

Anyone, EU or non-EU, moving to Spain to take up official residence gets a break if they want to bring with them a car they already own.

This car will be exempt from import duties, from Spanish IVA of 16 per cent, and from Spain's own special registration tax of 12 per cent or 7 per cent, a noteworthy saving of 28 per cent.

If the vehicle has less than 1600 cubic centimetres, the special tax is only seven per cent. The 7 per cent also applies to diesel vehicles under 2,000 cubic centimetres.

For Europeans, of course, there are no duties in any case, but for other nationalities the exemption from Spain's 10-per cent import duty comes in handy.

The conditions for the exemption are that you must have owned the car for at least six months, you must have paid VAT in the country of origin and you must obtain a certificate of *baja de residencia*, a certificate of non-residence, from the country you are leaving.

Some nationalities can obtain this certificate from the town hall where they live. It can also consist of a declaration made to the Spanish consulate in your home country, declaring your intention to leave your residence and reside officially in Spain. Or you can make the declaration to your own consulate inside Spain after you arrive, stating that you are taking up residence in Spain.

The consulate will then issue the certificate, allowing you to apply for tax-exempt importation of your car.

Warning: Procedures to import a car this way must be started within one month from the date of issue of the residence permit. Be careful here because you may very well receive your actual residence permit, which you must present, several months after the issue date stamped on it

Really, it is best to apply for the car exemption at the same time you apply for your residence card. Because of this complication and the rest of the red tape involved in this application, you will need the services of an expert *gestor*, but it can be done.

Even without paying any taxes, the procedure will cost you around €700 for the various papers involved.

Remember that any concession on the duty-free import of cars applies only to people who take out an official residence permit. Such persons have always been able to import their household effects and furniture into Spain free of duty (see section on "Importing Your Possessions"), but automobiles formerly were not included.

## CARS ON TOURIST PLATES

Real savings are available to non-EU persons who remain non-residents and purchase a new car on Spanish tourist plates. This is the "export" registration provided by a number of countries.

An American tourist, for example, can purchase his Mercedes-Benz directly from the factory in Germany, drive it around Europe for six months on the "Z" plates issued to him, without paying any of the normal German taxes.

He will finally import the car into the United States, pay duty on a used car, and have it definitively registered. This registration is designed, by its nature, to be temporary, lasting only until the car is taken to its new home, where taxes are paid.

An American who buys a €30,000 vehicle on Spanish tourist plates can save himself almost €10,000 by skipping Spain's total taxes of 28 per cent. He can have the car to use for a total of six months in any calendar year. These six months need not be continuous. He can make several visits as long as the total time does not exceed six months.

He is also required to have this tourist-plate car *precintado*, or sealed, if he is absent from Spain for more than two months. (See above).

If he wishes to have the car available for use twelve months of the year, he can renew this tourist registration every year indefinitely. One *gestoria* cited a total cost, including their fees, of around €600 for each renewal. This means twice a year. If the tourist plate has expired, the renewal fee is much higher. If you keep the car permanently in one town, they will charge you annual municipal vehicle tax as well.

123

The only requirements are that the car must be purchased with foreign currency and it cannot be bought on hire purchase.

Meanwhile, official residents and Spaniards themselves are paying the full freight of 28 per cent on each car they buy on normal Spanish registration.

## BUYING A CAR ON SPANISH PLATES

Buying a car on Spanish plates, just the way Spaniards do, can save a lot of complications and has certain advantages. You do not have to pay in foreign currency and you can purchase on the instalment plan. Britons in particular will find that new Spanish cars are priced much lower than the same models in the UK.

A foreigner may buy a car on Spanish plates if he meets one of the following qualifications:

1.  He holds an official residence permit.

2.  He presents the title deed - *escritura* - to a home he owns in Spain. The deed must be for a dwelling, not a place of business, and it must be in the personal name of the foreigner, not in the name of a company, especially an offshore company.

3.  He presents a *certificado de empadronamiento*, a certificate showing that he is a registered inhabitant of the municipality whose town hall issues the document. This is not a residence permit; it is only a registration certificate showing that the person lives in that municipality. You get this certificate by presenting your passport, a title deed or rental contract at your town hall.

4.  He presents a rental contract of one year's duration.

**Note of caution:** If you are a non-resident and you buy a car on Spanish registration, make sure that you obtain one of the following documents:

1.  An International Driving Permit to carry in addition to your home country licence.

2.  An official translation of your driving licence, often available through the Spanish Consulate in your home country.

124

3. A *Certificado de Equivalencia,* a "Certificate of Equivalence", which is prepared by Spain's Royal Automobile Club, the *RACE.*

This applies to both EU and non-EU citizens. The reason for this is that Spanish traffic police want somebody who is regularly on Spanish roads, and not merely a tourist visitor, to carry a licence they can read and understand. You can be fined 300 if you do not comply.

When you make the rounds of auto dealers in your part of Spain, collecting brochures and comparing prices, you will find many makes and models available, at prices in some cases a little lower than in the rest of Europe. Renaults, Fords, Opels, Seats, Citroëns, all manufactured in Spain, are among the best sellers. Dealers compete in offering guarantees, financing terms and special sales.

Besides these Spanish-manufactured cars, you can also find dealers specialising in imported cars on Spanish plates. Imported cars have actually captured 25 per cent of the Spanish market.

If you are a new arrival and don't own property, you may be asked to provide some financial certification that you can pay for the car, or even be required to find a Spanish co-signer to guarantee your payments.

You make a deposit on the car, which will vary from dealer to dealer, and agree terms from one to four years. Interest rates have come down on these plans as competition grows keener.

If you decide on a two-year scheme, for example, you will make your down payment and then sign a series of 24 *letras*, or bills of exchange, for the instalments. These *letras* oblige you to make the payments and are often addressed directly to your bank account for payment.

## GOVERNMENT OFFERS €721 OFF

If you have an older used car that is ready for the junk-heap, you can take advantage of a Spanish government offer to reduce your new-car costs.

Under the Prever plan, designed to encourage the scrapping of thousands of old cars circulating on Spanish roads, the

125

government will reduce your registration tax by • 480.80 when you buy a new car and junk the old one.

If your old clunker burns regular leaded gasoline and you scrap it to buy a new car that burns unleaded fuel, the offer goes up to €721.

You will usually find that the dealer can handle all the necessary paperwork for you, as well as sell you your car insurance. Full coverage is usually required if you buy your car on the instalment plan.

## MUNICIPAL VEHICLE TAX

You pay your vehicle tax each year at the town hall. If you are not paid up, you will not be able to sell or trade in the car later.

This is the *impuesto municipal sobre vehículos de tracción mecánica*, a municipal tax on vehicles registered in each town. Formerly this tax was charged at a single rate all over Spain, but now each municipality is free to charge whatever rate it sees fit, so the tax varies from town to town.

It is based on the *potencia fiscal* of the car, its horsepower as rated for tax purposes. Small cars pay something around €50 and large cars €100 and even more. Motor-cycles also pay this tax each year.

Your car will go on the books of the town where you live as soon as you are registered as the owner of the car with the traffic authorities in the provincial capital.

You pay the tax by going into the town hall and asking for the appropriate window. April and May are the usual times to pay it, but this varies from town to town. You will not necessarily receive an individual notification, but announcements will appear in banks, in the newspaper and on the municipal notice-board. It's best to ask when the tax is due. Late payment will draw a fine of 5 per cent during the first month and 20 per cent thereafter.

Many municipalities are now offering local taxpayers a carrot and stick progamme, in which those who pay their taxes early get a discount.

You can also arrange to have the tax paid by standing order at your bank.

126

This vehicle circulation tax receipt is one of the papers you should keep with you in your car, along with the car's official registration papers and insurance receipt, as the police may ask to see it at any time. You cannot sell your car or trade it in for a new model without the paid-up vehicle tax receipt.

## USED CARS

There is an active market in used cars in Spain, with many makes and models available. You now find used-car dealers in any town and the new-car dealers have their own used-car departments, where they recondition and sell older cars taken as trade-ins for new ones. Dealers offer widely varying guarantees, prices and service, so be sure to shop around.

A resident can purchase a second-hand car on Spanish plates, just as if he were a Spaniard. You may be unpleasantly surprised at the high prices for second-hand cars, but that is the way the market is in Spain. As we have seen, taxes on automobiles are higher than in most other European countries, and in most parts of Spain the good weather ensures that cars deteriorate less rapidly than they do in many other parts of the world.

Many of the used cars available here are former rental cars. The Costa del Sol in fact may be the world's capital of hire cars, as those thousands of tourists who pick up their cars every week at Málaga airport attest.

Sometimes you can find a real bargain directly from a car hire company disposing of its two-year-old cars, and sometimes you find a real lemon being passed off by a dealer as a privately-owned car. Be alert.

The dealer who sells you your second-hand car will probably be quite happy to arrange the transfer of title to you for a small fee. In a private sale, you and the seller can go to a *gestoría* that handles automobile transfers.

You can also go directly to the *Jefatura de Tráfico*, the motor vehicle department in your province, and handle the whole thing yourself, thus saving any intermediary's fees. To do this you will need:

1. The application form, which you obtain at the provincial traffic department.

2.  The Circulation Permit of the vehicle, with the transfer of owners listed on the back, including the seller's signature.

3.  The paid-up municipal vehicle tax receipt, along with a photocopy.

4.  Receipt for the payment of the vehicle transfer tax, charged at 4 per cent on the sale of second-hand vehicles. This tax is paid to Hacienda.

5.  A current ITV report and photocopy. This is the *Inspección Tecnica de Vehiculos*, the vehicle inspection certificate.

6.  Residence permit and photocopy.

You will have to pay a €40.20 fee and present all your documentation at the traffic department, including a stamped, self-addressed envelope for them to send you the finished documents.

## TAKE CARE WITH CAR TRANSFER

Be wary of handling the used-car transaction on your own, however. If you are selling your own old car to a new owner, make absolutely sure that the transfer is completed into the new owner's name. Otherwise, you may find that the new owner conveniently forgets to register the car in his own name, which leaves you as the still-registered owner liable for any parking tickets or road tax that come due on the car.

If you fear that this may be the case, you must then have the vehicle de-registered in your name. This is called a *baja de matricula*.

Again, you obtain the form from the traffic department, and you must present the receipt for the current year's municipal vehicle tax. If you no longer have the circulation permit and the inspection certificate, because they are with the new owner, you can make a sworn declaration of this.

You must also make this application for *baja* when you junk an old car. Sometimes you think that the car is off the road when it has in fact been repaired and someone totally unknown

128

to you is illegally operating it. Make the de-registration and you will be protected from later consequences.

## INSPECTION REQUIRED

Vehicle inspection of older cars is compulsory for Spanish-registered cars. Cars more than four years old must be inspected. So be alert when purchasing an older car, and ask for the *Inspección Técnica de Vehículos* certificate. If the car doesn't have one, you have to have the car tested yourself if you want to use it on public roads, and there's no guarantee it will pass the test. When you hear Spaniards say ITV, they mean MOT.

## BUYING USED CARS IN EUROPE

With Spain's entry into the Common Market, people begin to ask whether they can go to Belgium or any other EU country and buy a used car and import it into Spain, because Spanish used cars tend to be more expensive than used cars in most countries.

Automobile depreciation is much quicker in countries like Germany, Holland and Belgium. One estimate calculated that a mid-level BMW about two years old could be bought and imported from Germany at a saving of about 25 per cent, including the payment of Spain's special registration tax of 12 per cent.

Be warned, however, that there is plenty of paperwork and delay. Experienced *gestores* report that the process takes more than three months; that the testing and registration fees can easily reach €600, in addition to the special tax.

They also advise the prospective importer to make sure the original factory invoice for the car is available and to have the vehicle inspected and certified roadworthy in its country of origin even before it enters Spain.

## BOATS, CARAVANS, MOTOR-CYCLES

Boats, caravans and motor-cycles with engines of more than 49 c.c. are treated basically the same as cars, but with a few differences.

## Boats

You can enter a Spanish port with your foreign-registered yacht and keep it there and use it in Spanish waters for six months of a calendar year, just as with cars. The six-month period need not be continuous; an advantage for people who want to keep their yacht in a Spanish port, but can only use it for a month or two at a time on extended visits.

The customs authorities in the marina can seal the boat *(precintar)* while its owner is away, and unseal it when he wishes to use it. Thus, the non-resident can keep his boat in a Spanish port all year and use it for six months of that year.

Like cars, yachts are also available from dealers in Spain on a Spanish tourist flag registration, under which they do not pay normal Spanish taxes. Such a yacht can be used six months of the year, and an extension of its tourist registration requested each year to permit its owner to use it all year.

One useful provision of the sealing process for the non-resident yacht owner is that he can have his boat sealed for the last six months of the year and continue to live aboard it. He may not sail it out of the harbour, but he can use it as his home.

Import duties on a used yacht still come to something more than half the value of the boat, depending on the evaluation the customs authorities make. In addition, you can only import the boat if you are taking up official residence in Spain.

## Caravans

Caravans are treated almost exactly like cars. That is, if you enter Spain with your caravan pulled by your car, you have six months in the calendar year to circulate freely as a tourist. You can also have the caravan sealed by the customs officials should you wish to leave it behind and drive out with your car.

## Motor-Cycles

Motor cycles with engines of more than 49 c.c. are treated exactly like cars, with the same six-month time limit.

The small 49 c.c. motor bikes are a different story. You do not need a *certificado de empadronamiento* or any other document to purchase one, and you can even import your foreign-registered bike duty-free as part of your personal possessions when you take up residence in Spain.

Initially your foreign licence and, later, your foreign licence with its translation, or an international permit, will be valid for these bikes. Your Spanish driving licence will also be valid.

If, like some people, you have no driving licence at all but want to operate one of these convenient little bikes for dashing around town, you can get a special licence to do so by taking a simple examination. Most driving schools can steer you through the process for a small fee.

Even a child of 14 can get this licence and operate his own bike, a boon for parents who are tired of driving their offspring into town and back. The child will have to show that he possesses a school certificate and must pass a simple examination, in Spanish, on the rules of the road. The child of 14 to 16 years also requires a statement of parental consent.

After the age of 16, the child gets this *moto* licence the same way as an adult. At 18, he can get a regular driving licence. And don't forget to warn him that he must wear a helmet both in town and on the highway, or he will be fined.

## INSURING YOUR CAR

If you are visiting Spain, either for a short or extended stay, and you are still on tourist status and driving your foreign-registered car, all the auto insurance you need is the coverage by your insurance company in your home country, extended to cover travel in Spain.

Your own company can issue you a "green card", as the international insurance certificate is popularly known. If you are from an EU country, you no longer need to present this to the Spanish border officials when you enter, but it is still a good idea to have it even if there are no longer any border guards at all, because some insurance companies limit their coverage to the legal minimum outside their own national borders, unless the policy holder has arranged for his green card.

## Spanish Cars

Let's suppose that you have just purchased your Spanish car, on tourist plates or on normal Spanish registration, new or second-hand. The dealer who sells it to you will either have an insurance company representative as part of his organisation or will be happy to steer you to his brother-in-law who sells auto insurance. His brother-in-law's company may be fine, but it also pays to shop around, or at least ask among other foreign residents in your area to recommend a company.

If you are buying a new car on instalments, you may have little choice in what insurance you want. The dealer usually requires you to have full-coverage insurance on the car until it is paid off.

For a small car, this all-risk - *todo riesgo* - insurance will cost you between €1,200 and €1,800, depending on whether you are an excitable young man or a prudent woman of mature years.

These personal details are factored into your premium as insurance companies become more sophisticated. On the other hand, you can drive legally for as little as €400 a year, or even less, with a 50 per cent discount as a no-claims bonus. This price will cover the obligatory insurance, required by Spanish law. It now covers you for claims by third parties up to the amount of €360,000 for bodily harm and €100,000 for damages.

A "third party" is anyone who makes a claim against you for injury or damage caused by your car. It includes driver and passengers in another car with which you may collide. It may include even passengers in your own car who are not members of your family. It includes pedestrians, and the owners of any property you may damage. If you drive your car into someone's wall and knock it down, the wall's owner can make a claim against you.

This minimum insurance does not cover you or your car at all. It covers only other persons and their property, and only up to the limits above. This coverage is the legal minimum.

If you are injured by a driver who has no insurance at all, the Spanish insurance consortium, which backs the entire industry, will pay out amounts up to these limits. The Spanish limits used to be even lower but they are gradually being raised. This of course means a corresponding rise in premiums.

If you want further coverage, you can take out additional insurance, and most people do. For a few hundred euros more, you can get the same third-party coverage, but up to much higher sums or even unlimited, which means no ceiling on what the company will pay in the case of a terrible accident with very high claims.

You can choose just what you need to insure - yourself and your family, for example, who do not count as third parties, or your shiny new car. You can buy coverage against theft, fire, damage, death or injury, and even insurance to pay for legal costs involved in court proceedings brought against you or which you have to bring against another driver when claiming damages. You can get comprehensive insurance covering all these or a policy covering only part.

Let's look at a few possibilities. Total coverage can cost you €1,000 or more depending on the size and age of your car, but you can get quite a lot of protection by taking out a policy under which you yourself pay the first €200 or so of any small damage to your car. This exemption is called a *franquicia*. Because you promise to pay this much, the company saves quite a lot of expense in administration and paperwork, and you get your major coverage more cheaply.

A typical policy might be one in which you pay the first €300 of any claim against you and you are insured for:

1. The full value of the car in cases of fire or accident.

2. Up to 80 per cent of its value in case of theft.

3. Coverage for you and your family in case of death or permanent injury.

4. Coverage of your legal expenses.

5. Unlimited coverage for third-party claims against you.

This should cost around €700 a year for a mid-sized car. Over the years you will get a discount on your premiums as a "no-claims bonus" if there are no claims against your policy.

Finally, if your car is insured in Spain and you wish to drive it to an EU country, your Spanish insurance will cover you, but only for the legal minimum in each country, so it is a good idea to take out a green card for your trip out of Spain. Some companies charge extra for the green cards. Others offer it as a free service.

## FOREIGN CARS IN SPAIN

Many foreigners stay for long periods in Spain as non-residents, keeping their foreign-plated cars with them.

Legally, a foreign-registered car can stay on Spanish roads for six months in a calendar year without any formalities at all. In fact, the car itself can remain in Spain permanently, although it can only be operated on the road for six months of that year and must be garaged for the other six months.

The new problem for these cars comes from European Union regulations that now require all cars to be insured in their country of registration. Formerly, the owners of these British or other cars simply insured them with Spanish companies. They can no longer do this. Nor can they obtain insurance from the UK because the car has never been returned for its MOT and it is no longer a UK resident, as it were.

Some insurance companies have come up with a sort of off-shore insurance that will cover the car in any country except its original home. If you are in this situation, ask your insurance broker. With the European liberalisation of insurance companies, there are also Spanish branches of UK companies that will insure the car on UK plates.

These companies will require your car to pass the Spanish vehicle safety inspection, the ITV, to make sure it is in sound operating condition. You get your ITV sticker, which satisfies the insurance company but has no other legal force. Your car, if it is British-registered, remains illegal in the UK because it has no British MOT. Technically, the car is not legal in Spain either without its UK MOT, but police seldom ask. If you take it back to the UK, you will have to pass the MOT immediately.

What you really want to know is what happens when you make a claim? Will the Spanish insurance company pay you? The short answer is Spanish insurance companies are just as reluctant to pay out as most other companies, but they are also prepared to live up to their legal obligations.

If you have full coverage and someone dents your new car in the parking lot and departs without leaving his name, you will probably find that your insurance company pays up quickly and without a murmur for the repairs, but you may lose any credit you have been getting as a no-claims bonus. If the claim is not your fault, many companies will continue your credit.

On the other hand, if there is an accident and you feel the other driver is at fault but he chooses to contest this, you may have to wait as long as three years for a court decision in back logged Spanish courts.

## IF YOU HAVE AN ACCIDENT

So some idiot has darted out of a side street without looking and pranged your new car. Or perhaps you yourself were careless, following too close, and banged into the car in front of you.

In Spain procedures to follow after an accident are much the same as in any country. The police may appear and take all the details of both drivers. Or, in the case of smaller accidents, the two drivers can settle the matter between themselves.

You must be sure to get the licence number, the name and the insurance company of the other driver. Do not be intimidated by any shouted threats. It is an upsetting situation, but try to keep your wits about you.

Remember that you have two months in order to bring a charge against the other driver. If you are sure that he is at fault, it is better to do this immediately, but it is not absolutely necessary. If you live in Spain, the normal procedure will be to contact your insurance agent quickly. He will lead you through the process.

If you wish to make a charge, you go to the local police station, make a declaration and then let the insurance companies sort it out. Even if it seems clear that the fault is yours, do not be too quick to admit it. Again, let the insurance company handle it.

The Spanish courts do function. A friend of mine saw a car back into her own car in a parking lot, crumpling the door. As the offending driver fled, she was able to get the licence number of the car. She traced the owner through this number, went to the police station and made a charge against him.

Two years later, she was summoned to a court hearing, where the other driver denied everything. The court ruled in her favour, however, and ordered the other driver to pay for all damages plus court costs, which his insurance company paid. Two years was a long time to wait, but there is a satisfaction when justice is done.

## ON THE ROAD

A genuine tourist visiting Spain and driving either his own car from his own country or a Spanish rental car can do so on the licence issued to him in his home country. He needs no translation or official certification to do this, and the privilege is good for a visit up to six months.

After that it gets more complicated.

## WHO NEEDS WHAT LICENCE?

### EU citizen, non-resident

If you are driving a vehicle you own on normal Spanish registration, you must have one of the following extra documents:

1.  An International Driving Permit in addition to your home country licence.

2.  An official translation of your driving licence, often available through the Spanish Consulate in your home country.

3.  A *Certificado de Equivalencia,* a "Certificate of Equivalence", prepared by Spain's Royal Automobile Club, the *RACE.*

This applies to both EU and non-EU citizens who own cars on normal Spanish registration. The reason for the exercise is that Spanish traffic police want somebody who is regularly on Spanish roads and not merely a tourist visitor, to carry a licence they can read and understand.

If you do not have one of these extra documents, you can be fined €300 for carrying an improper licence.

## EU citizen, resident

If you are an EU citizen who is resident in Spain you will need one of the following documents:
1. Spanish driving licence.

2. Your home driving licence stamped by the Spanish traffic department.

It is very easy now to exchange your EU driving licence for a Spanish permit. Go to your provincial traffic headquarters with your present licence and a photocopy, one photograph and your residence card and photocopy. If you are lucky and the line is short, you can get your Spanish licence within a few hours. The cost is only €16.20. This exchange procedure is called *canje*.

If you later return to your home country, you can re-exchange your Spanish licence for a home country licence, just as you did here, only in reverse. Your home country licence must be stamped by the provincial traffic department, the *Jefatura de Trafico*.

Spain allows EU citizens who take out a Spanish residence permit to continue using their original licences. However, the driver must take this licence to his provincial traffic headquarters, where it is registered in the Spanish list of drivers and violators, in the computer, and is stamped.

If he does not do this, and simply continues using his home licence, he can be fined €300 for improper licence.

## Non-EU citizen, non-resident

For the first six months of your stay in Spain, driving your car on its home country registration or driving a rental car, you can simply use your home country licence with no problem. If you cannot document your absence from Spain in the past six months, you can be fined €300 for improper licence. Spanish traffic police know that many foreigners are staying in Spain over their legal time limit, and they are starting to crack down on this practice.

If you are driving a vehicle that you own on Spanish registration, you must have:
1. An International Driving Permit to carry in addition to your home country licence.

137

2. Or an official translation of your driving licence, often available through the Spanish Consulate in your home country.

3. Or a *Certificado de Equivalencia,* a "Certificate of Equivalence", which is prepared by Spain's Royal Automobile Club, the *RACE.*

This applies to both EU and non-EU citizens. The reason for the exercise is that Spanish traffic police want somebody who is regularly on Spanish roads and not merely a tourist visitor, to carry a licence they can read and understand.

**Non-EU citizen, resident**

Now things start to get tough for the non-European Union citizen. He absolutely must have a Spanish driving licence when he becomes a resident of Spain. There is no alternative.

Furthermore, he cannot exchange his home country licence for a Spanish one. Because the European Union is still working out its international agreements on driving licences, no non-EU licence can be exchanged at this time, and for the immediate future.

This means that Americans, Swiss, Australians, and so on must take the Spanish driving examination, both written and practical, just as beginning Spanish drivers do.

Furthermore, they must take the written exam in Spanish. Formerly the exam could be taken in several languages but now it is only in Spanish. Really, it is only logical. A person who does not know that *peligro* means "danger" could get into trouble.

Furthermore, the non-EU citizen must attend a Spanish driving school, and pay its fees, in order to take the exam. The Spanish *autoescuelas* have got a hammer lock on the system and have become semi-official bodies. You cannot go for the exam without the school.

A rock-bottom price for a few classes on the rules of the road, and a few driving classes, plus the exam cost, would be about €500. And of course you must take the eye and reaction test as well.

The minimum age for a B licence, the most usual sort, is 18 and the maximum age is 65, if you have never held a licence before. If you are 68 years old when you arrive in Spain, don't worry. The 65-year figure applies only to first-timers. You can continue to renew your existing permit as long as you are physically able to drive safely. If you are under 45, your licence will be issued for 10 years; between 45 and 70, for five years. Those over 70 will have to renew their licence every two years, which means a medical examination each time.

## REVISED LAW REQUIRES REFLECTING VEST

Spain's 2004 revised traffic code for the first time requires all vehicles to carry reflecting vests or jackets for night safety, as well as the two red triangles previously required. As of July, 2004, all cars must carry one vest. They come in various colours and cost less than 10 euros.

The law also stiffens penalties for speeding and for drunk driving. For the first time, police can retain the licence of a driver they estimate is not in condition to operate a vehicle. Drunk drivers face maximum penalties of licence suspended for one year, and even a possible six months in jail.

Exceeding the speed limit by 50 per cent (and at least 30 kph) becomes a "very serious" infraction, with fines up to €602 and suspension of driving licence for three months.

This would include someone driving at 150 kph on a normal highway with a limit of 100 kph, for example. Or someone blasting his brand-new BMW at 180 on the motorway, where the limit is 120 kph. Speeding violations that do not exceed the limit by 50 per cent remain in the merely "serious" category.

Violations are divided into three categories: very serious (*muy grave*), serious (*grave*), and minor (*menor*).

**Very serious** violations, incurring fines from €302 to €602 and suspension of licence up to three months, include:

- driving under the influence of alcohol or drugs.

- Refusing to take the breathalyser test

- Exceeding posted speed limit by 50 per cent or at least 30kph.

- Reckless driving

- Driving in the wrong direction against traffic

- Professional drivers exceeding the permitted time at the wheel by 50 per cent, or not completing the programmed rest period by 50 per cent.

- Racing

- Carrying 50 per cent more passengers than passenger seats.

**Serious** violations, incurring fines from €92 to €301 and possible suspension of licence, include:
- Speeding of less than 50 per cent over the limit.

- Parking vehicle in dangerous position.

- Negligent driving such as driving without lights

- Throwing from the car any object that could produce fire or accident.

**Minor** violations, incurring fines up to €91, include:
- Parking violations and a host of others.

Offenders can obtain a discount of 30 per cent for prompt payment of fines. This is up from 20 per cent under the old law. If you choose, you can pay the policeman on the spot, or you can send a postal money order available at the post office.

Any driver who accumulates three "very serious" violations in a two-year period will have his driving privileges permanently revoked. This is not exactly a point system, such as some other countries have, but it has the same result.

### Special cases

The new law also provides for "special cases", incurring fines of up to €1,503 and suspension of licence for up to one year. These include:
- Driving without proper licence.

- Driving an unregistered or improperly registered vehicle

- Using mobile phones while driving. (The only permitted use of either phones or radios is by a completely hands-off system. No headsets, microphones, helmets or similar rig may be used).

Radar detectors that warn drivers of the presence of police radar checks are also prohibited, and you can be fined if you attempt to warn other drivers of police presence by flashing your headlights or making other signals.

The 2004 code puts stricter controls on infants and children in cars. A child up to three years of age cannot ride in the front seat under any circumstances. It must ride in the back, in a seat with restraints designed for its size. A child from four to twelve years old who is shorter than 1.5 metres may ride in the front passenger seat with a special seat or restraint system. If none is available, the child must ride in the back seat.

A 12-year-old taller than 1.5 metres must use the adult seat belt in the front passenger seat. Any person at all shorter than 1.5 metres must be treated the same as a child.

For the first time, the law makes parents of minor children responsible for paying fines incurred when these children ride motor-bikes, which they can do at 16, although they must wait until they are 18 to obtain a normal driving licence.

A driver is required to maintain a safe distance behind the vehicle he is following, and he is obliged to leave enough space for another vehicle safely to pass him and pull in.

If you have ever thought of reporting a driver who follows too closely, you are perfectly within your rights. Any citizen may report a traffic violation. You must be prepared to testify in court, however, to make your accusation stick.

All Spanish cars must be fitted with seat-belts in the front seats and they must be worn. You can be fined €90 for not wearing them, so be alert. Cars made after 1997 must have rear seat belts as well.

If the traffic police have reason to think a driver has been drinking they can require him to take a breath test to analyse the amount of alcohol in his blood. If it exceeds the minimum permitted, he can be heavily fined and have his licence revoked. It is your right to demand a blood test as well.

Refusal to take the breath test can lead to a charge of disobeying a police officer, which can bring a penalty of six months in gaol.

## Non-residents can be fined on the spot

If you are a non-resident tourist driving through Spain, you may be disturbed to discover that the Spanish police are empowered to demand payment on the spot for any traffic violation you commit.

The police can order your car impounded if you are unable to pay up. They do this because a tourist usually has no property or other assets in Spain, which could be seized if he does not pay the fine

You will have to pay the fine but if you feel you have been unfairly charged and wish to protest, you can fill in the space for contesting the ticket and mark *garantía* in the area where your payment is noted. This means that you consider your payment only a guarantee, necessary for the policeman to permit you to continue your trip, but that you intend to contest the ticket.

Just like the resident, you will be informed after a few months, when your court hearing is scheduled. You will have to list an address inside Spain for this purpose. You can then go to the Spanish court and make your case.

## GLOSSARY

**Aduana** – Customs

**Baja de Matricula** – De-registration of motor vehicle

**Baja de Residencia** – Non-residence certificate required for duty-free import.

**Canje** – Exchange of EU driving permit for Spanish permit.

**Certificado de Equivalencia** – Certificate of equivalence of foreign licence

142

**Certificado de Empadronamiento** – Registration in municipality

**Coche** – Car, automobile

**Franquicia** – Automobile insurance policy excluding first part of claim.

**Impuesto Municipal sobre Vehiculos de Tracción Mecánia** – Municipal Motor Vehicle Tax

**Inspección Técnica de Vehiculos** – Vehicle inspection, MOT

**Jefatura de Tráfico** – Traffic department headquarters

**Letra** – Bill of Exchange, signed for monthly car payments.

**Matricula** – Registration

**Matrícula Turistica** – Tax-free tourist registration

**Multa** – Fine, traffic or otherwise

**Permiso de Circulación** – Permit for vehicle to circulate on public roads

**Permiso de Conducir** – Driving Licence

**Potencia Fiscal** – Tax-rated horsepower

**Precintar** – To seal, as in automobile or yacht

**Todo Riesgo** – Comprehensive insurance covering all risks.

# 8    You and your money

**F**or many European Union citizens in Spain, cross-border transactions have been greatly simplified by the introduction of the euro, with no more exchange rates and conversion tables to worry about.

UK citizens, however, still have to deal with exchanging pounds for euros. So far, this is working greatly in their favour. The strong pound has in fact made Spanish property look so cheap that many Britons are buying in Spain.

The answer to your first question is yes, you can take out of Spain all the money you bring in, and more. If you have made money by selling property at a profit or by working or investing, you are free to take your profits out of the country. There are forms to fill out and the normal Spanish taxes to pay, but you can do it.

Spain has free conversion of currency but it also has a complex reporting system by which most transactions between residents and non-residents involving foreign exchange and having a value in excess of €600 must be declared to the bank on Forms B-1, B-

2 and B-3.

This declaration does not mean that the Spanish authorities can deny the exchange, only that it must be reported. Spanish banks have complained about the added paperwork, and it has been reflected in higher bank commissions for routine operations.

Both Spaniards and resident foreigners may hold bank accounts in foreign currencies, either inside Spain or abroad. If a resident opens such an account, he must inform the authorities within 30 days, however, and he must regularly present a form to the Bank of Spain detailing the movements in this account.

This measure makes it convenient for those expatriate residents who wish to retain bank accounts in their home countries, or who do business abroad, or who wish to keep their bank deposit certificates inside Spain but denominated in pounds or dollars. It also helps Spaniards who are doing business with other countries.

## IF YOU SELL YOUR PROPERTY

Whether you are resident or non-resident, if you sell your property in Spain and receive payment in Spain, you have the right to take out the money and send it wherever you like.

If the amount is more than €600, however, you must have your bank fill in one of the "B" forms to report the transaction. These forms list full identification, details of the source of the funds and reason for the transaction. The forms are required in order to keep some control over money laundering operations of black funds, where the source is not known.

The "B" form does not give Spanish authorities the power to refuse the transfer; it is only for information. In fact, our property seller does not need to present the form until 15 days after the transfer has taken place.

So, you can sell your property for €120,000, then change euros into pounds, and send them to your British bank account immediately. Or sell for euros. You can have a bank cheque made out in your name or you can have the bank transfer the funds

146

to your British bank.

When a non-resident purchases Spanish property, he must also fill in the proper form. This is only to show that he originally imported the foreign currency into Spain and is not using black money - undeclared profits inside Spain - to make the purchase.

The non-resident buyer can also present a certified cheque in foreign currency if he is paying in another country's money. This is perfectly legal if the seller prefers to be paid in his own currency and avoids the need to fill in any forms at all.

The important element here is the identification. As long as the DGTE, the *Dirección General de Transacciones Exteriores*, the General Directorate of Foreign Transactions, knows who you are, which means that Hacienda, the tax ministry, also knows who you are and what you have done, then they are satisfied.

If the taxes on the transactions are not paid, at least they know the name of the dodger and where to find him. The Spanish tax agency has another control on non-resident property sellers as well.

If you are a non-resident thinking you can take the money and run without paying your Spanish capital gains tax of 35 per cent on the profit, be warned that the purchaser of your property must pay five per cent of the total purchase price directly to Hacienda in your name, as a guarantee that taxes will be paid. (See tax section for details)

If you are tempted to obtain payment in some more portable and less traceable form, such as cash, bearer cheques, or gold coins, be warned that any such exportation over €30,000 is illegal unless the exporter obtains prior authorisation from the DGTE.

To do this legally, you must fill in form B-2, which contains all the pertinent information, and then await permission from the authorities to export the cash. This is routinely granted.You then present the authorisation at the border to be stamped by the Spanish customs agents.

Falsification of any of the information on the form is an offence, as is attempting to take out of Spain more than €30,000 in cash or gold or bearer cheques.

Requiring this authorisation to export money does not square with European Council directives regarding free circulation of money and the European High Court has ruled that Spain may require notification but cannot limit the amount to be taken out.

Those caught taking out too much cash without authorisation can face prison sentences of up to 12 years. Spain so far has refused to change its legislation.

So Spain maintains a check on the amounts of foreign exchange passing across its borders, but you can transfer any amount of funds you choose in any form you choose. In practice the government does not deny the authorisation, but you are warned that Spain is keeping an eye on you for your tax obligations.

## LOANS IN FOREIGN CURRENCY

A Spaniard or a resident can borrow freely from abroad in foreign currency for sums up to €1.5 million without any authorisation. Above that amount, permission is needed. The only condition is that the lender not be based in a "tax haven" according to the Spanish government list.

This means that a home-buyer in Spain can obtain his mortgage from a lending institution in the UK or any other country, denominated in any currency he likes.

For some people, of course, such loans or mortgages are the perfect solution. When your income is denominated in pounds, it is not a bad idea to have your loan in pounds as well, so you know that any currency fluctuations will not change your payment situation.

On the other hand, Spanish interest rates are lower than most and the banks are competing to offer mortgages that are competitive by any nation's standard. Furthermore, with the euro down against the pound, a Spanish mortgage in euros looks attractive.

Keep in mind also that foreign lenders are always reluctant to lend against property located in another country. European unity has not yet reached the stage where it is easy for a bank in the UK to repossess a Spanish property.

## TRANSFERS OF CASH, GOLD AND BEARER CHEQUES

Let's take a closer look at the regulations regarding transfers of funds in and out of Spain.

First we will take the rules regarding cash in any currency, gold bars, precious metals and bearer cheques, which you can carry in your attaché case across the border quite legally if you observe the regulations.

Any amount under the value of €6,000 is completely unregulated. You can carry this amount in or out of Spain without mentioning it, whether you are resident or non-resident.

Whether you are resident or non-resident, and you are bringing into Spain more than €6,000 in cash or bearer cheques, you are required to declare the sum to the customs authorities where you enter Spain, on form B-1. This form includes your personal details and a statement of what you intend to do with the funds.

If you are taking out of Spain a sum more than €6,000 but less than €30,000, you must also fill in form B-1. You can do this at the bank where you obtain the cash or cheque, which will give you one copy for presentation to the customs agent at your point of departure, or you can make the declaration directly at the customs.

If you want to take out in cash a sum of more than €30,000, you must fill in form B-2 and request permission from the DGTE. This is routinely granted.

Both of these forms have a validity of 15 days only, so you will want to plan your trip accordingly.

If you are re-importing or re-exporting sums which you have previously imported or exported, you must also make the declarations, as long as they are more than €6,000.

## TRANSACTIONS THROUGH BANKS

The above refers only to cash, gold and bearer cheques. Transactions made through banks - the great majority of all money transfers in and out of Spain - are regulated more closely.

149

The top limit for absolutely free transfers is €600. That is, a resident or non-resident may obtain a bank cheque in foreign currency from his bank or effect a transfer in Sterling pounds or US dollars up to this amount without any control at all, simply exchanging his euros for the foreign money.

In order to make a payment abroad of more than €600, the Spanish resident must declare to the bank the name and address of the recipient of the transfer or payment, and state the reason for the payment.

The resident must make this declaration to the bank before the payment is made, unless the payment is being made by a cheque in the name of the recipient, drawn on the resident's account, in which case the declaration may be made up to 15 days after the transfer. So, even if you are just sending a cheque for €1,000 for an encyclopaedia you have ordered from London, you must fill in the form.

A resident who is receiving payments or transfers from abroad must also supply full information to the bank where the transfer arrives, including the name and address of the non-resident who sends the sum, and the reason for the operation.

This means that, if your pension cheque each month is more than €600, you must declare it each time. It takes only a moment to fill up the form at the bank.

The same declaration applies for transfers affected by debits and credits in your bank account to or from another bank account.

Residents who receive payments from non-residents or make payments to them of more than €600 in cash or bearer cheques, must declare these payments, made or received, on form B-3.

This form includes the name, address and NIE of the resident and details of the non-resident and states the reason for the operation.

Note here that the resident who receives or makes the payment must make the declaration even when he is not the final recipient or the person responsible for the operation. This would include a fiscal representative who is receiving funds from abroad to pay his client's tax bill, for example, or a person who is acting as agent for another in making a payment abroad.

So, we see that transactions between residents and non-residents are documented for sums above €600 when they involve bank transfers, but cash and bearer cheques can be freely imported and exported up to €6,000.

We can begin to see why the banks have already complained about the paperwork involved. Even where it is not a question of permission being denied, the simple reporting takes a lot of time.

## OPERATIONS BETWEEN NON-RESIDENTS

Operations between non-residents transferring bearer cheques, euros or foreign currency must be authorised in advance. The original importation of the means of payment must be justified on form B-1, or declared on form B-3 if such means come from a resident, before the bank can carry out the operation.

This means that, when a non-resident buys a Spanish property from another non-resident, the purchaser must declare his importation of the foreign currency and its exchange into euros, or pay by a cheque on a non-Spanish bank in a foreign currency. This is perfectly legal, and many sellers prefer to be paid in their own currency.

For purposes of foreign exchange transfers, the resident may accredit his status by showing his residence card. If you have to prove that you are a non-resident, you must obtain a certificate from the Ministry of the Interior declaring that you are not listed as a resident, and this certificate must be dated at least two months before it is presented.

## BANK ACCOUNTS IN SPAIN

Both residents and non-residents may freely open bank accounts in euros. The accounts of residents and non-residents are distinguished from each other, because different regulations apply to taxation for the resident and the non-resident. The non-resident account is called a *cuenta extranjera*, but for all internal purposes, is exactly the same as the resident's account.

In addition to your normal current account from which you write euro cheques to pay your normal bills in Spain, you may

151

wish to take out a Deposit Certificate in euros or other currency. The interest rates will vary, because Spanish banks have cut back their interest on deposit certificates, in line with the general drop in Spanish interest rates. In fact, the banks cut back their own rates of interest before they cut back the interest rates they charge on mortgages.

Those residents who presently hold time deposit accounts in Spanish banks should check their interest payments now if they are on a variable-rate scheme. It might be time to discuss this with your investment advisors.

If you are a resident, 15 per cent of your interest earnings will be withheld and paid to the Spanish tax man in your name, just the same as for Spaniards. You may be eligible for a refund on this tax. (See section on You and Your Taxes). If you are a non-resident, no tax will be withheld, but you will be liable for tax in your country of residence.

Any bank operation involving more than €3,000 requires that the payer and the receiver of the amount be identified.

Your normal current account may be paying as low as a miserable one-tenth of one per cent (0.1 per cent) on its average balance, and you will be paying some of the highest bank charges in Europe for routine services. You may be irritated when you discover that your bank has charged you €5 to make a draft for €60 worth of pounds in order to pay for a magazine subscription in your home country, so be sure to ask in advance what these charges will be.

And remember what we said in the first chapter about making sure of just how your pension cheque or funds from abroad will be transferred to you in Spain, and just how long it will take from the time of sending to the moment you can write a new cheque.

Many, many people have suffered greatly from delays in the transfer of funds, even when they are sent from a British bank to its branch in Spain, so ask the bank manager how long it will take. You may wish to use one of the rapid bank transfer systems such as SWIFT, which assures you of having the money sent quickly. It costs a little more, but it is probably worth it.

There have been many complaints about high commissions

charged on these transfers as well. Some people have been charged more than 4 per cent when sending money out of Spain. This would be €4,200 on a transfer of €120,000. Other banks charge fees of around €21 per €6,000 of transfer, a total of €420 on the same operation, or one-tenth of the charge.

## NO COMMISSION ON PENSIONS

Spanish banks have even charged exchange commission on direct transfer of British pensions. This is against European Union banking regulations, especially when the British send the pension cheques directly in euros to the Spanish bank.

If your bank is charging commission on your pension cheques, make sure that you are receiving them by direct transfer in euros. If not, arrange to do this - a simple letter is sufficient - and tell your Spanish bank that charging commission on pension transfers is against the EU regulations.

Having said the above, many Spanish bank services function very well. Spain has one of the most complete and modern networks of electronic banking services, for example, where you can be sure of using your bank card to obtain cash from the electronic teller in all parts of the country, and in other countries as well.

Remember that, if you lose your Visa card and it is used by the thief before you report it, you are liable for the first €150 charged.

If you have a complaint with your bank service and your local manager does not give you satisfaction, you will find that almost all banks have a *Defensor del Cliente*, who will hear your case and who must respond within two months.

More than half of all such complaints are resolved in favour of the client, reports the banking association. If you don't get any joy from your own bank, you can also complain to the Bank of Spain's *Servicio de Reclamaciones* in Madrid.

You will have to try your bank manager first, then the bank's own client department, and present your case in writing but the Bank of Spain helps hundreds of depositors every year. You can telephone them on 91-338 5068 for detailed information.

153

## WRITING CHEQUES

Once you begin writing cheques on your normal Spanish account, you will find that many Spaniards prefer a cheque made out to *portador* ("bearer" or, as the Americans say, "cash"). The *portador* cheque is preferred by many because there is no record of who cashes it. You can either accept this practice or insist on making the cheque out in the name of the person for whom it is meant.

The post-dated cheque is no longer effective in Spain. That is, if you put a date one month or so in the future on your cheque, the receiver of it will be able to cash it at the bank immediately regardless of the future date you have written.

If you have a cheque written by a person with insufficient funds in the bank, you will be able to collect a partial amount up to the total of funds available. That is, if you have a cheque for €600 and the issuer has only €300 in his account, you can collect the €300 and the bank will note this on the cheque, which you can present again later in the hopes that the rest of the money has arrived.

You will also find that personal cheques are not used quite as much as they are in most European countries for routine payments. Spaniards are still not quite used to the idea of personal cheques, though charge cards and credit cards are widely accepted. For many payments, especially instalment purchases of automobiles or major home appliances, the Spanish system prefers to use *letras,* or bills of exchange.

## TAKE CARE WITH *LETRAS*

For example, when you buy a car on instalments, you might sign 24 *letras* of €180 each, one to be paid each month. The auto dealer may send each *letra* directly to your bank, where it will be paid directly from your account, a system often used. Or you can go round and pay it yourself in person each month. The *letra* that you sign is a personal debt, so you want to be cautious.

And you want to make sure the *letra* is paying for what you think it is paying. There have been cases where someone selling property insisted that the buyer pay in *letras*, but had them made out to him personally and not to the company selling the property. So our buyer paid the *letras*, which the seller's agent was converting to his own use, and the poor buyer wound up having to pay for the property again, as the company had never received any money.

In another case, a man working for a company signed *letras* for a piece of machinery. The company went out of business but the man had to finish paying for the machinery, as he had signed the *letras*.

In yet another case, a man signed *letras* to pay for his new computer. He sent the computer back to the company because it was defective. The company made no problem, but the distributor who had sold him the computer went out of business, having already disposed of the *letras* to a bank.

The bank now held the bills of exchange and expected payment from the signer. Our buyer's only recourse was to bring a lawsuit against the bankrupt distributor, because the computer company had received no money from him, hence could not return it to him, and the bank had made a deal in perfectly good faith to purchase the *letras* from the distribution company.

This practice of purchasing other peoples' *letras* is quite legal and normal. The bank or other institution buys them at a discount, because they will have to wait for payment, and the company accepts this in return for immediate cash. In the case above, however, it leaves our purchaser out in the cold.

Another useful service available from your bank will be the *domiciliación de pagos* or the "domiciling of payments".

The word "domicile" simply means home, and the domiciling of a payment is a standing order at your bank to pay your electricity bill, for example, or your IBI. This service is very useful for people who do not spend the whole year at their property in Spain, as it assures payment of necessary bills while they are away.

You fill up a form at the bank. A copy goes to whoever is sending the bill and the bank keeps another copy as their authorisation to pay out directly from your account.

The disadvantage, of course, is that a bill may be paid which you do not want to be paid. The electric company or the tax authorities may make an error, which you would normally protest and refuse to pay. The bank will pay it unless they notice something terribly wrong.

The idea of *domiciliación* also applies when you are investing in Spain. This sort is a bit different, however. This official "home account" is one through which all your foreign transactions must pass. When you bring foreign exchange into Spain to make your investment, it comes into the officially domiciled account, and when you wish to repatriate your profits, you also do it through the same account. The *Dirección General de Transacciones Exteriores* can thus keep an eye on all cash movements related to your investment.

## INVESTING IN SPAIN

One of the simplest ways to invest in Spain, whether you are a resident or not, is with bank deposit certificates for varying periods of time. These pay different rates of interest depending on the amount invested, the time period fixed and the currency in which they are held. An official resident may now hold his deposit certificates in any currency he likes.

With interest rates down at last in Spain, however, you will not achieve a very high rate of return on your investment.

An official resident will also find that the bank withholds 18 per cent of the interest to cover income tax. You get a receipt for this and when you go to pay your Spanish income tax, you deduct this prepaid tax from any income tax you may owe. (See section on "You and Your Taxes".)

If you are not a resident, you may hold these deposit certificates in any currency and no tax will be withheld. The problem of withholding tax is one of the knottiest facing EU negotiators, who are trying to convince all member states to impose a 15 per cent withholding tax on bank interest.

You can also, resident or non-resident, purchase shares in Spanish companies on the Bolsa, or stock exchange, and you can purchase Spanish government bonds.

## SPAIN DOES NOT TAX
## STOCK-MARKET PROFITS

Spain does not tax profits made by an EU non-resident investor in the Spanish stock market. These profits from sale and income from interest on bonds are now considered as not arising in Spain. Dividends, however, remain taxable, when paid by Spanish companies.

But even dividends are free of Spanish tax when the EU investor puts his money into a foreign company that is quoted on the Spanish stock-market, and there are many.

This freedom applies only to individuals, not companies, who are resident in other EU countries. It supposes that the non-resident investor is paying his taxes in the country where he resides.

You may also find new investment opportunities open up for you as a non-resident of your home country, such as certain British government stocks that are not taxed at source when the holder is a non-resident.

Expats find new hazards as well as new opportunities, however. If you are tempted to invest your pension capital in offshore funds that promise rapid growth, be warned that the "Independent Financial Advisor" is completely unregulated in Spain.

Investments in the Spanish stock market are controlled by the *Comision Nacional del Mercado de Valores,* a board that oversees the stock market. Insurance investment products are regulated by the national insurance board.

The offshore funds, however, manage to fall outside the control of these bodies. Many of the funds provide good returns but the investor should be warned that he has no comeback if things go wrong.

## INVESTING IN PROPERTY

You can do what thousands of Europeans have done and invest in real estate, especially on the Spanish coastline. This can take the form of buying large tracts of undeveloped land and waiting for the price to go up.

Or perhaps you want to develop it yourself and create your own urbanisation. You might chance across one of the last empty building lots in a town by the sea and put up your own apartment block. The Spanish real estate market is booming in the new millennium.

Perhaps you want to purchase a few apartments and make some income by letting them to holiday-makers while you wait for them to increase in value in today's rising property market. With stocks and shares down, rental property begins to seem like an attractive alternative even though it involves much more administrative work.

You will be allowed, as a non-resident, to take out of Spain the rents you receive for your property. Of course, you have to pay Spanish tax on this income arising in Spain. Legally, 25 per cent should be declared on form 210 and paid to Hacienda before you are allowed to take the rest out of Spain.

If you rent regularly to tourists on a short-term basis, providing linens and cleaning services to holiday-makers, you must also charge IVA, or value added tax, at 16 per cent, and register your business as tourist letting.

Your accountant or property consultant or management company can steer you right on these taxes. You also get to make a number of deductions for property maintenance on your income tax that are not available to home-owners who inhabit their property.

Now that you are a rather international sort of person, you may find that offshore banking and investment have advantages. There are perfectly legal ways to increase your income and avoid certain taxes by keeping your assets in investments located in tax havens such as the Channel Islands or Gibraltar.

There is a big push in Gibraltar to offer banking services and the formation of "offshore" companies that are non-resident in Spain. These companies are legally empowered to own property in Spain. They offer the advantages of secrecy and the legal avoidance of some Spanish transfer taxes, because when the time comes to sell, one does not sell the property, but only the company. Hence, no transfer has taken place in Spain, as the same company continues to own the property.

This system can also avoid Spanish - or any other - death duties and can be useful where property is bequeathed to a non-relative (see chapter on "Making A Will" and "You and Your Taxes" for more information on off-shore companies and their taxation.)

"Avoiding" taxes, by the way, does not mean "evading" taxes. To evade a tax that you are legally liable to pay is a crime. But to take advantage of your change of residency in order to avoid taxes is only sensible.

In any case, you must look into the possibility of an offshore company before you purchase property. And remember, the formation of the company also incurs expenses. Such offshore ownership is not for everyone. You'll need expert advice to determine what's best for you.

For example, British emigrants should establish both residency and legal domicile (two different things) in Spain before they sell up their business in Great Britain. They can often, though not always, avoid British capital gains tax this way. There are similar advantages for those of other nationalities, but you need to take expert counsel.

This book cannot replace an individual investment adviser who studies your particular circumstances and plans the wisest course for you. Each person's situation and needs are different, requiring different strategies. The formation of a family trust or corporation based in Andorra or another tax haven, which would own all your property and pay you an income, might be best for some people. Such a family corporation has great advantages in tax reduction and also attracts no death duties.

## GLOSSARY

**Acciones** – shares, stocks

**Bolsa** – Spanish stock market

**Cheque** – Cheque (see Talon)

**Comisión Nacional del Mercado de Valores** – National board regulating investments in companies registered with Spanish stock market.

**Cuenta Corriente** – Current account

**Defensor del Cliente** – Defender of the Client, bank ombudsman

**Dirección General de Transacciones Exteriores** – General Directorate of Foreign Transactions

**Divisas** – Foreign exchange

**Domiciliación de Pago** – Standing order to pay a bill

**Efectivo** – Cash

**Letra** – Bill of Exchange

**Portador** – Bearer, check made out to "cash"

**Talón** – Cheque (See Cheque)

**Talonario** – Chequebook

**Transferencia** – Transfer

# 9 Taxes on property

## CAPITAL GAINS TAX

Anyone who buys property in Spain today will be liable to pay
Spanish capital gains tax when he sells his flat or
villa in the future.  This applies to residents and non-
residents alike.

Residents pay a maximum of 15 per cent and their capital gains are calculated as part of their Spanish income tax.

Non-residents pay a flat rate of 35 per cent. Buyers from non-resident sellers are required to withhold five per cent of the total purchase price and pay it directly to the Spanish Tax Agency, thus making sure that the seller does not take the money and run.

Until December 31, 1996, both residents and non-residents could deduct 11.11 per cent per year from their profits, after the first two years of ownership, and pay no tax at all after 10 years. This favourable picture has ended.

There are four special situations in which a property seller is not liable for capital gains tax. Let's see if you are among the lucky ones.

## RESIDENTS OVER 65 EXEMPT

An official resident of Spain 65 years of age and over, who has lived in his principal residence for three years, is not subject to capital gains tax when he sells the residence.

If you are 65 or over and hold a Spanish residence permit, you can buy a principal residence this year and sell it in three years for a fat profit in today's brisk real estate market, and have no capital gains tax to pay.

## RESIDENTS GET ROLLOVER CREDIT FOR NEW HOME

An official resident of Spain who reinvests all of the proceeds of his house sale to purchase another Spanish home as his principal residence will get complete relief from this tax. He must have lived in the home for three years to qualify. If he uses only a portion of the total amount of his house sale, he will get a percentage of relief up to the amount reinvested.

One typical situation is where an older couple sell their large villa, which they no longer need, and move into a smaller apartment, using the rest of their profits to improve their life style. If we suppose that the couple originally bought the villa for €120,000 and sell it today for €180,000, they have a profit of €60,000.

162

If they buy a new flat for the whole of the €180,000 selling price, they will have no Spanish capital gains tax to pay. But if they buy a small flat for €90,000, and keep the remaining €90,000 in cash, they will have used only one-half of their sale proceeds to purchase a new principal residence. Thus, they get to deduct only one-half of their profits. Half of €60,000 is €30,000 free of tax.

## BUYERS BEFORE DECEMBER 31, 1986

If you bought your Spanish property before December 31, 1986, you are free of capital gains tax. This applies to both residents and non-residents.

As we noted above, under the previous capital gains regulations, those who owned their property for 10 years were free of tax. This provision ended in 1996, making 1986 the final cut-off date for exemption.

## HOLDERS OF USUFRUCT

A recent change in capital gains regulations exempts elderly persons who use the "inherit from yourself" schemes in which you sell your house but retain the right to live in it until your death.

A person 65 or older who contracts with a company to sell his principal residence in exchange for the lifetime right to inhabit the dwelling, along with a monthly payment, will not be taxed on any capital gain involved. This makes such deals to turn your home ownership into lifetime income more attractive for older persons of modest means. The right to inhabit the property is called a *usufructo*.

If you do not fall into one of these groups, you will be liable for capital gains tax when you sell your property.

We can distinguish three possible situations for sellers of Spanish property today. These are:

**1. Long-term Owners:** The fortunate long-term owners who bought their homes before December 31, 1986, meaning they have owned them for 10 years before December 31, 1996. They have no Spanish capital gains tax to pay when they sell

163

now. If they are non-residents, they are not subject to the five per cent retention.

**2. Transitional Sellers:** Those who bought in the period from 1987 through 1994. They have the right to the 11.11 per cent per year reduction, starting after the first two years of ownership, but only up to 1996. Those who bought in 1995 have no reduction because their initial two-year period of no reduction runs up against the December 31, 1996, cut-off point. These sellers can also apply the inflation correction factor (see below).

**3. Today's Buyers:** Those who purchase today (and really, since 1995) will have no 11.11 per cent reductions at all. Their only help is the application of a coefficient that corrects for inflation. Nevertheless, it is a help because it is applied to the entire amount of your original purchase price, rather than to the amount of your profit, so you don't pay much more tax than under the old system.

If you sell your Spanish property today, you will fall into one of these categories. Let's take them one by one.

### Long-term owners

If you are one of the fortunate long-term owners who bought before December 31, 1986, you have no tax to pay, so you may skip this section.

### Transitional sellers

If you are a "transitional seller" in Group 2, you have the most complicated calculation. Here is a step-by-step example.

1.  Find the price you paid for your property originally. This will be the price entered on your *escritura*. If you did as many other Spanish buyers did a few years ago and entered a price lower than the price you actually paid, you will suffer for it now. Let's suppose you bought in 1990 and your registered price is 15 million pesetas.

2.  Convert this price into euros. It comes to just over €90,000.

3.  Now add onto your price all the official expenses you had

in acquiring the property. After your purchase was complete, you should have attached the receipts for the taxes, fees and other expenses to your title deed for your files. Add to your original purchase price the amount of property transfer tax you paid at the time, at 6 per cent, or at 7.5 per cent if you bought a new property from a developer, thus paying IVA instead of transfer tax. Enter expenses for notary, property registration, the *plus valía* tax if you as the buyer had to pay it, and lawyer. You need the official receipts for these payments in order to claim them.

4.  Convert these peseta expenses into euros.

5.  Let's suppose that these expenses total just over 10 per cent of your price, or €10,000. You add them in, making a total acquisition cost of €100,000.

6.  Apply inflation corrector. Your purchase was in 1990 and the money has become worth less today because of inflation. You can apply the inflation correction factor from the table below to bring that €100,000 to today's values. Looking at the table we see that any purchase before 1994 has a factor of 1.1461. Multiply this by €100,000 and you get €114,610. Those of you who are mathematically minded will notice that this does not really correct for all the inflation since 1990. However, the taxman knows that transitional sellers will also have the reduction factor of 11.11 per cent per year to apply. I told you it was complicated.

7.  In order to apply your reductions, you have to calculate your profit. You are selling today for €330,000, tripling your money in 14 years. Not too bad. And you are declaring the full amount on the contract. Subtract selling expenses from your total. You can reduce your total selling price by any justified expenses. If you have a bill from your estate agent, with IVA, you can deduct this. If the commission is five per cent, let's call that a nice round €15,000. If your total acquisition cost, corrected for

165

inflation, is €114,670 and your reduced selling price, as declared, is €315,000, this makes your profit on paper a round €200,000.

8. Now you get to apply the reduction percentage to this profit. If you bought in 1990, your factor starts in 1992, after your first two years of ownership. The factor ends in 1996, so you get four years worth. Four times 11.11 per cent is, rounding off, 44 per cent. Apply this to €200,000 and let's say you have €88,000 worth of reduction. Subtract this from €200,000 and you have a corrected and taxable profit of €112,000. So far, this operation applies to residents and non-residents alike, but now we see a difference in their taxation.

## RESIDENT PAYS AS INCOME TAX

A resident pays his capital gains tax as part of his income tax. If you sell in 2004, you do not declare this until May of 2005, when you file for Spanish income tax.

If you are of modest income, paying Spanish income tax somewhere around 15 per cent, you will also pay your capital gains tax at 15 per cent.In the present case, 15 per cent of €112,000 is €16,800 tax you will pay on a real profit of more than €200,000, having owned the property for 14 years.

Even if your income is very high, the absolute limit on capital gains tax for a resident is 15 per cent. This means that you could never pay more than €15,000 on a profit of €100,000.

In Spanish, capital gain is called *incremento de patrimonio*, and there is a section of the tax form especially designed for it.

## NON RESIDENT PAYS 35 PER CENT

The non-resident, however, faces a tax of 35 per cent. In our example, this gives a tax of €39,000, more than twice the resident's tax.

If the non-resident is tempted to take the money and run, remember that the buyer does not pay him the full price. He must withhold five per cent of the total purchase price and pay it directly to the Spanish Tax Agency, filing form 211. The Notary demands to see the paid-up form 211 at the signing of the deeds, so there is no escape.

In the example, five per cent of €330,000 is €16,500. The seller still owes another €28,500 on top of this. He is required to file Form 212 within 30 days and pay the rest of his tax. If he decides to become a tax dodger, he can leave Spain, owing the Tax Agency €28,500, not a big profit for the risk.

If the deposit of five per cent turns out to be greater than the amount of tax owed by the non-resident, he can also claim a refund on the same Form 212, which should be filed within 30 days of the transaction. The Tax Agency promises to return the over-payment within 90 days, but many report that they take as long as a year.

## COEFICIENTE DE ACTUALIZACIÓN
## INFLATION CORRECTION TABLE

| PURCHASE DATE | 2004 SALE |
| --- | --- |
| 1994 and earlier | 1.1461 |
| 1995 | 1.2108 |
| 1996 | 1.1694 |
| 1997 | 1.1461 |
| 1998 | 1.1238 |
| 1999 | 1.1036 |
| 2000 | 1.0824 |
| 2001 | 1.0612 |
| 2002 | 1.0404 |
| 2003 | 1.0200 |
| 2004 | 1.0000 |

**Today's sellers**

Well, we told you it was complicated. If you fall into the third category of seller, those who bought after 1994, you have only the inflation correction factor to apply.

That is, if you bought in 1996 and you sell today for €200,000, you look at the table and see that the factor is 1.1694. After you have added in all your acquisition costs, let's suppose that your total cost in 1996 is a nice round €100,000.

Apply the factor and you get €116,940. This reduces your taxable profit from €100,000 to €83,000 and saves you about €6,000 in capital gains tax if you are a non-resident. It doesn't look like a great savings, but it's better than nothing.

## SECTION 2

### TAXES YOU PAY EVERY YEAR

All property owners in Spain are liable for three separate taxes every year. These taxes are:

1. Property owners' imputed income tax

2. Wealth Tax (non-resident tax form 214)

3. Annual Real Estate Tax

### Property Owners' Imputed Income Tax

The good news for residents is that Spain's property owners' imputed income tax is no longer payable on the owner's principal residence.

A non-resident must continue to pay the yearly tax, however, because he is not resident in Spain, so his principal dwelling cannot be here. Residents who own more than one dwelling will also continue to be subject to the tax on their second home or other property.

Persons subject to this tax have two per cent of the *valor catastral*, the official rated value, of their property attributed to them as a sort of imaginary income. This is 1.1 per cent if your rated value has been raised sharply since 1994.

Residents pay their tax on this notional income by having it added to their other income as if it were more earnings. This means that they pay tax at their normal income tax rate. If their incomes are modest they will pay 15 per cent and if their incomes are high they will pay 30 or even 40 per cent.

The non-resident is taxed always at the flat rate of 25 per cent on any income arising in Spain. Do not confuse this tax of 25 per cent on earnings with the capital gains tax of 35 per cent, which applies to profits from the sale of assets, such as a house or shares in a company.

168

If a non-resident husband and wife own a villa which has a *valor catastral* of €120,000 and a real value of €180,000, we find that the Spanish Tax Agency imputes to them separately an ownership of €60,000 each, half of the *valor catastral*. We then calculate that 2 per cent of €60,000 is €1,200 of imaginary income. Taxed at 25 per cent, this gives a bill of €300.

## "Wealth Tax"

In addition to his income tax the Spanish resident - and non-resident property owner - is liable for Spain's tax on capital assets, known as the *patrimonio* tax. The name "wealth tax" may not sound like proper legal terminology, but it is an adequate translation of the Spanish name, as it's exactly that, a tax on all your assets and property, your total wealth.

In Spanish, the name is *impuesto extraordinario sobre el patrimonio,* the extraordinary tax on assets. This tax started in 1978 as a special measure to force many Spanish citizens who had been hiding their wealth, especially property, to bring these assets into the open.

Hacienda placed a very small tax on these assets, amounting to only .002, that is two-tenths of one per cent, or two-thousandths of the taxable base, up to assets of €167,129. After that, the rate goes up as assets go up.

Wealth tax is based on the real sale value declared in the contract, which is almost always higher than the *valor catastral.* You declare for this tax when you declare for your income tax, on the simplified Form 214 if you are a non-resident with only one property or on the separate Form 714.

Wealth tax affects residents and non-residents differently. A resident is required to declare his world-wide assets while the non-resident declares only his property and assets in Spain.

These taxable assets can include bank deposits, stocks, shares, bonds, ownership of a business, gold bars under the mattress, automobiles, yachts, private airplanes, works of art unless they are owned by the maker, jewels, luxury fur coats or anything else that can be considered wealth. Your home furnishings are exempt unless they are valuable antiques. There are deductions available for debts against your business, mortgages on your property, and any tax of a similar nature paid in a foreign country.

The principal deduction for a resident of Spain is that he pays nothing on the first €108,182. A husband and wife each have an exemption of €108,182, and each must make an individual declaration. Further, if the asset in question is a principal residence, each person has an exemption of €150,253.

If a husband and wife own together a property valued at almost €300,000, they each declare half the value, take their exemption of more than €300,000, and have no *patrimonio* tax to pay.

## PATRIMONIO TAX RATES 2004

(In euros, rounded to nearest euro)

| Taxable Base | Tax | Rate Band | Marginal rate% |
|---|---|---|---|
| 0 | 0 | 167,129 | 0.20 |
| 167,129 | 334 | 167,123 | 0.30 |
| 334,253 | 836 | 334,247 | 0.50 |
| 716,581 | 2,507 | 668,500 | 0.90 |
| 1,337,000 | 8,523 | 1,337,000 | 1.30 |
| 2,673,999 | 25,904 | 2,673,999 | 1.70 |
| 5,347,998 | 71,362 | 5,347998 | 2.10 |
| 10,695,996 | 183,670 | excess | 2.50 |

As Spanish law views property as individually owned, for wealth tax purposes, this means that a husband and wife who own their home together, must each file a wealth tax declaration declaring 50 per cent of the value as their property.

None of the exemptions above apply to non-residents. They must pay from the first euro of valuation. The non-resident, however, is taxed only on his assets located in Spain.

Non-residents declare on their own special tax Form 214 every year (see forms at end of chapter) and can declare at any time during the year. In our example above for non-resident property tax, the sale value of the property is €180,000. Two-tenths of one per cent of this is €360, or €180 for each of the husband and wife half-owners.

Add to that €600 of Spanish non-resident property owner imputed income tax, divided into €300 each, and you get a total of €480 due to the Spanish taxman from each of the co-owning spouses, or €960 total from both spouses. This is in addition to your annual real estate tax. (see below)

If we imagine that your annual real estate tax, IBI, on the villa is €240 pesetas, this means that it will cost you €1,200 a year in Spanish taxes simply to own the place.

Keep in mind that, if you own two properties in Spain, you cannot use Form 214 and must declare on Form 714 for wealth tax and Form 210 for imputed income tax, and you must declare in the period between May 1 and June 20.

If you own two properties, you are still required to name an official *representante fiscal,* a tax representative in Spain. If you fail to name a representative, you can be fined up to €6,000.

One owner who applied for Form 214 was annoyed to discover that he was not eligible because he had purchased his garage separately from his house. Because he has two separate title deeds, he must fill out the standard forms, declare in the regular time period and name an official tax representative.

In addition to this, both residents and non-residents pay the annual real estate tax.

## ANNUAL REAL ESTATE TAX (IBI)

The annual real estate tax on your Spanish property must also be paid. This tax, based on your *valor catastral,* can vary widely from town to town for the same type of property because it is a municipal tax. You can expect to pay much more for a townhouse in Marbella than you would pay for the same accommodation in an inland provincial town. If you live in a typical village house set back from the coast, your annual real estate tax could be as little as €60. If you have a well-positioned villa on a large plot you could pay as much as €3,000.

This real estate tax is called the IBI, the *Impuesto sobre Bienes Inmuebles.* The tax is raised every year, as a result of inflation.

If you are a non-resident, the best solution for you is to have the tax *domiciliado* in your bank. This is a standing order to the bank to pay the tax - and you can include any other municipal charges as well. You obtain a form at the bank that authorises them to pay the tax bill, and you deposit a copy of the form with your *ayuntamiento*. This tells them where to send the bill. You are thus assured that your taxes are paid when they are due, the same as the telephone, water and electric bills.

If you prefer to pay the bill in person, you will have to go to your town hall and pay it each year. Some towns offer a discount for early payment, so be sure to ask.

In addition to the *valor catastral,* the assessed value of your property for tax purposes, the IBI also lists your *referencia catastral* number, which will locate your property at the *Catastro* office, along with its officially measured dimensions. This can be important in buying and selling property because sometimes the physical description does not agree with the description given in the property title.

If you think that you can simply forget about these three taxes because you are not a Spanish resident and someday will sell your home in the sun anyway, think again.

The Spanish tax agency, Hacienda, will check the books at the time of the property sale. They will be holding that deposit of 5 per cent of your total sale price, remember. It is a guarantee against the owner's imputed income tax and wealth tax obligations for the last four years, as well as against the capital gains liability. You will also be required to present the current real estate tax receipt, the IBI, when you sign the sale contract.

## RENTAL OR BUSINESS INCOME (FORM 210)

All non-residents who are making money by renting out their Spanish property are subject to tax on this income arising in Spain. They are required to declare their Spanish income on Form 210. They are supposed to declare within 30 days of receiving the income, but they can apply to make their declarations quarterly to save paperwork. Such non-resident income is taxed at the flat rate of 25 per cent.

If you are a non-resident but you own and operate a business in Spain, such as a restaurant, or a bar, or a cement factory, you are also liable for Spanish tax on your profits.

## COMMUNITY CHARGES

The fees charged annually by your Community of Property Owners, to pay for your share of maintaining the community property, are not taxes of course, but they need to be factored into your totals when you are calculating the annual running costs of your Spanish property. These fees might be as little as €400 a year for a small flat or more like €4,000 a year for a luxury villa on an elegant estate in Marbella.

## YOUR FISCAL REPRESENTATIVE

The non-resident property owner of only one property is no longer required by Spanish law to name a fiscal representative who is resident in Spain. Those who own two or more properties must do so, however, under penalty of fines that can go as high as €5,000 if he does not comply.

The fiscal representative assures the Spanish tax authorities that they can have a reliable contact inside Spain for the non-resident taxpayer. Although most non-residents name their tax consultant or lawyer as their fiscal representative, it can be anyone, even a foreigner, as long as he is officially resident in Spain. Any *gestoría* or tax office has the simple forms necessary.

## NON-RESIDENT'S FISCAL IDENTIFICATION NUMBER

If you are a non-resident property owner, you will have the above-mentioned taxes to pay and perhaps a fiscal representative to name. In order to pay these taxes, you must apply for a *número de identificación de extranjero,* a NIE, which is your Spanish tax identification number. Residents, of course, have a number as well, and Spaniards do, too.

In fact, you should apply for this number when you purchase your property. The number identifies you to the Spanish taxman and is required when you pay your taxes or have any dealings with Hacienda.

To obtain it, simply present yourself at the nearest police *comisaría* with a foreigners' department, along with a photocopy of the first pages of your passport. Fill in the form and wait a few weeks for your number to be assigned. You can also have your *gestoría* do this for you. Then you will be registered with Hacienda's central computers just like the rest of us in today's electronically observed society.

## SPECIAL TAX ON OFFSHORE COMPANIES

During the property boom of the 1980s thousands of luxury homes on the Spanish Costas were sold on the basis of ownership through a non-resident company. Many of these offshore companies are located in the so-called "tax havens" where little or no local taxes are charged and the names of the owners are confidential.

On the Costa del Sol, entire urbanisations were marketed with Gibraltar companies already formed to own the property. The buyer purchased the Gibraltar company, in Gibraltar, and his real name never appeared on any Spanish documents, only the name of the Gibraltar company.

Estimates are that at least 12,000 companies exist, in Gibraltar alone, without mentioning other offshore tax havens, for the sole purpose of owning property in Spain. These companies were created, quite legally, as a means to slide around a number of Spanish taxes while concealing the identity of the true owners of the property.

Other non-resident companies are located in European countries where they are subject to tax like any other company, including tax on their assets in Spain.

There is nothing incorrect about this sort of operation, and it means that all Spanish transfer taxes - which can amount to 10 per cent of the price - are bypassed when property owned by such companies changes hands. This is because only the offshore company is bought and sold, a transaction that takes place outside of Spain. As far as the Spanish government is concerned, the property is still owned by the same company, and no change has taken place, so no tax is due.

This offshore company ownership also avoids Spanish inheritance tax. The company is not registered in Spain, even though it possesses an asset here, so no Spanish inheritance tax is charged when the company is bequeathed to its inheritor, who then continues to own the company through Gibraltar, the Channel Islands, or some other country.

This is all perfectly legal. Nevertheless, it is not quite cricket and finally the loss of tax revenue has irritated the Spanish authorities so much that they have enacted a special tax on offshore companies. They are not the first to do so. In fact they were just about the last country in Europe to permit these operations.

This special tax on offshore companies is 3 per cent of the *valor catastral*. This means that, if your property is valued at €100,000 (with a real market value of perhaps €150,000), your annual tax is €3,000.

For companies registered in Gibraltar or other tax havens around the world, there are absolutely no exemptions. Spain's tax ministry has a list of jurisdictions regarded as "tax havens".

When both the company and its real owners are fiscal residents of "normal" countries which have taxation treaties with Spain, the company can claim exemption from the tax of 3 per cent by revealing all details of the owners, and presenting certification that the company pays its taxes in its country of registration.

The law is designed to crack down on those persons taking advantage of secrecy provisions in tax havens while permitting normal EU companies to continue to own property in Spain as long as they pay their taxes at home.

This leaves perfectly legitimate owners of tax haven companies, however, in the position of either having to pay the stiff tax or divest themselves of their companies.

If they "sell" the property to themselves as the new individual owners, this operation attracts tax at about 10 per cent of the total operation, just like any normal property sale. Some lawyers have been able to wind up the Gibraltar company and distribute its assets to the owners, under a small business tax of one per cent, plus a few other charges that bring the total expense to about three per cent.

This leaves you as an individual owning your home in Spain, just like almost everyone else, and subject to all the usual Spanish taxes we have discussed.

As the tax is based on the *valor catastral,* the assessed value, paying the tax might be a viable option in situations where this value is much lower than the real value. There are still cases where properties that are worth €200,000 on the market have an assessed value of €50,000.

In such cases and where the individual has special need for confidentiality in his ownership, it could be a possible course of action. Be warned, however, that Spain continues its process of raising the *valor catastral* towards normal market prices. Furthermore, European Union commissions are now studying the possibility of stricter controls over tax havens as part of the EU campaign to discover the hiding places of black money obtained through various types of illegal operations.

Each case will need individual study and some careful planning.

## GLOSSARY

**Ayuntamiento** – Town Hall, where you pay IBI

**Coeficiente de Actualización** – Inflation correction factor

**Contribuyente** – Taxpayer

**Formulario** – Form, as in taxes

**Impuesto** – Tax

**IBI Impuesto sobre Bienes Inmuebles** – Annual real estate tax

**Impuesto sobre el Patrimonio** – Capital gains tax

**Incremento de Patrimonio** – Capital gain

**Modelo** – Form, as in taxes

**NIE (Numero de Identificación de Extranjero)** - Foreigner's tax identification number.

**Paraiso Fiscal** – Tax haven

**Patrimonio** – Capital assets, wealth

**Referencia Catastral** – Reference number for property inscription in the Castastro Registry

**Representante Fiscal** – Official tax representative of foreigner

**Valor Catastral** – Rated value of property for tax purposes

**Usufructo** – Usufruct, right to inhabit property

# 10    Spanish income tax

The big news for tax year 2004, payable in May and June of 2005, is that Spain's Hacienda ministry has made no changes whatsoever in the tax scale or the deductions. After the series of changes introduced in 2003, which cut taxes by an average 11 per cent. they apparently are taking a rest. If your income for the year 2004 was exactly the same as your income for 2003, you could simply re-cycle your declaration.

In one of those 2003 changes, they decided that working mothers with children under three should receive a monthly payment of €100 instead of a tax reduction, and more than 800,000 mothers have signed up for the plan.

They also promise to make refunds within two weeks.

## SIMPLIFIED SYSTEM FOR WAGE EARNERS

Spain has also introduced a simplified system for wage earners, bringing their withholding tax more into line with the tax they actually owe, so that fewer workers have to make a tax declaration at all.

179

If you are a salaried worker earning less than €22,000, you probably don't need to make a tax declaration. As a result, almost 80 per cent of taxpayers do not need to file a return this year, nor in the immediate future.

This does not mean they are not paying income tax. It means that their withholding tax, taken out of their wage during the year, has been carefully calculated to match their liability by taking into account the number of dependants in the family and other factors.

Workers earning up to €22,000 a year can escape making the tax declaration under this plan.

The Spanish tax agency itself calculates their tax, sends them a special form to sign, and makes any refunds to them by the end of April, before the rest of us even get a chance to make our declaration.

If you are in this situation, the Tax Agency should send you a Form 105 to fill in early in 2004 for the 2003 tax year. If you agree with the calculations presented, you simply check the right box and return the form.

## FOREIGN RESIDENTS MUST DECLARE

Foreigners with incomes from outside Spain, but under €22,000, should not get over-excited, however. Any foreign resident who has the right to apply a double taxation treaty cannot take advantage of the plan and this includes almost every foreigner in Spain.

Another of the conditions for the €22,000 limit is that all the income must proceed from one source only, and it must have been subject to prior Spanish withholding tax.

The Spanish tax ministry, which is now known as the *Agencia Estatal de Administración Tributaria* - Agencia Tributaria for short - has been making efforts to ease the taxpayer's burden when he goes to declare.

The Agency, which we still call Hacienda, has inaugurated new telephone information services and has beefed up its own assistance to taxpayers who declare early and use Hacienda's own computer program. This program is ominously called title deed and real estate tax receipt for your house directly to the tax office, where staffers will help you plug the data into the PADRE program, just as they did for millions of taxpayers last year.

You can rest assured that your declaration is in proper form and Hacienda also declares that users of the PADRE program will be first on the list to receive any refunds - *devolución* - coming to them.

In many areas, taxpayers can make a previous appointment by telephone to make their PADRE declaration. You will be assigned a time to meet with a tax agency staffer, who will help you to plug your declaration into the program. You must take all necessary papers with you. (See below). In tourist areas, there is usually someone who speaks English. The general number to telephone in order to make this appointment is 901-223344.

Furthermore, you don't have to go in person to your tax office. The forms can be presented directly at your bank, whether they require payment or not. Your own bank, in many cases, has the PADRE forms in its computer, and a bank staffer will help you to make your declaration, as part of the bank's service.

If your tax picture is complicated, however, do not hesitate to consult a Spanish tax consultant, the *asesor fiscal*, who will be able to advise you in detail on the circumstances of the foreign resident in Spain. Most of these tax consultants use the PADRE program as well. You don't have to go to the tax office to take advantage of it.

And whether you are resident or non-resident, you can telephone Hacienda's own consultation number 900-333555 to have your doubts settled by the taxman's own consultants. This telephone call is completely free, but users report that the number is often engaged. In other cases of telephone consultations, callers are sometimes asked to leave a message describing their problem, and Hacienda will call back with the answer. Try also 901-200345.

All these user-friendly innovations at the tax ministry sound just fine but they don't mean that Hacienda is not serious about enforcing the law and collecting its money. Let's hear a word of warning.

181

As recently as 10 years ago, tax evasion was a way of life in Spain. People put ridiculously low values on their assets for property taxes, and anyone who talked about paying income tax on his real income was regarded as a kind of innocent fool.

Well, those good old days are gone forever. Spanish show business stars, football players and high-flying business tycoons find the taxman at their doors with a list of embarrassing questions.

Some Scandinavian governments have been known to inform the Spanish tax authorities that certain taxpayers have gone off their books and they have even included specific income information. Many new British residents of modest income have found they pay just as much tax in Spain as they paid in the UK.

The Spanish taxman has slammed the door on single-premium insurance policies and secret bank accounts; has exposed a gigantic ring of IVA (VAT) fraud; will tax offshore companies owning property in Spain when the ownership is not revealed, and requires a five per cent deposit when non-residents sell property.

Tax consultants and accountants who used to advise their clients to bury income and not declare dividends are now warning people that Big Brother, aided by the most modern computers in Madrid, really is watching everyone. This means you, so let's take a look at your possible tax obligations in Spain.

## AVOIDING DOUBLE TAXATION

When you stay in Spain for 183 days in one calendar year, you become legally liable for Spanish income tax, whether or not you take out a formal residence permit. On the morning of the 184th day, the Spanish treasury ministry, Hacienda, considers you a resident for tax purposes, and this means income tax on all your income, wherever in the world it may arise.

You also become liable for Spanish tax on your worldwide income when you take out a residence permit.

But what if you've just left the United Kingdom or Germany, where your pension has already been taxed? Do not worry too much. Spanish income tax regulations provide relief in cases where double taxation may arise. Spain has agreements with many countries to avoid double taxation and, where there is no specific agreement, relief is available through direct deduction of foreign tax paid or by a formula called *compensación extranjera,* or foreign compensation.

Even if you are not a resident of Spain and spend less than 183 days in the country, you are still liable for Spanish tax on any income arising in Spain, such as from the letting of your flat on the Costa Blanca. In this case, you may be taxed in Spain and will have to apply for relief when you pay income tax in your home country.

Scandinavians, Dutch and Belgians find Spanish income tax a relief. Most other Europeans will pay about the same as they paid at home. United States citizens will find that they still have to file for their US taxes because it is one of the few countries in the world that bases tax liability on nationality rather than on place of residence. Americans will also find that they have some Spanish income tax to pay on top of their US tax because Spanish rates are a bit higher than the American rates. They can, however, turn around and deduct most of the Spanish tax from their US tax.

The Spanish authorities make adjustments to avoid double taxation in this way: if you have already paid abroad a tax much higher than the one you would pay in Spain, you will not have to pay more. But if your income tax in your home country is less than it would be on the same income in Spain, you will have to pay the Spanish government the difference.

So you are taxed in Spain at Spanish rates. But you are not doubly taxed. It seems fair enough. These are general principles, and you can read all about them in a Spanish Ministry of the Treasury booklet called "Taxation Regulations for Foreigners."

If you are now liable to pay income tax in Spain, you will find that international agreements make all your income taxable, including your old-age pension, investments, interest, and any other source of income. The only exceptions to this are the pensions of civil servants. They are taxable in the home country that pays them.

However, the type of tax-free status varies from country to country because of the differences in Spain's treaties with each nation. UK civil servant pensions are totally tax-free in Spain. A tax office information officer has declared that, as far as Hacienda is concerned, these UK civil service pensions "do not exist", and need not be declared. They include the pensions of municipal employees as well.

For the Dutch, however, a retired civil servant will find that the amount of his civil service pension must be declared to the tax agency, which will add the sum of the pension to the declarer's other income, in order to calculate his tax percentage bracket. Then the amount of the pension will be deducted, but the remaining income will be taxed at the new and higher tax percentage.

Retired United Nations civil servants do not receive the benefits of this exemption, but they have formed an association to protest this apparent discrimination.

And so it goes, with other variations for other countries. If you are a retired civil servant, obtain a copy of your double taxation agreement with Spain in order to find your particular situation.

## How to Avoid Double Taxation

For British citizens who have recently arrived to take up residence in Spain, a double taxation problem arises almost immediately. The British tax inspector requires that a person be absent from the United Kingdom for a full tax year at least, before he is no longer liable for British income tax.

The UK tax year runs from April 6 to April 6, whereas the Spanish tax year is the natural year, from January 1 to January 1. This overlapping of dates often means that a Briton is subject to tax both in the UK and in Spain during the first year of his Spanish residence.

If you have suffered income tax in both Spain and the UK, you can claim a return of your British tax from:

Inland Revenue, Inspector of Funds
Lynwood Road, Thames Ditton,
Surrey KT7 0DP, England.

From this address you may also obtain forms on which to claim exemption from British income tax once you are an official

184

resident of Spain. The form comes in both Spanish and English.

You present the two forms to the Spanish Hacienda when you pay your Spanish tax and one is stamped by Hacienda for return to the British tax authorities as proof you have paid your Spanish tax.

You may also need to claim exemption for interest payments in the UK, where tax has been deducted at source, and on other investment income.

A number of shares and bonds are taxed differently when a Briton becomes non-resident in the UK. Great savings may be available if you get professional advice. Remember that you will not get any exemptions or reductions unless you apply for them.

## HOW TO DECLARE YOUR INCOME TAX

You do not have to file a declaration if your income for 2004 is less then €8,000 a year. This applies to married couples and retired people as well. The only condition on these limits is that no more than €1,600 of this income is from investments. If your income is less than €8,000 but it all comes from investments rather than work or pension, you will have to declare.

If you are running a business or working as a self-employed professional in Spain, you will have to declare no matter how low your income is.

Foreigners resident in Spain will need to present a Spanish tax declaration when they renew their residence card. Not to worry. You can present your declaration even if you do not owe any tax and this will meet the requirement.

The €8,000 limit includes total income of husband and wife and any children still living at home. Remember, this is worldwide income, not just Spanish income.

Let us suppose that you are retired and a resident for tax purposes in Spain, and you are legally bound to make a tax declaration. In many cases, it is best to consult a tax adviser. This may be a lawyer who specialises in tax matters, an *asesor fiscal*, who is an accountant and tax consultant, or a *gestor* who is experienced in tax matters.

These advisers will be up to date on new regulations and current practice. They will charge you a fee ranging upwards from €60 for this service, depending on how complex your return is, but their advice can save you many times that.

If your situation is simple and your income is from one basic source, such as a pension from your former employer, with perhaps a little income from stocks, you can do what millions of Spaniards do every spring, and walk into your local Hacienda office - which in major resort towns will be modern and well-equipped and staffed by young and helpful people - and ask for the *información al contribuyente* section. Here you will probably find an English-speaking staffer who will advise on the preparation of your tax return and help you plug into the PADRE program.

The usual dates for declaring Spanish income tax are from May 1 to June 30. You need to present the following documents:

1. Your pension slips showing the amount of your income.

2. Your end-of-year bank statement, which will show any interest you have been paid and your *saldo medio*, your average balance.The interest is part of your income and the average balance, or your balance on December 31, whichever is larger, is counted as part of your assets for Spanish wealth tax (see section on wealth tax). You probably will not be liable for wealth tax, as residents have an exemption on the first €108,182 of assets.

3. Take any papers relating to deposit certificates, stocks or bonds or any other asset you own, wherever such assets may be located. Remember that you as a resident are subject to Spanish income tax on your worldwide income.

4. Of course you need your passport or your residence permit.

5. If you are claiming any deductions for invalid relatives living with you, for mortgage payments and interest on the purchase of your Spanish home, or for any other reason, take the appropriate documents.

6. If you have paid income tax in another country and are seeking relief from Spanish tax on that account, take the receipts or copies of your foreign declaration.

## NO IMPUTED INCOME TAX ON PRINCIPAL RESIDENCE

Residents are no longer subject to the property owners' imputed income tax on their principal dwelling. For this tax, two per cent of the official rated value of your property, the *valor catastral,* is calculated as if it were income and added to your total. If your rated value has recently been raised sharply, the figure will be 1.1 per cent.

This tax on imaginary income ended in 1999 for the taxpayer's principal residence. If, however, you own two homes in Spain, as do many Spaniards, you will have to pay the tax on the second residence.

Non-residents remain subject to the tax because, by definition, Spain is not their principal residence. They file on Form 214 as described in the preceding chapter on Property Taxes.

The two per cent or 1.1 per cent of value is not a tax. It is added to your other income just as if you had received the cash. If your property is valued at €120,000, for example, two per cent will be €2,400. If your income is modest, €12,000 a year, you add this sum to it. Now your income is €14,400. You are paying Spanish income tax at about 20 per cent, so the extra €2,400 of income produces an extra tax bill of €480.

If you are fortunate enough to own two properties in Spain, take along your receipt for this year's IBI, the *Impuesto sobre Bienes Inmuebles*, the annual real estate tax. This slip shows the official rated value of the property that is not your principal residence, so the tax officials can calculate your imputed income tax.

The Hacienda staff will counsel you on the proper way to fill in the forms, on your basic deductions, any credit for foreign tax paid, and so forth. But they cannot work miracles for you if your situation is complicated, and you may need the services of a professional tax consultant.

## HOW MUCH IT WILL COST YOU

As Spain continues its de-centralisation, it passes many areas of public administration to the individual regions. To pay for this, a part of the national income tax is also assigned to the autonomous regions. This regional share is 15 per cent, which goes into their individual annual budgets. We are not dividing the tax table into two sections, however, in order to simplify our calculations.

## SPANISH INCOME TAX RATES FOR 2004

(In euros, rounded to nearest euro)

| Taxable Base | Tax | Rate Band | Marginal rate% |
|---|---|---|---|
| 0 | 0 | 4,000 | 15 |
| 4,000 | 600 | 9,800 | 24 |
| 13,800 | 2,952 | 12,000 | 28 |
| 25,800 | 6,312 | 19,200 | 37 |
| 45,000 | 13,416 | excess | 45 |

The tax table refers to the year 2004, payable in May and June, 2005. Although it is divided into 85 per cent for the Spanish State and 15 per cent for the autonomous regions, we present the total scale. The same scale is used for individual or joint declaration. This is balanced by providing greater family deductions in the joint declaration.

In the year 2000 tax revision, an entire series of time-honoured tax deductions, for medical expenses and others, disappeared. They were replaced by a reduction directly from income on the philosophy that each human being needs a €3,400 a year "survival minimum", not subject to tax.

Thus, a single person of modest income can reduce his tax base by €3,400, while a married couple can combine their survival minimums and take €6,800 off, plus €1,400 or more for each child.

In this way, the system favours - just a little - married couples of modest incomes declaring jointly. The rates are about the same as most European rates, though the complex marginal system of taxing the difference between the successive rate bands is different.

To find your tax before you take your deductions, you can consult the table. The first column lists your taxable income. The next column gives the amount of tax for that bracket. The third column refers to the amount of excess income until you reach the next step, and the last column tells what percentage is applied to that excess amount. It works like this:

If your income is €28,800 per year and you are declaring as a married couple, you first take your reduction of €6,800. This gives you a tax base of €22,000.

We look at the scale and we see that an income of €13,800 pays a tax of €2,952, and the excess over that pays at a rate of 28 per cent all the way up to €25,800. Our excess is €8,200, so we multiply that by 28 per cent. This gives us €1,968. We add that to €2,952 and we get a total of €4,920 we owe the government, about 16 per cent.

If you are 65 or over (see below), your personal minimum has an extra €800. If you are paying off a mortgage on your principal residence, you can take 15 per cent of that, which would help your bill.

## DEDUCTIONS FROM INCOME

From your total income you can deduct:

1. The total amount of your payments into the Spanish Social Security system during this year.

2. Seventy-five per cent of any *plus valia* tax you may have paid during the year on a property transfer.

3. Your personal or family minimum exempt from tax. This minimum varies according to the person and the family. For example:

   - For the first child, €1,400.

   - For the second child, €1,500.

   - For the third child, €2,200.

   - For each child more than three, €2,300.

Further deductions for handicapped children range from

189

€2,000 to €5,000 depending on the seriousness of the handicap. The children draw this deduction until they are 25 years old, as long as they are living at home and not earning themselves more than €8,000 in a year.

Any aged parents over 65 living in the family unit draw a deduction of €800 as long as they do not earn more than €8000. Any person over 65 has a reduction of €4,200 personal minimum instead of the normal €3,400. A handicapped person may have a personal minimum exempt from tax up to €8,000. One-parent families have a higher range of all these personal minimums.

## Wage Earner Deductions

The wage earner can deduct €3,500 from income up to incomes of €8,200. This deduction goes down on a sliding scale as income rises to €13,000, when it is fixed at €2,400. It is also fixed at €2,400 when there is income from other sources, such as investments, of €6,000.

Pension income counts as wage earnings, so nearly all pensioners would have the benefit of this deduction. If both husband and wife receive pensions, they each can deduct. Handicapped workers have higher deductions. Dividends have a general deduction of 40 per cent.

## Better Rate for Annuities

There are tax reductions for those who receive regular payments from lifetime annuities, called in Spanish *renta vitalicia*. Reductions depend on the age at which you begin receiving payments.

The amount to be taxed goes by the following table:

- 45% when the recipient began receiving payments at the age of 39 or less.

- 40% when he started between 40 and 49.

- 35% between 50 and 59.

- 25% between 60 and 69.

- 20% over the age of 69.

190

So, if you began receiving your annuity payments at the age of 65, for example, you declare the entire amount but you are taxed on only 25 per cent of the income. This applies only to annuities constituted by purchase on your part. It does not apply to other pension plans.

A five-year annuity pays on only 15 per cent of the income, a five to 10-year annuity at 25 per cent, an annuity of 10 to 15 years will be taxed on 35 per cent of the income, and any annuity of a longer period will be charged on 42 per cent of the payments.

## Mortgage deduction made from tax due

The only one remaining is the deduction for purchase of your principal residence. This is basically 15 per cent of all expenses involved in buying your home, including mortgage repayments and the interest on the mortgage, up to a limit of 15 per cent of €9,000 per year.

If the mortgage loan exceeds half the value of the dwelling and no more than 40 per cent of it is to be paid back in the first three years, the deduction can be 25 per cent of the first €4,508 and 20 per cent of the rest, up to €9,000.

This means a maximum deduction of €2,028 per year. Remember, however, that this comes off your tax payable, not from your income, so it has a large effect.

## Foreign Tax Deduction

If you have already paid income tax abroad, you can also deduct that from your Spanish tax bill. The procedure is to calculate the amount of Spanish tax you would pay on your income.

If you can show the amount of tax you have already paid abroad, this is entered as a possible deduction. But first, your tax consultant or adviser in Hacienda will make a little calculation, to find out what your *compensación extranjera* will be. It involves some complicated arithmetic.

This calculation is made by dividing your *base imponible,* or tax base, into your *cuota líquida*, the amount of tax actually payable, times 100.

This gives a percentage called the *tipo medio*, or average rate,

191

which is then, in turn, applied to the tax base, giving a new tax payable figure. You then deduct from your Spanish income tax either the full amount of the tax you have paid abroad, or the results of the *compensación extranjera* calculation, whichever is less.

The reason for this tricky arithmetic is to make certain that the Spanish tax authorities do not find themselves in the position of having to refund to you tax money, which you have paid to the Swedish treasury ministry, for example.

Taxes in Sweden are higher than they are in Spain and the Spanish treasury department simply cannot permit you to deduct that very high payment, which would mean that Spain would have to pay you back money that Spain never received.

The application of that calculated *tipo medio* means that your Spanish tax payable never falls below zero. This does not mean that people never get money back from the Spanish treasury. Millions of people do every year, foreigners among them.

This refund is called a *devolución*, and more than half of all Spanish taxpayers get money back at the end of the year.

## "WEALTH TAX" FOR RESIDENTS

In addition to his income tax the Spanish resident - and non-resident property owner - is liable for Spain's tax on capital assets - *patrimonio* tax. The name "wealth tax" may not sound like proper legal terminology, but it is an adequate translation of the Spanish name, as it's exactly that: a tax on all your assets and property.

Do not be alarmed, however. A resident of Spain has an exemption of €108,182 of valuation, which rises to €150,253 when the asset is the principal residence. This means that a husband and wife whose principal asset in Spain is their home are exempt from the tax up to €300,506 if both their names are on the title deed.

In Spanish, the name is *impuesto extraordinario sobre el patrimonio*, the extraordinary tax on assets. This tax started in 1978 as a special measure to force many Spanish citizens who had been hiding their wealth, especially property, to bring these assets into the open.

Hacienda placed a very small tax on these assets, amounting to only 0.2 per cent, that is two-tenths of one per cent, or two-thousandths of the taxable base, up to assets of €167,129. After that, the rate goes up as assets go up. (See tax table).

The idea was that anyone who did not then declare his assets would be in violation and subject to fines. Further, any difference between assets declared at that time and such assets as later came to light would be treated as income for that year and taxed as such, at the much higher income tax rate, of course, going as high as 48 per cent.

The "extraordinary" tax worked more or less as projected, and many formerly hidden assets came to light. However, the State found it a good means of keeping track of people's wealth, so they have not yet discontinued it and it has become all-too ordinary and normal.

You declare for this tax when you declare for your income tax, on the separate Form 714.

## PATRIMONIO TAX RATES 2004

(In euros, rounded to nearest euro)

| Taxable Base | Tax | Rate Band | Marginal rate% |
|---|---|---|---|
| 0 | 0 | 167,129 | 0.20 |
| 167,129 | 334 | 167,123 | 0.30 |
| 334,253 | 836 | 334,247 | 0.50 |
| 716,581 | 2,507 | 668,500 | 0.90 |
| 1,337,000 | 8,523 | 1,337,000 | 1.30 |
| 2,673,999 | 25,904 | 2,673,999 | 1.70 |
| 5,347,998 | 71,362 | 5,347998 | 2.10 |
| 10,695,996 | 183,670 | excess | 2.50 |

Wealth tax affects residents and non-residents differently. A resident is required to declare his worldwide assets while the non-resident declares only his property and assets in Spain.

These taxable assets include anything he owns, not just real estate. They can include bank deposits, stocks, shares, bonds, ownership of a business, gold bars under the mattress, automobiles, yachts, private air-planes, works of art unless they are owned by the maker, jewels, luxury fur coats or anything else that can be considered wealth.

Your home furnishings are exempt unless they are valuable antiques. There are deductions available for debts against your business, mortgages on your property, and any tax of a similar nature paid in a foreign country.

Real market value is used as the basis for Spanish capital assets tax. Unlike the property owner's imputed income tax, where the rated value is used, wealth tax is based on the current market value, or the declared price on property deeds.

## RESIDENTS EXEMPT FOR €108,102

A resident of Spain pays nothing on the first €108,102 of valuation. In 2001, this exemption was raised to €150,253 for the resident's home.

A husband and wife each have the exemption and each must make an individual declaration. If they own together a property valued at almost €300,000, they each declare half the value, take their exemption of €150,000, and have no *patrimonio* tax to pay.

For most of us, our principal wealth is our home so most residents wind up paying nothing under this tax. In fact, of 14 million Spanish residents declaring for income tax, only 800,000 of them had to pay anything in wealth tax.

But, as you see from the table, if you have worldwide assets of about a million pounds Sterling, that is, over 1.6 million euros and you are a Spanish resident, you will have to pay wealth tax of almost €12,000 each year.

## GLOSSARY

**Agencia Estatal de Administración Tributaria** – Spanish State tax agency

**Base imponible** – taxable base

**Compensación extranjera** – compensation for foreign tax paid

**Contribuyente** – tax payer

**Cuota liquida** – tax payable

**Declaración de la renta** – income tax declaration

**Devolución** – refund

**Hacienda** – Ministry of the Ecomomy

**Impuesto sobre el Patrimonio** – capital assets tax

**IRPF – Impuesto sobre la renta de las personas fisicas** – income tax for individuals

**PADRE** – tax payers' help programme

**Plus Valia** – municipal capital gains tax

**Renta Vitalicia** – lifetime income, annuity

**Saldo Medio** – average bank balance

**Tipo Medio** – average tax rate

**Valor Catastral** – rated value of property for tax purposes.

# 11 Working and starting a business

Council of Europe regulations provide that European Union citizens can work in Spain under exactly the same conditions as Spaniards.

The key words of the regulations are "equal treatment" and "non-discrimination". The *autorización de residencia y trabajo,* which is a work and residence document, is still required but it is now much easier to obtain if you are an EU citizen.

And Spain cannot refuse a work or residence permit to any family members of the EU worker. Spouses and children under 21 years of age, or who are dependent on the worker, have full rights both to reside in the country and to obtain employment, either as hired persons or self-employed.

This right applies even to family members who are not EU nationals. If a Briton working in Spain is married to a US national, for example, the non-EU spouse will have full rights to residence and employment in Spain.

All of these rights, and more, are set out in the EU Regulation 1612/68, regarding the free circulation of workers within the European Union. Among these rights are:

- The children of foreign workers will have the same rights to trade school education and apprenticeship programmes run by the State as nationals of that State.

- Any clause in the employment contract or in any trade union agreement that is discriminatory against EU citizens will be considered null and void. EU workers in other countries may vote and be elected to office in unions at a local level.

- Article 9 of Title II of the Regulation notes that such EU workers will enjoy the same priority of access to public or subsidised housing as Spanish nationals. That is, where low-cost housing is available to workers, the EU member will be able to enter his name on the waiting list under the same conditions as a national.

- Title I of the Regulation specifically prohibits any country from applying rules that limit or put unusual conditions on the employment of EU foreigners, or that set out any different or special rules for hiring foreigners, or that oblige employers to advertise jobs differently for foreigners and nationals, or that force foreigners to register with employment offices before they can obtain work, or that make any obstacles for the hiring of EU nationals who may not yet reside officially in that country.

- Article 5 of Title I requires that any EU foreigner looking for work in another EU country shall receive the same help from State employment offices as its own nationals seeking work.

All of these regulations add up to non-discrimination and equal treatment for all workers throughout the EU. They even mean that the foreign worker, should he lose his employment in Spain for reasons beyond his control, can have access to unemployment payments just like a Spanish worker.

Once he has found employment, he will then need to register

for his work and residence permit. Employees require a work permit called *cuenta ajena*, which means "on another person's account". Those seeking to work on a self-employed basis need another sort of permit, called *autonomo, or cuenta propia,* "on your own account".

## CUENTA AJENA

In practice this means that an EU citizen who is looking for a job may enter Spain without any more formalities than the presentation of his passport, and remain as a "tourist" for a time, until he finds work. The EU job seeker should present himself at the nearest office of the INEM, the *Instituto Nacional de Empleo,* the National Employment Institute, where he registers as a *demandante de empleo,* a person looking for work. This is exactly the way Spaniards do it. The time limit for this is the normal tourist visit of six months.

When our job seeker obtains employment, he must present his work contract and Social Security registration to the Spanish police and to the national government's sub-delegate office of the province, as well as to the *Delegado de Trabajo,* the provincial director of the Labour Ministry, who should routinely issue his *tarjeta comunitaria,* his EU citizen's residence and work permit.

The first work permit will be for one year and renewals will be for five years. Your new employer will make the arrangements for your registration and payment into the Spanish Social Security scheme. Remember that it is illegal to work in Spain without being registered for Social Security.

There are short-term permits as well, called *Permiso A,* running for three-month, six-month, or nine-month periods. The normal work permit is called *Permiso B.*

Those who have found jobs in Spain should also read the next chapter on Employing Others for a full discussion of their rights as workers.

## CUENTA PROPIA OR AUTONOMO

The other sort of work permit applies to persons such as plumbers, carpenters or business operators, who wish to work as self-employed. This is called working "on your own account" the *cuenta propia*. It is often called *autonomo* as well, because the worker pays into the Spanish Social Security system under a different plan from the employee.

Unfortunately for these self-employed persons, their situation is a little more complicated, but it is no more complicated than it is for Spaniards themselves. Remember that "equal treatment" means that those persons applying for self-employed permits will have to go through a series of fiscal licences, opening permits and inspections just like Spaniards trying to start a business. The red tape has driven more than one Spaniard round the bend and foreigners will find the same frustrations. (See the section of this chapter entitled How to Start a Business for more details).

European professionals who want to work in Spain now find it much easier to have their professional qualifications standardised to Spanish regulations and to set up their practice in Spain.

Doctors, dentists, nurses, veterinarians, architects, lawyers, insurance agents and hairdressers now experience fewer difficulties when they want to render their services in Spain. Other professions also will find restrictions relaxed.

The recognition of foreign qualifications has been greatly simplified and speeded up. Even the professional Colleges can no longer act as either open or covert obstacles to the practice of professions by EU citizens who hold the proper titles in their home countries.

## NON-EU WORK PERMITS

Unfortunately for those citizens of non-EU nations, the situation has remained the same as before. Such third-nation citizens as Americans and Canadians still need the *visado de residencia,* the special visa they must obtain from the Spanish consulate in their home country even before they come to Spain.

There are seven classifications of these visas, so be sure you get the right one when you apply. There are visas for people who only want to retire in Spain, visas for people who are going to start a business, visas for those who have found employment, visas for top-level executives, visas for students and visas for teachers.

Applicants who intend to take up employment will have to show a proper work contract, along with proof that the position has been advertised with the Spanish employment institute and that no adequate Spanish candidate can be found for the job.

In many areas this is a serious obstacle, but in specialised fields such as computers the Spanish authorities accept that the outside worker can make a positive contribution to Spain's development. Executives in sensitive positions and teachers usually have few problems in obtaining work permits.

Those non-EU applicants who wish to go into business will have to demonstrate that they have about US $18,000 to invest in their Spanish business and that they will provide work for Spanish nationals. Often enough, the Spanish consulate will insist that the investment be made, the employees hired and the business ready to operate before they will grant the visa. Remember that you need this visa even before you go to Spain to apply for the work permit itself, so things can get complicated.

These restrictions seem harsh, but try to understand the point of view of the Spanish labour authorities. Unemployment has been as high as 20 per cent until recently, so the Ministry of Labour is very concerned with the creation of employment for Spanish nationals. If your business idea will bring employment to three or four Spaniards, your application will be looked upon most favourably.

Is there any way you can either earn a living or stretch your pension without having a work permit? Not really. The law says that anyone who carries out any activity with *fines lucrativos*, a lucrative purpose, and gains money by it, is required to have a permit.

Painters may paint in Spain without a work permit but if they start making money by selling their paintings they should have a work permit. An established painter selling his work through a Madrid gallery will have no problem getting a permit. A young street artist who peddles his works to the tourists in the restaurants will probably never get a permit.

A musician contracted to give one concert does not need a work permit, though he is liable for Spanish income tax on any

201

money he earns in Spain. A musician who is contracted to perform regularly in a night spot will be required to have a work permit.

There are also temporary work permits up to six months for people such as tour guides and specialists who work in Spain for short periods without intending to take up residence. This is the sort of permit often arranged for timeshare sales people. The company that hires you should provide you with this permit.

## HOW TO APPLY FOR A WORK PERMIT

If you are an EU citizen, you can enter Spain as a tourist, go to the INEM (the National Institute of Employment) and register as a job-seeker just the same as a Spaniard. Then you look for work.

Once you have found your job, you go to the nearest Spanish police station which has a *departamento de extranjeros*, taking your job contract, social security card, passport, medical certificate issued by an authorised examination centre, and four photos. Fill in the application forms and wait for your permit to be granted. Along with the *tarjeta comunitaria*, you will be issued a NIE, a *número de identificación de extranjeros,* your Spanish tax identification number.

In fact, your employer will steer you through the entire process. If you later change jobs, your new employer will handle the paperwork.

If you are opening your own business, things will be more complicated, so be prepared to face a jungle of permits if you want to open a bar on the Costa Blanca. However, once you have obtained your *licencia de apertura*, your opening licence, you will be issued a work permit. For more details on starting a business, see next below.

If you are seeking a self-employed work permit, you will have to register yourself with the Spanish Social Security.

## NON-EU CITIZENS

If you are a non-EU citizen, first you obtain your visa from the Spanish consulate in your home country. Without the visa, you will never obtain the work permit.

You will need to obtain from your home province or state a police certificate stating that you have no prison record. This is called a *certificado penal*. If it is not in Spanish, it must be translated into Spanish and legalised by a certificate of *apostille* before the Spanish authorities will accept it. Ask the Spanish consulate in your country for the proper forms.

Once in Spain, you need to get your health certificate, the *certificado médico*. It shows that you have no contagious diseases. Forms are available from the *gestorías* and government offices, as well as the authorised medical centres.

You need a certificate of registration with the consulate of your home country in Spain, showing that you are registered with their office.

Then you need the ever-present photos, five of them if you are a non-EU citizen. One photo stays with the police, one with the *Sub-Delegado del Gobierno* office of your province, one with the *Delegación de Trabajo* file, one goes on the document itself, and I forget what happens to the other one.

As one veteran resident of the Costa del Sol remarked: "They must have nearly a hundred photos of me by now. I wonder what they do with them?"

This application is a complicated, time-consuming and frustrating procedure. You will probably need some expert advice from a *gestoría* or a lawyer.

### *AUTONOMO* WORK PERMIT LIST

Not all the items on this list will be required in every case, thank goodness, but it gives you an idea.

1. Title or degree. If you wish to practice medicine or architecture, you must present your titles and certificates from EU institutions. If your titles are from outside the EU, they will have to undergo a lengthy process to be validated.

2. I.A.E. *Impuesto de Actividades Economicas,* the Tax on Economic Activities. Until this year, the IAE was a municipal tax, but it has now been taken over by the central tax administration. You apply at your Hacienda

203

office. The IAE now costs nothing if your turn-over is less than €600,000 a year, but you must register for your specific activity in any case to have your code number *(epigrafe)* assigned.

3. Your registration with the Spanish Social Security as a *trabajador autonomo,* a self-employed worker. You register at your nearest Social Security office, and you pay a minimum €225,11 every month. It is illegal to work in Spain without paying into the Spanish Social Security system.

4. A *licencia de apertura,* an opening licence, will be necessary if you have business premises, such as a shop or a workshop installation. This municipal licence comes from your town hall and authorises you to operate your particular business in that particular location.

5. A written explanation of the activity you will carry out. This is called a *memoria de actividades*, and it describes just what work you will do as a self-employed person.

6. Passport and photocopy.

7. Four photos.

8. Title deed and lease contract for business premises and photocopy.

9. Incorporation charter, If a company has been formed.

10. Filled-in form *(solicitúd)* requesting permit

11. Any other permits relating to your special profession. If you are going to work as a cook in a restaurant, you will need a food handler's certificate, for example.

## WHAT IT WILL COST

The cost of a work permit depends on a number of factors, principally on whether you use a *gestoría* or a lawyer or you handle the application on your own, and whether you have found a job or will work on your own account.

If you have a job, your employer will pay most of the expenses and will probably steer you through the entire process. If you are self-employed, you had better figure €500 to €700, including all the taxes and fees.

If your Spanish is reasonably good, you can probably handle the matter yourself. Obtain the forms from your local police station or from the *Delegación de Trabajo,* fill them out, present them and wait to see what happens.

The first step is for the police to clear your residence permit application. This can take a month or more. Then the papers go to the Labour ministry office in your province, where they rule on your work permit request. The Government Sub-Delegate (formerly Civil Governor) office also vets it. If granted, you then receive a combined work and residence permit.

The application forms themselves, the solicitud, are free, but they are the only item on your list that is. By the time you have added your first Social Security payment of €225,11, plus any possible costs for opening permits and other fees, you are looking at a real expense.

Few foreigners, however, will feel confident enough with their Spanish and their familiarity with bureaucratic ins and outs to handle their work permit application on their own.

They will turn to a competent *gestoría.* The only way to find one is to make enquiries among people who have work permits and who can recommend a particular *gestor.* Their advice can be invaluable.

As in any country, there are right ways and wrong ways to go about things, and a good *gestor* will know the right way. He will also be up to date on recent rulings of the Labour ministry, and can advise you on whether or not you are likely to get a permit. He may suggest that you word the application in a certain way, for example.

For a work permit, one gestor recently charged the rock-bottom figure of €200, with the taxes and fees added to this. Or you can use a lawyer. This, of course, can cost you €300 or more, in addition to the fees and taxes, but if you are starting a business, employing others, purchasing property for commercial use, or if you feel your particular case may need a little extra explaining, this fee can seem quite reasonable.

205

A lawyer will be able to advise you on many questions outside the competence of the *gestoría*, such as aspects of investment procedures. Again, make enquiries among people working already to find a lawyer who has given satisfaction.

## SPANISH SOCIAL SECURITY

All those European workers who are now free to seek employment in Spain on equal terms with Spaniards will want to know what the Spanish Social Security system will cost them and what it has to offer. It's never too soon to start thinking about your old age.

Many complications arise in the calculation of Social Security payments and benefits, depending on the age of the worker, time of payment, dependents and other factors, but the short version goes like this:

## SELF-EMPLOYED

If you are a self-employed worker such as a plumber or a business operator, you are required by law to pay into the Spanish Social Security system in the *autónomo* scheme, which will cost you a minimum of €225,11 a month.

The minimum time to qualify for a minimum retirement pension is 15 years but you need to pay for 35 years to get a full pension. The minimum is half the full pension.

If you had paid into the Spanish system at this minimum rate for the last 35 years, reached the age of 65, had a spouse under your support who received no other State pension, you would receive a pension of just under €500 a month.

If you paid only 15 years, you still qualify for a pension but it is reduced by the number of years less than 35 that you have paid into the system. So, a person who paid 15 years will get half the full pension.

Remember that you will receive 14 payments a year, not 12. It's just like the workers' pay. You get an extra month each at Christmas and in the summer.

206

## EMPLOYEES

If you are a normal salaried worker, your Social Security payments and benefits can vary widely.

The minimum salary base for paying into the system is €755,40 and a basic percentage of 28.8 per cent of this is calculated as the monthly payment for Social Security.

A very small part of this is deducted from the worker's salary. The employer pays the greater part directly to the Social Security system in the name of the worker. These payments, with their extra charges, come to a minimum of about €185 a month for a low-salaried worker.

The system is much more complicated than the outline above and amounts and percentages vary according to the type of employment.

Once the salaried worker has paid into the system at the minimum rate for the same period of 35 years, he also will receive the same minimum pension of €500 a month as the self-employed worker who retires at 65 with a spouse to feed.

The employed worker's monthly contributions include the possibility of unemployment payments if he should lose his job for reasons beyond his control. Self-employed workers only receive these payments if they are medically incapacitated for work.

Recent cutbacks in benefits mean that many unemployed workers receive only 75 per cent of the minimum wage as their unemployment benefit. The minimum wage for 2004 is €460.50 so this means that the unemployed who have not paid into the system for a full year will receive only €320 a month. What is worse, they lose their credit towards a retirement pension as well.

Both *autónomo* and *cuenta ajena* workers are entitled to medical benefits through the Spanish National Health scheme, which is going through the same sort of financial and overburden crisis as national health plans in most European countries.

Nevertheless, Spanish Social Security hospitals are just as modern and well-equipped as those in other countries and their medical staff are just as well trained. If the Social Security hospital on the Costa del Sol was good enough for Melanie

Griffith to have her baby there, it should be good enough for the rest of us.

If a worker is ill, he will also continue to receive a portion of his salary, depending on various factors. The self-employed person can also receive sickness pay, at the same rate of 75 per cent of the minimum wage, as long as he can present a doctor's certificate testifying that he is incapacitated for carrying out his profession.

Domestic workers have a special scheme, in which they pay at a lower rate, but receive the same minimum benefits as other workers after 15 years. That is if they are working on their own account, for two or three families. If they are employed full-time with one family, then they must be paid the minimum wage and have their Social Security under the normal scheme. (See next chapter Employing Others for details)

## SPAIN HAS TREATIES WITH OTHER NATIONS

For most foreign workers in Spain, not only EU citizens, there are treaty agreements with many nations to ensure that a worker who has laboured in several different countries does not wind up without enough years of paying Social Security to qualify for a pension in any country.

These agreements usually provide that the total number of years paid into the Social Security systems in the various countries be added together to enable the worker to qualify for a pension, which usually is paid proportionally by each country.

So far we have discussed only the minimum payments and benefits of Spain's Social Security system, but workers may pay more into the system and qualify for higher pensions at 65.

A self-employed worker can choose to set his salary base as high as €2,500 a month, meaning he would pay €900 a month into the system, in order to qualify for the maximum permitted pension of more than €1,500 a month after 35 years. A salaried worker earning that sum can also make maximum payments in order to get the maximum pension.

Those fortunate enough to be earning higher incomes find that no more Social Security payments can be made on the additional income.

The Spanish Social Security system also sets out a schedule of payments for major disability, such as losing your legs in an industrial accident, for orphans and for other areas, and generally functions much like the system in other European nations.

It has much the same worries about how the system will continue to work in the future, with the population having more and more retired people to be supported by a smaller percentage of active workers.

## STARTING A BUSINESS

The first thing you should do if you are starting a business is bring money - lots of it - and open a bank account.

Make contact with a good *gestoría* to advise you on all bureaucratic procedures. Find a good *asesor fiscal*, tax consultant, to handle your bookkeeping. Consult a lawyer to make sure you understand your contracts. A good adviser in one of these categories will save you time, trouble and money, and many of them speak English.

Locate your premises and arrange to purchase, rent or lease. The Spanish lease was formerly called a *traspaso* and is now called a *cesión*. It can be bought and sold under certain conditions.

When you buy a going business with a *traspaso* or *cesión* for the premises, be aware that the operator of the business who sells you the leasehold may very well not be the actual owner of the premises. The actual owner will have a right to re-negotiate the *traspaso* when the lease is up. If you lease directly from the owner, you have the right to renewal when the term is up.

Should you wish to sell the lease for the business premises, you must offer it to the landlord first at the same price as your prospective purchaser has offered. The landlord always has first refusal. The whole business of *traspasos* and *cesiones* has many ins and outs and you will need expert legal advice to avoid pitfalls.

Keep careful records of your start-up expenses because the costs and the IVA that you have paid out will become deductible from the taxes on your business earnings later.

Apply for your *Licencia de Apertura,* your opening licence for the business, which is granted by the town hall. This can cost you as little as €100 for a small shop; €200 for a bar or restaurant, and up to €5,000 if you are opening a plush real estate office. Be prepared for sanitary and technical inspections, and in some localities be ready for long waits as well.

In the city of Málaga, some establishments have waited as long as six months before receiving their licences. Many of them, of course, simply opened without the licence after a time. In fact, in Benalmádena on the Costa del Sol, it was recently discovered that more than 1,000 of the 5,000 businesses operating there had no licence at all. That's all right for Spaniards, but you as a foreigner will need your licence to apply for your work and residence document.

In addition to the other papers, you may need a food handler's medical certificate or other document, depending on the business you choose. You will also be assigned your NIE, your foreigner's tax identification number, which identifies you to the Spanish tax authorities. Spaniards have a number, too. You can obtain this NIE without having a residence permit if you need it for your operations before your final permit is issued.

You need to acquire two more documents at this time. One is your Spanish Social Security card. As a self-employed businessman you will be called a *trabajador autónomo* (see above). You also need to register yourself as a businessman or professional for the IAE - the *Impuesto Sobre Actividades Económicas* - the tax on economic activities.

The IAE replaced the former *licencia fiscal,* or business licence, though many people continue to refer to it by this name.

In a move to stimulate small business, the government has:
1.  Reduced this tax to zero for professionals or business that turn over less than €600,000 per year.

2.  Removed the administration of this tax from the municipalities and returned it to the central Tax Agency. Now you must apply to register at your Hacienda office.

You must still register for IAE, even though it will probably cost nothing, because you must have a tax category assigned to you for your business or profession. A dentist has a different

210

code number – *epigrafe* - to a plumber or travel agency.

If you are employing others, you will find that a worker costs you at least €900 a month. This is based on the low salary of €560, plus Social Security payments of about 30 per cent of that, plus extra payments at Christmas and in the summer, and assorted other expenses. See next section on Employing Others for more details.

There are many complications with hiring workers and making contracts. Remember it is illegal to hire any worker without paying his Social Security. Perhaps you can take advantage of some of the tax breaks offered in 2004 to those who create new jobs for younger or older workers or for workers who have been unemployed for long periods.

Be alert as to how much it will cost you to make the worker redundant if your business fails to prosper.

Keep accurate books of expenses and income, noting all your payments of IVA, Spain's Value Added Tax, plus your expenses for the *gestoría,* accounting and legal advice, and get ready to make your first quarterly tax payment, your *pago fraccionado.*

Most small businesses will find that there are two options for paying their business tax, one of which is called *modulos,* or modules, and the other *estimación directa,* or direct estimation.

A small business is obliged to start by using the modular system. In the case of bars and restaurants the tax agency itself decides what your income should be, based on a complex analysis of how many tables you have, how many waiters you employ, your location, the square metres of your premises, and other factors.

You will be charged business tax on this assigned amount each quarter. At the end of the year you file your complete return of actual income and take you deductions for business expenses. If the tax agency owes you money in return, and they probably will, you claim the refund.

The only advantage of this system is that you do not have to maintain a detailed set of accounts in order to present your quarterly statements. This is helpful for small operations dealing in hundreds or thousands of little transactions. Of course, you must present your totals at the end of each year.

After the first year, you can decide if you wish to pass to the direct estimation system, which requires complete bookkeeping, with every *factura* in its place. The advantage, of course, is that you are paying tax on your real business earnings each quarter. If you choose this system, you must continue to use it for three years.

Spain's company tax is charged at 35 per cent. Again, you can claim return of any overpayment, but Hacienda will have had the use of your money for a year or so. These tax rates apply to professionals as well as to businesses and any other self-employed persons.

It begins to sound as if you definitely need the services of a tax consultant and business specialist here. Very few can handle this paperwork on their own.

## FORMING A SPANISH COMPANY

If you intend to carry out any large-scale activity, you may wish to form a Spanish company, or a branch of a foreign company, in order to do business in Spain. You are permitted to do this as either a resident or a non-resident. If you have €60,000 to put up in capital, you can form a Spanish *Sociedad Anónima,* which is the equivalent of a British limited company (a plc), or an American corporation (an Inc.), where liability is limited to the amount of capital each investor has subscribed. These companies have "S.A." after their names.

S.A. companies must now have their books audited yearly and register these audited accounts with the Mercantile Registry as public documents, available for inspection by any citizen. This means that you may consult the Mercantile Registry for information about any Spanish company with which you intend to do business. You can find out the names and addresses of the principal officers of the company and see its profits and losses for the previous year. Failure to file such an audited statement or to falsify any information it contains is an offence, punishable by fines.

Under the old system, which required very little capital for the formation of a company, hundreds of thousands of companies were constituted, under no obligation to publish their accounts. It was easy for an unscrupulous businessman to form a company, conceal its profits, and later disappear, owing money to his creditors, which they had no way of recovering. The present system is designed to correct these abuses.

You can also form in Spain a *Sociedad Limitada*, a simpler form of incorporation with a reduced number of shareholders and capital, or you can undertake a legal partnership or make a Spanish branch company, a sucursal, of a parent company already existing in your home country.

If you form a company, its Articles of Association must be signed and registered with a Spanish Notary and of course the Mercantile Registry. Formerly, one needed three shareholders and three directors to form a company, but under the new legislation, a single person can incorporate himself.

If you form a company, you may be employed by it as a director, even if you own the company completely. The company will be liable for Spain's corporate tax of 35 per cent on its profits.

You will need the best legal advice you can get, both in your home country before you start your Spanish company and in Spain before you form the company, to make sure that you are getting the best tax and business breaks available to you when you transfer funds. There are many tax complications and opportunities when you set up a company, so study it carefully before you begin.

Such questions as whether you set up your company while you are still a non-resident of Spain and whether you liquidate your foreign holdings before or after you become a resident of Spain will become important considerations.

There is a maze of regulations and opportunities around foreign investment, and you will need a lawyer skilled in these matters. The foreign investment will be vetted by the *Dirección General de Transacciones Exteriores*, the general directorate of foreign transactions, better known as the DGTE, the authority which continues to keep a controlling eye on foreign exchange, even though it has fewer powers to deny money transfers.

You want to be sure that your Spanish company will be able to take its legal profits out of Spain, and also that it will have access to bank credit just like any Spanish company.

Spain's *Ministerio de Economía y Hacienda* publishes several booklets in English that are "must" reading for anyone thinking of starting a business here. The series is called "A Guide to Business in Spain". Among the titles are Foreign Investments, Forms of Business Organisations, and Labour Legislation. The Spanish consulate in your home country may be able to supply you with copies, or you can write directly to the Dirección General de Transacciones Exteriores, Calle Almagro 34, 28010 Madrid.

## GLOSSARY

**Autonomo** – Self-employed

**Certificado de Antecedentes Penales** – Certificate of prison record

**Certificado Medico** – Medical certificate, for work permit application

**Cesión** – Leasing of any sort

**Cuenta Ajena** – "On another's account", an employed worker

**Cuenta Propia** – "On your own account", a self-employed worker

**Delegación de Trabajo** – Provincial office of Ministry of Labour

**Demandante de Trabajo** – Jobseeker

**Dirección General de Transacciones Exteriores** – General Directorate of Foreign Transactions, regulates foreign investment

**Epigrafe** – Tax Code Number for business or professional activity

**Estimación Directa** – Direct calculation of income for tax purposes

**Impuesto sobre Actividades Economicas** – Tax on business activities

**Instituto Nacional de Empleo** – National Employment Institute

**Licencia de Apertura** – Opening licence

**Memoria de Actividades** – Description of activities, when applying for business licence or permit

**Ministerio de Economia y Hacienda** – Ministry of Economy and Finance

**Modulos** – Modules, a form of estimating business income for tax purposes

**NIE (Número de Identificación de Extranjero)** – Foreigner's tax identification number

**Pago Fraccionado** – Quarterly tax payment for businesses

**Registro Mercantil** – Mercantile Registry, where companies are inscribed

**Sociedad Anonima** – Limited liability public company, plc, or corporation

**Sociedad Limitada** – Limited liability company, less than S.A.

**Solicitúd** – Application

**Sub-Delegado del Gobierno** – Provincial representative of national government

**Sucursal** – Branch office

# 12    Employing Others

**M**ost foreigners will at some point employ Spanish or other foreign workers. Property owners need odd jobs done and the growing number of foreign residents starting their own businesses need employees. Here are a few things you should know about labour relations in Spain.

## MAIDS AND GARDENERS

Though Spain is no longer the low-priced paradise it once was for northern Europeans, many new residents find they are still able to afford at least a part-time maid and gardener.

Just as in any country, the vast majority of part-time maids, cleaning women and garden workers in Spain are working illegally, whether they are employed by foreigners or Spaniards.

By "illegally", we mean they are not covered by Social Security, and are not making payments into the system. This is probably true of part-time domestic help in most countries. These workers do not make a lot of money anywhere, and their work is easy to hide.

In Spain the law says that all workers - absolutely all - must be covered by Social Security.

A full-time employee has most of his Social Security paid by his employer under the terms of his employment contract.

A worker such as a handyman, maid or gardener, who provides services to several employers, must be covered by Social Security as a *trabajador autónomo*, a self-employed worker, or under a special scheme for domestic workers.

## MINIMUM WAGE

The law stipulates that all full-time domestic workers shall be paid at least the *salario mínimo interprofesional* (€460.50 a month in 2004). You may, of course, pay more if you wish. The law also stipulates a 40-hour work week.

This minimum wage, less than €3 an hour, will seem low to most foreign residents who cannot find a part-time cleaning woman for less than €6 an hour, but remember it is a minimum for full-time workers.

When employment is less than 40 hours a week, payment should be proportional. That is, if the maid works 30 hours a week, she should get three-quarters of the wage, and if she works 20 hours a week, she gets half of it.

A domestic employee has 30 days of paid vacation each year. This means a month's holiday, in addition to weekends. Full-time maids receive two extra payments each year, of 15 days' salary each.

An employer and a domestic employee may make a written contract. If the employer chooses not to renew the contract at its expiry, he must pay the employee seven days of salary for each year worked.

If there is no written contract, the law assumes that the verbal agreement is for one year. At the end of this year, or at any other time, the employer can dismiss the worker, giving at least seven days' notice and paying the seven days' salary for each year or part of a year worked.

The law provides a 15-day trial period for new employees. It sets a 3 per cent increase in salary for every three years worked, or one per cent per year, which seems very little. The minimum wage itself rises more than that to keep up with inflation.

An employer who provides a live-in maid or other domestic

employee with housing and food may deduct as much as 45 per cent from the cash payment to cover this food and lodging.

Labour legislation requires that all workers have Spanish Social Security. Some foreigners have been slapped with stiff fines and been forced to pay Social Security payments for years back when reported by the maid or gardener who seemed so nice at first, so be wary.

In one case, a home-owner who employed a gardener in his village for many years without any papers at all, decided to sell his property and dismiss the gardener.

The gardener, who had always seemed so pleasant, and so ignorant, went to the Labour Court on the basis of the implicit verbal contract and obtained a settlement of almost €18,000. The owner could not sell his property until this was paid.

## WARNING TO EMPLOYERS

One veteran labour expert at a Gestoria in Marbella warned employers of maids and gardeners in the following way:

"Let's imagine that a villa owner decides to sell up and leave Spain. He has a maid and gardener who have never had a contract or in fact anything at all written down. He simply paid them in cash each month or each week.

Now the maid and gardener come to see a *gestor*. To be blunt, he might suggest to them that not only do they put in their case for Social Security payments, they sue the owner for a year's wages.

In reality, they have been paid these wages, but there are no receipts to indicate this. The gestor might take a commission of 20 per cent of whatever they are able to get. Unscrupulous agents do this every day.

"And that is why I urge all employers of Spanish domestic help at least to require that the employee sign a receipt for his pay each time, even if he doesn't have a contract."

## DOMESTIC WORKERS SPECIAL SOCIAL SECURITY SCHEME

For their Social Security, domestic employees have special regulations.

A full-time maid, for example, need pay only about €120 per month for complete Social Security health coverage and a minimum pension after 15 years. For a full pension, 35 years is required. The law says that the employer should pay 83 per cent of this and the employee 17 per cent. In practice, the employer usually pays it all.

If two or three families share a maid, she can enter herself on the Social Security books under the *Régimen Especial de Empleados de Hogar*, the special scheme for domestic employees, and the employer pays nothing.

She herself is responsible for her Social Security payments, but they are also €120 a month under this scheme, against about €185 for a normal industrial worker making a low salary.

Her Social Security card will state that her work is to supply *servicios domésticos de carácter parcial o discontinuo,* domestic services of a partial or discontinuous nature. In this way, she is protected in case of accident or illness.

The gardener or chauffeur is in a similar situation. If he works for several employers, he must be a *trabajador autónomo* also, but he comes under the general regulations and each month he pays €225,11.

## HOME OWNERS INSURANCE

One great disadvantage of employing an uninsured maid is if she has an accident while working on your property. You, as the owner, can be held responsible if she sues you for damages. Your home owners' insurance policy will not cover any claims from a person working on your property. It covers visitors and passers-by, but not workers.

## HANDYMAN NEEDS INSURANCE

You may also become an employer of Spanish nationals when you have some work done around your property, such as building a wall in a corner of your garden. If you hire a man on an hourly basis to carry out this work, as is often done, you will probably have no problem.

But take care. Such hiring in theory makes you an employer

and the worker an employee, and can make you liable if there is an accident on the job.

Your best protection is to ask any such worker for a *presupuesto,* a bid, for the job you want done. This bid should include the worker's NIF, which is his tax identification number, and it should specify the price, along with the amount of IVA, or value added tax.

That, technically at least, makes him an independent contractor, responsible for his own insurance and Social Security. This written *presupuesto* is a good idea in any case to make sure that both parties understand the terms of your agreement.

As with the maid or gardener, the hitch here is accident insurance. As the property owner, you could find yourself sued if the worker suffers an accident.

Your home owner's insurance policy will not cover a worker injured on your property. Your protection against this is to ask to see the worker's Social Security card when you contract him for the job. Even better, deal with a registered building contractor. This will surely cost you more, but it is the only way to be completely safe.

Remember also that you must have a proper bill or *factura,* including the fiscal identification number of the contractor, the price and the IVA, if you wish to deduct the cost of home improvements from your profits when you sell your Spanish property.

Sometimes the friendly offer of "no bill, no IVA" represents a false saving in the end.

## BUSINESS EMPLOYEES

Spain's entry into the European Union means that an EU citizen starting a business in Spain no longer must provide employment for Spanish nationals in order to obtain a work permit and business licence. He can hire any workers he chooses.

Even so, a foreigner new to doing business in Spain may very well decide he needs at least one Spanish employee to assist in serving his Spanish clients. Keep in mind that just as many Spaniards spend their holidays on the Spanish Costas as do foreigners.

Whether your employees are Spanish or foreign, they will be entitled to all the benefits of Spanish labour legislation. This means, under Spanish law, that you will pay Social Security payments for your employee, and redundancy pay if you let him go and you are confronted with all the changing complexity of Spanish labour law.

Just one surprise for employers from other countries is that Spaniards are often paid 14 months' salary for 11 months' work. This is because the Spanish custom of an extra month's pay at Christmas and again in July still persists in many cases, with the employee being entitled to a month's vacation, of course. This is in addition to his 14 paid holidays.

Another of the principal problems of employing workers in Spain is the difficulty of firing a worker. Spain is only beginning to relax its strong protection of the worker's right to job security. Many workers are protected and cannot be fired for any reason other than gross incompetence, without being paid a large redundancy sum.

Many Spanish businessmen have pointed out that the rigidity of this system actually works against full employment because it makes bosses reluctant to take on extra employees when things are going well for fear of being stuck with them later.

It also makes life difficult in seasonal businesses like hotels, and generally cramps enterprise, especially in small concerns where the wages of one or two employees make the difference between profit and loss.

The government has passed a series of measures to make the labour market "more flexible". They include provisions for hiring workers on short-term contracts. The employer must pay the usual Social Security contributions, but he is liable only for a very small redundancy payment should he choose to let the worker go.

So many Spanish employers have taken advantage of these plans that 75 per cent of all labour contracts at one point were such "provisional" hirings. The trades unions call these *basura* contracts, "garbage" contracts, because the worker can be thrown out like rubbish.

Further measures were then enacted to discourage the short-term contracts and encourage long-term hirings. They added an indemnity of eight days pay for each year worked on such temporary contracts, and relaxed the indemnity for workers let go from long-term contracts from 45 days pay per year worked to 33 days pay per year.

Another plan provides tax breaks for employers who take on workers over 45 years of age who have been out of a job for more than one year.

There are many plans designed to help small businesses, and the foreigner starting an enterprise in Spain could find them quite useful. Unless you get competent legal advice, however, you could miss out on the benefits.

In many cases, Spanish labour law continues to regard the relation between employer and employee as legally binding, even if there is no written contract, and the worker becomes protected from dismissal, no matter how poorly your business goes. Make sure your contract is clearly understood when you take on any new employees

## BEWARE OF "INDEFINITE" CONTRACTS

Be wary, in particular, of "temporary" contracts that do not give a definite time period or state a date on which the contract lapses unless renewed. In some cases Spanish employees have taken advantage of this type of contract in the following way:

The employee works for a time at his new job. One day he simply fails to show up for work and the employer is unable to contact him. Months later the employer receives a notice from the Spanish labour court that he is being charged with unfair dismissal by the missing employee.

The former employee wants his Social Security paid for six months or a year and he wants an indemnity of €10,000 or so to make up for his suffering.

All this is an invention of course, but the labour court (see below) has a long history of favouring the employee against the employer, so some unscrupulous workers have learned to take advantage of this, and the employer faces a long and expensive process to prove he is right.

Very often the employer will simply give up, even though he is being taken for a ride, and will make an out-of-court settlement to the "worker".

The employer's only protection here is to formally dismiss the worker when he fails to appear. He must be informed at his home address - a telegram constitutes legally acceptable notice - that he has been fired for failing to appear at his job.

Whether he responds or not, a copy of this telegram will help the employer in his court case later. Some employers have failed to make this official dismissal, to their later sorrow.

You will be right if you think that situations like the above have produced a sort of paranoia in small business owners, who in turn are tempted to hire workers without any contracts or Social Security or any papers whatsoever.

This is illegal, however, even though thousands of Spanish as well as foreign employers are doing it right at this moment.

## FINES FOR EMPLOYING UNREGISTERED WORKERS

Labour inspectors do check on establishments and fines start at €3,000 for employing unregistered employees, whether they are Spaniards or foreigners. Especially in coastal bars and restaurants, inspectors find hundreds of cases every year, and fine the owners.

## RIGHTS OF EMPLOYEES

Among the rights of employees is included the payment of the official minimum wage, which is different for different sorts of work. The absolute minimum is €460.50 per month. It is quite low, however, and most employees are paid more.

The standard work week is 40 hours, though this varies from one occupation to another. There is an official 40 per cent increase for overtime, with double time for Sundays and national holidays.

In a changing Spain, one is never quite certain what the national holidays will be next year. They even differ from Catalonia to Andalusia.

224

Workers are entitled to 14 paid holidays a year, 12 of them national and two of them local, such as the town's fiesta. The annual vacation is a minimum 23 days. In many cases, "fixed" workers are entitled to a leave of absence with pay of 15 days should they get married, and two days when a relative dies or is seriously ill.

A woman may be entitled to 16 weeks' leave for child-bearing, but the Spanish Social Security system will pay a large portion of her salary during this time. A new father gets two days off and the mother can choose to pass up to two weeks of her maternity leave to the father.

These are guidelines which do not apply to all workers and you should consult a competent gestoría or lawyer who is an expert in labour law to find out just what applies in your individual field.

The Spanish custom of special payments in July and at Christmas, or even more often in some cases, continues to apply. These are called *pagas extraordinarias* and their original purpose was to make sure that workers had some funds in hand for Christmas and summer holidays. These payments are often stated as one month's pay each time, but the actual amount depends on a number of factors, such as seniority, the type of work, and individual contract.

## EMPLOYER PAYS SOCIAL SECURITY

The principal expense you will have with any worker you employ in your business, whether on one-year contracts or "fixed", will be the payment of his or her Spanish Social Security contributions. As an employer, you will have to pay this for yourself, as well.

The payments are split between the employer and the worker, but the employer pays by far the greater share. Your payment is based on the *nómina*, the official salary for your type of work. If you employ a waiter or a shop girl, paying the absolute minimum wage of €460.50, you will find that your payments are still based on the lowest official *nómina* for paying Social Security.

This minimum base is €755,40, and you will pay about 35 per cent of this, meaning you pay more than €255 each and every month in addition to your worker's salary. This is a rock-bottom figure. Most employers pay higher wages and higher Social Security payments.

Remember that this includes complete health care, accident and disability insurance, unemployment payments, and the worker's State retirement pension.

Spain, like most other modern industrial nations, is concerned about its Social Security system and where the money will come from as the number of pensioners in the population steadily increases.

## LABOUR DISPUTES

An employer can fire a worker without compensation if the worker is repeatedly absent or late, if he does not obey reasonable orders or if he is drunk or otherwise in a condition which affects his work.

A worker can quit and seek compensation if he feels that the employer has not held to the contract, has substantially altered working conditions for the worse, or has not paid the agreed wages.

Disputes about these matters are taken to the *Magistratura de Trabajo*, the labour court, which will decide who it thinks has the right and make judgement accordingly. Compensation payable to a worker varies, but he might get 33 days' pay for each year he has worked if the court rules he has been unfairly dismissed.

If a company goes out of business, one guideline holds that its employees are entitled to 20 days' pay for each year they have worked.

## GLOSSARY

**Factura** – bill, invoice

**Fijo** – "Fixed", a worker on an indefinite contract

**IVA** – VAT, Value Added Tax

**Jardinero** – gardener

**Magistratura de Trabajo** – Labour tribunal

**Mujer de limpieza** – cleaning woman

**Obrero** – worker, labourer

**Paga Extraordinaria** – Special payment

**Presupuesto** – Bid or estimate for a job of work

**Regimen Especial de Empleados de Hogar** – Social Security Special Scheme for Domestic Employees

**Salario Minimo Interprofesional** – Minimum wage

**Seguridad Social** – Social Security

**Trabajador Autonomo** – Self-employed worker

# 13  Birth, death, marriage and nationality

**J**ust as all nations do, Spain requires that births, marriages, divorces and deaths be officially registered.

A baby born in Spain needs a Spanish birth certificate, regardless of the nationality of its parents. If the parents are not Spanish, they should also register the birth at the consulate of their own country.

A death must also be registered, both in Spain and with the consulate of the country of the deceased.

A civil marriage between foreigners can be celebrated in Spain and will be recognised in other countries as valid.

Married foreigners can be divorced in Spain, regardless of where they were married, as long as one of the parties is resident.

Let's take a look at each of these events and the necessary formalities in Spain.

## BIRTH IN SPAIN

By law, all births in Spain must be reported and registered. If you unexpectedly have your baby while you are on holiday in Spain, the birth must be reported here. This is done at the *Registro Civil*, the Civil Registry, of the town where the birth takes place.

The attending physician or other official of the hospital certifies the birth, though a registered midwife may also do this if the birth takes place at home with only the midwife in attendance.

The report must be made within eight days and include the hour, date and place of birth, the child's first and last names, the full names of both parents, and the doctor's certificate. This information will go on file at the civil registry.

> ### CHILD BORN IN SPAIN HAS TWO LAST NAMES
>
> When you register the birth of your child, you will come in contact with the peculiarly Spanish practice of using two last names. If you are John Smith and your wife's maiden name was Betty Jones, your son will be registered in Spain as James Smith Jones. The Spanish rule is that the last name of the father comes first, followed by the last name of the mother. Recent changes in law allow a child to choose to use his mother's last name first if he desires when he comes of age.

The parents can then request for their own records one of two forms of the birth certificate. One is called the *Extracto de Inscripción de Nacimiento,* which gives the birth date and inscription number and the names of child and parents. This abbreviated "extract" form is sufficient for most legal purposes.

You can also get a *Certificación Literal,* which is more complete and contains all of the items in the declaration, such as the exact place and hour, the attending physician, and so on. This one will cost you a little more, but neither of the forms is expensive.

Armed with this certificate of birth in Spain, you can then go to the consulate of your home country in Spain and report the birth. Some countries, such as Great Britain, require the literal certificate before they will issue a birth certificate of their own country. You may also need your passport, your own parents' birth certificates and your marriage certificate.

Procedure and documents required vary somewhat depending on your country of origin.

Your Consulate will then issue a certificate of the birth of a citizen abroad.

## NATIONALITY OF CHILD BORN IN SPAIN

A child born to foreign parents in Spain does not automatically acquire Spanish nationality. If both parents are foreigners, the child will be a foreigner even if the parents are residents.

However, if the child should, between its 18th and 19th birthdays, choose to apply for Spanish nationality, it will certainly be granted, particularly if the child has been living in Spain during most of that time.

If either of the child's parents is Spanish, a child born in Spain is automatically entitled to Spanish nationality. A child born in Spain out of wedlock, where the paternity is not disclosed, is also entitled to Spanish nationality, regardless of the nationality of the mother.

Laws about nationality vary from country to country and can be quite complicated. Make enquiries at your own consulate. Sometimes a country requires that a child of its own nationals who is born abroad must return to his parents' country for a certain time period in order to justify his nationality, for example.

## DEATH IN SPAIN

If you are resident in Spain and have no plans to return to your home country near the end of your life, you should take these steps:

1.  Make your Spanish will.

2.  Select a cemetery where you wish to be buried.

3. Make contact with a Spanish funeral director.

4. Share your arrangements with your partner and family members.

5. Perhaps take out Spanish burial insurance if you are not already covered.

Procedures in Spain are similar to those in your home country, but it helps to be familiar with them.

If the death occurs in a hospital, a doctor on the staff will prepare and sign the death certificate, which must be officially issued by a Spanish judge. If death occurs at home, the attending physician can prepare the certificate.

## THE FUNERAL DIRECTOR

The funeral director is probably the first person you'll want to contact if you are in charge of arrangements for a death.

Funeral directors in Spain, just as in other countries, are aware that family members are distraught when a loved one has died. So they aim to provide full service, including all the necessary paperwork. You may need to make only one telephone call to set the process in motion.

Funeral directors in areas with many foreign residents usually have at least one English-speaking staff member. When they receive a call, they respond quickly.

If no doctor has officially pronounced the person dead, they will locate a doctor to do so and they will inform both the Spanish judge who officially issues the death certificate and the consulate of the person's nationality, as the consulate must issue a death certificate for that country.

You need both these death certificates for any insurance forms and for executing the will of the deceased. The funeral director takes the passport data of the deceased and of the person who is responsible for the body in order to prepare his own reports. He sees that the necessary official certificates are delivered to the family.

If necessary, the funeral director can then take the body to the nearest cold-storage vault. Such vaults exist in most larger towns in Spain.

Cemeteries are usually owned by the towns where they are located and a foreigner can be buried in most of them, whether or not he or she is Catholic.

Perhaps we shouldn't say "buried" as the majority of cemeteries in Spain are, in fact, above ground and the bodies are placed in niches. At a burial, the casket is eased into the niche and a pair of masons brick it in.

You will probably need to be registered as an inhabitant of your municipality in order to be buried in the local cemetery. This is another reason to obtain that *certificado de empadronamiento,* or municipal registration, which we have mentioned before.

This does not represent any discrimination against foreigners. A Spaniard may not usually be buried in the municipal cemetery if he is not registered, either.

If your new home-town cemetery doesn't suit you, there are others available.

In Malaga, for example, there is a British Cemetery and in Benalmadena there is an International Cemetery. This has the sort of burial plots to which northern Europeans are more accustomed.

Funeral directors will make arrangements for the cemetery plot or niche. They can also contact a British, Danish, Swedish or German pastor, as appropriate, to perform the burial service.

If the body is to be returned to the deceased's home country, most funeral directors can make the arrangements for the air transport as well as the embalming. Embalming is not a standard practice in Spain, but it can be done.

The Spanish funeral director will see to the body's transport to the airport in the home country, after which you will have to make other arrangements to have the body picked up. A few funeral directors have corresponding agents in other countries who will see to it that the body is delivered to any town in that country.

## CREMATION AVAILABLE IN MANY AREAS

If your preference is cremation, you will find crematoriums available in many areas of Spain. Cremation - *incineración -*

almost unknown a few years ago, has grown greatly in popularity.

One peculiarity of the cremation procedure is that family members are not allowed to attend the cremation itself. They may hold a religious service before the cremation, with the body present, or after it, with the urn.

Cremation costs around 300 euros as a minimum.

For those who choose to donate their bodies to medical science, any medical school in Spain will be very pleased to make the arrangements in advance. Simply telephone the medical school and declare your intentions. You can either visit them to fill out the forms or they will send a representative to you. They will arrange with your funeral director for collection of the body.

Their only conditions are that the body be available within 24 hours of death and that the death was not caused by an infectious disease or an accident that requires autopsy.

---

**FACT:** *In the Province of Malaga, more than half of all bodies, Spanish or foreign, are cremated.*

---

The usual custom in Spain, where bodies are seldom embalmed, is to bury the day after death.

This is custom, not law. The law says only that a body may not be interred sooner than 24 hours after the death has occurred. Where there is no cold storage, it must be buried within 72 hours. Where there is cold storage available, this limit does not apply.

What will all this funeral service cost you? A basic rate would be around €1,500 but this can rise quickly when transport costs, embalming fees, cold storage and cemetery fees are added in.

You should know that most Spanish cemeteries usually rent their niches for varying time periods. The municipal cemetery rates are quite inexpensive, but it isn't the same as purchasing the plot forever. One Malaga cemetery quoted rates of €300 for the first five years, dropping to about half that rate thereafter, around €30 per year, or €1,500 for 50 years. If the rent is not paid, after a time the body may be removed to a common grave-site within the consecrated cemetery grounds.

If you wish to purchase a plot, it can cost more than €3,000 for a double plot at the Benalmadena International Cemetery on the Costa del Sol, for example. Ask at your own town hall for prices *'en perpetuidad'*.

If you wish to repatriate a body to its home country, you will find that prices for air transport of bodies are high. They go as freight and are charged by the kilo. Air transport costs within Europe can range from €1,000 to €2,500.

Prolonged storage will also add to your costs. Embalming costs around €1,500.

It pays to plan ahead. Check now with a Spanish funeral director for his rates and services.If the first price quoted you seems high, don't hesitate to visit another funeral director and compare rates.

Burial insurance is also available in Spain.

## MARRIAGE IN SPAIN

It is perfectly possible to be married in Spain. People do it every day.

Foreigners can be married in Spain, in a civil ceremony, provided that one of them is either resident or registered in the municipality – *empadronado*. This marriage will be recognised in other countries.

There is quite a lot of paperwork, however. Some evidence must be provided that the two parties are single, such as a certificate from the Civil Registry of your home country. Birth certificates are required. A widow or widower will have to present both the original marriage certificate and a death certificate for the deceased spouse. A divorced person will need to present evidence that there is a valid divorce.

All of these documents must be officially translated into Spanish and accompanied by the Certificate of Apostille, which verifies to one country that another country's document is valid. This internationally recognised certificate is issued by different authorities in different countries, so you will have to ask.

The marriage is held at the court building, the Spanish Civil Registry office, or perhaps the Town Hall, with the local judge presiding, although town Mayors and deputised municipal councillors are also authorised to perform civil wedding ceremonies. It has become rather trendy, in fact, for couples to be married in places like Marbella, where the Town Hall has arranged an attractive wedding site in a municipal park.

If you are interested in being married in Spain, be warned that you will have to come in person to present and sign all the forms and it will take about 30 days before these are processed and you can be married.

Roman Catholics, even though not Spanish, may also be married in church, following the practice outlined above for civil marriage along with the usual practice of the Roman Catholic church.

Each partner will present a baptismal certificate and a declaration from their former parish priest that they adhere to the Roman Catholic faith and they are free to marry. After the ceremony, the priest gives the couple a certificate of marriage, which makes them man and wife, but they must still present this certificate at the Civil Registry to get an official marriage certificate.

If you marry a Spaniard, you receive a *Libro de Familia*, the "Family Book", which is a very important document in Spanish life. It is the official registration of husband and wife and their children. Spaniards present it on various occasions: when they come of age and apply their own identity card, when they marry and when they die.

If you marry a Spanish subject, you do not automatically become Spanish. A husband or wife will have to apply for Spanish nationality, which should be routinely granted, but does not come automatically.

## MARRYING IN GIBRALTAR

Gibraltar is an easy alternative for wedding-bound couples of most nationalities.

Forms are available at Consulates in Spain, or in your home country on which the parties to the marriage enter their personal details and apply for a special marriage licence from the Governor of Gibraltar. The divorced or widowed will need to produce the appropriate certificates.

When the licence is granted, the couple may go to Gibraltar and be married in the registry office there, or you can present your papers personally at the civil registry office and get married the next day. They will need two witnesses.

## DIVORCE IN SPAIN

Through the Franco years there was no divorce in Spain. This was out of deference to the regime's special relationship with the Roman Catholic Church.

In 1981, however, the divorce law went into effect and it is now possible to obtain a divorce in Spain on various grounds. Even foreigners who have been married in other countries can, if they are now residents in Spain, obtain a divorce here that will be recognised in their home country. In fact, only one of the parties need be resident in Spain.

If a man's wife leaves him and returns to her home in Belgium, for example, he can, after a time, petition in Spain for a divorce. The couple must have been married for one full year before a petition for divorce will be heard, which seems reasonable enough.

The simplest procedure is divorce by mutual consent or for one of the pair to request with the formal consent of the other a legal separation. This must be carried out before a Spanish *notario*. They will need a lawyer. When they have lived apart for one full year after that, the divorce will be granted.

At the time of requesting this legal separation, the couple will be required to settle their financial arrangements about who gets what share of their property, any child support or maintenance payments, visiting rights of children, and so on.

At the end of the separation period, there is a brief hearing. If nothing has changed, the final divorce will be processed.

In addition to this "no-fault" sort of procedure, the standard grounds for divorce familiar to most Europeans also apply. They include adultery, desertion, cruelty, alcohol or drug addiction and mental problems. You will want to consult a Spanish lawyer when seeking divorce on these grounds.

If your income is modest, you may be entitled to free legal assistance, which you can find out by inquiring at your area's

*Colegio de Abogados*, the law society. (See chapter on Your Legal Advisers for more details)

## COMMON LAW COUPLES

There is no "common law" marriage in Spain. That is, a couple may live together for many years as man and wife and have children together, but this establishes no legal rights for either the man or the woman.

If the man dies, the woman has no claim to inherit any share of his property. In the eyes of the law, there is no legal relationship.

Unless the man has formally recognised the children as his own, he is not required to leave his property to them.

The law regards these children as offspring of a single mother. Their births must be registered as such and they take their mother's two last names because she is their only legal parent.

If the unmarried father of the children chooses to leave parts of his estate to his unrecognised children, they will not have the right to apply the lower inheritance tax rate enjoyed by children of married parents, except in some regions. (See page 246).

## SAME-SEX COUPLES

This situation also applies to same sex couples. They cannot legally marry in Spain. A number of municipalities have established a special registry for *Parejas de Hecho,* partners, same sex or opposite sex, living together as families.

Registration in this list confers no legal rights, however. Same sex pairs have the same inheritance problem as unmarried parents. That is, they can bequeath their property to their partners, but the partners will be subject to inheritance tax at twice the percentage that an immediate family member pays, except in some regions. (See page 246).

## NATIONALITY

If you move to Spain, install yourself here, take out a Spanish residence permit, pay taxes in Spain, raise your children here and do business here, that still does not make you or your children Spanish.

You remain a Norwegian, American or Briton, unless you choose to formally renounce your nationality in order to take another. At this point, complications arise. Some countries permit dual nationality and do not mind if one of their citizens takes on another nationality in addition to the one he was born with.

A British citizen, for example, can take another nationality without renouncing his British citizenship. The United States of America formerly did not permit dual nationality but has now changed. If one of its citizens takes Spanish nationality, this is no longer grounds for loss of his United States citizenship.

An American woman who marries a Spaniard does not lose her American citizenship, nor does she automatically become Spanish. It is also possible for a child born in Spain of a Spanish father and American mother to have Spanish nationality through his father and place of birth, and American nationality through his mother.

Until he reaches the age of 18, that is. Then he must make a choice. Spanish law does not recognise dual nationality for adults, so the child must then either renounce his American nationality, making a declaration to the authorities, or he will lose his Spanish nationality.

But if Spain does not recognize dual nationality, what about the British citizens who take Spanish nationality but still are regarded as British in the UK? Well, Spain does not regard them as even the slightest bit British. They are now Spanish, all Spanish and only Spanish. If the UK chooses to regard them as British, that is no business of Spain's.

Marriage is another tricky area. In general, marriage to a foreigner does not automatically change the nationality of the partner. So a British woman who marries a Spaniard remains British unless she applies for Spanish nationality, which she can do immediately after the marriage and which will routinely be granted. A British man who marries a Spanish woman, however, will have to wait out a two-year residence requirement before he can apply.

Each nation has somewhat different rules regarding the retention and loss of nationality, and where marriage partners of two different nationalities are involved, perhaps living for long periods in yet a third country, it is best to make careful enquiries at your own Consulate. When there are children, it can be even more complex, so it is best to get good advice.

The basic requirement for applying for Spanish nationality is a residence period in Spain of 10 years, even if you are a European Union citizen. This varies for South Americans, for example, who need not wait so long, and in the case of marriage.

A number of Europeans who have settled here have taken out Spanish nationality, although members of fellow European Union nations have practically the same rights as Spaniards, and can now even vote in municipal elections.

If you decide to apply for Spanish citizenship, you will need your own birth certificate, your parents' birth certificates and marriage certificate, all translated into Spanish by official translators and authenticated by your own Consulate.

You will need to show, by means of previous residence permits, that you have held a *residencia* for 10 years. The process will take up to a year before everything is cleared, and you will do well to have a skilled *gestor* or *abogado* handle your application, as they know the ins and outs of the paperwork.

Finally, you will be required to renounce your former nationality and you will swear an oath of allegiance to the Spanish Crown.

Then you will be Spanish, a citizen of a proud nation that once ruled vast portions of the globe and is today the world's ninth largest industrial power.

Your last will and testament must provide for your family according to Spanish law.

## GLOSSARY

**Certificate of Apostille** – Internationally recognised form on which an authority of one country validates a document to another country

**Incineración** – Cremation

**Inscripción de Nacimiento** – Birth certificate, comes in two versions, a short form called an «**extracto**» and a complete form called **"literal"**

**Libro de Familia** – "Family Book" in which husband and wife and children are inscribed

**Pareja de Hecho** – Unmarried partners living together as families

**Registro Civil** – Spanish civil registry, where births, deaths and marriages are recorded

# 14   Spanish Wills and Inheritance Tax

## SPANISH WILLS

There are four points to bear in mind in connection with Spanish wills:

1.  You should make a Spanish will disposing of your Spanish property in order to avoid time-consuming and expensive legal problems for your heirs. Make a separate will disposing of assets located outside of Spain.

2.  As a foreigner, you will probably find that Spanish authorities do not oblige you to follow the Spanish law of compulsory heirs, in which you must leave two-thirds of your estate to your children. You can leave your estate to whomever you choose, as long as your own national law permits this. Your estate, however, will be subject to Spanish inheritance tax, which can be high when property is left to non-relatives.

3.  There are very few ways around Spanish inheritance taxes and these legal ways require careful advance planning. With the exception of the reduction referred to in point four below, Spanish law provides no large exemption from inheritance tax, such as most countries have when the family home is transferred. The tax is due after the first €16,000.

4.  However, if you are an official resident of Spain leaving your property to a spouse or child who is also a resident, you may be eligible for a 95 per cent reduction in the value of the property for inheritance tax calculation for the first €120,000. This is not available to non-residents.

Let's look at these points in more detail.

244

In order to protect the family and provide for the children, Spanish inheritance laws restrict the testator's freedom to leave his property to anyone he pleases.

It is almost impossible for a Spanish parent to make the classic threat that he will cut the no-good son out of his will. This is because Spanish law requires a parent to leave two-thirds of his estate to his children, even by-passing the surviving spouse.

In general, most people wish to provide for their children, so they have no problem in making a Spanish will in accordance with those provisions.

But let us first establish just what the estate consists of when a person dies.

In Spanish law, a surviving spouse keeps all assets acquired before the marriage, half of the goods acquired during marriage, and all personal gifts or inheritances which have come directly to this spouse.

Assuming that most of the couple's assets were acquired during their marriage, this means that about half of their assets do not really form part of the deceased person's estate. Half of the property continues to belong to the surviving spouse.

## CHILDREN ARE COMPULSORY HEIRS

Of the rest of the assets, only one-third can be freely disposed of, under the Spanish law of *herederos forzosos,* or obligatory heirs. When a person dies leaving children, the estate is divided into three equal parts.

One of these thirds must be left to the children in equal parts. Another third must also be left to the children, but the testator may decide how to divide it. That is, he can choose to leave all of this third to only one of his children or grandchildren. A surviving spouse has a life interest in this third. If the estate is a house or a piece of property, the child who inherits it cannot dispose of it freely until his surviving parent dies, because the surviving parent holds an usufruct or *usofructo* over the property.

The final third of the estate can be freely willed to anyone the testator chooses.

245

## ANDALUSIANS GET TAX BREAK

Andalusian tax authorities have eliminated inheritance tax for family inheritors who are official residents of Andalusia and who receive less than €125,000. There are four conditions.

1.  The inheritor must be a direct family member.

2.  The total amount of the estate may not exceed €500,000.

3.  The already-existing registered assets of each inheritor may not exceed €402,678.

4.  Each inheritor may not inherit more than €125,000.

But once the total amount of the estate exceeds €500,000, or each inheritor's share exceeds €125,000, the exemption disappears, and normal inheritance tax must be paid on the full amount.

Andalusia already applies a hefty reduction of 95 per cent on the testator's habitual residence when left to family members who are also residents. This reduction rises to 99.99 per cent when the home is also the main residence of the inheritor. This reduction applies only to the first €120,000 of value.

Unmarried and same-sex couples registered with the Andalusian registry of de facto couples can also get this reduction.

## DYING WITHOUT LEAVING A WILL

If a foreign resident dies in Spain without a will, his estate in Spain will be distributed according to the Spanish laws of succession.

**Example:** When a husband dies, leaving a widow and three children and the only property is the house, the widow continues to own her half the house. The other half of the house constitutes the estate. This is divided equally among the three children. When the estate is settled, each child will have one-third title to half of the house, meaning that each one now owns one-sixth of the house, and the title deed has four names on it, the widow and each of the three children. The widow also holds an usufruct on the children's share. This means she can use their half of the property until she dies, as well as her own half. They must all agree and sign the deed if the house is to be sold.

246

## ARE YOU BOUND BY SPANISH LAW?

This Spanish law of obligatory heirs in theory applies to foreigners with property in Spain, restricting the disposal of this property just as it restricts such disposal for Spaniards. This is because most nations apply the law of the place where the property is located.

However, Article 9 of the Spanish Civil Code provides that, when a foreign property owner dies, even if he holds an official residence permit, the disposal of any assets he has in Spain will be governed by his own national law, not Spanish law.

If his own country's law permits free disposal of the estate, this frees him from the Spanish law of "compulsory heirs" explained above. English law and United States law provide free disposition of assets. German law and Scottish law require that some portion of the estate go to surviving children. You must check your own national law here.

This article does not free the foreigner from Spanish inheritance taxes, however. (See next section)

This freedom applies only when such foreigner has an existing foreign will or Spanish will. If he dies intestate, without having made a will, Spanish law will be applied to his assets in Spain and they will be divided equally among his children.

This is a powerful argument for making a Spanish will disposing of your assets in Spain according to your wishes.

For citizens of the United Kingdom, the first complication arises here. A number of countries, including Great Britain, have laws stating that the disposition of real property such as land, houses and apartments will be governed by the law of the country where such property is located. English law - which applies to Wales and Northern Ireland in this case, but not to Scotland - also states that other assets, such as investments, will be governed by the law of the country where the deceased is legally domiciled at the time of his death.

So Spanish law says that English law will apply, and English law sends the ball right back, saying that *Spanish* law will apply, because that is where the property is located. An Englishman in theory is subject to the Spanish law, which may mean he can freely dispose of only one-third of his assets in Spain.

247

A number of other countries have laws similar to the English law. Investigate in your home country to find out what law applies to the disposition of real estate, the law of your home country or the law of the country where the immovable asset is located.

All this is the theory. But what happens in practice?

## MOST FOREIGNERS HAVE FREE DISPOSITION

In practice, any foreigner can make a Spanish will bequeathing his Spanish property to any person of his choice as long as his own national law is ruled by the principle of free disposition of property by testament. The Spanish registrar of wills accepts this. When the time comes, the will is executed and the inheritor takes possession of his new property. Spanish lawyers routinely make such wills.

This means that, even if you are British, you can make a Spanish will leaving your Spanish property to whomever you choose.

The law also says that any foreigner officially resident in Spain is subject to Spanish inheritance law on his world-wide estate.

In practice the authorities simply do not ask whether the testator is an official resident or not. They accept as valid the Spanish will disposing of only the Spanish property. The only requirement enforced by Spain is the payment of Spanish inheritance tax on property or assets located in Spain.

So most foreigners will find no problem in making a separate Spanish will to dispose of their immovable property in Spain, even though the law seems to say otherwise, whether they are residents or non-residents.

## LEGITIMATE INHERITORS CAN CONTEST SPANISH WILL

One note of warning: All of the above relating to a foreignerP253-254 making a will that permits him to leave his Spanish property to anyone he chooses, thus avoiding Spanish inheritance law which requires him to leave at least two-thirds of his estate to his children, works perfectly well in most cases. But, as we have said, it is not exactly in agreement with the law as written. It is more a matter of the Spanish authorities choosing not to enforce their own laws too strictly.

This means that, if you write your Spanish will leaving your lovely villa to your favourite daughter and cutting out your no-good son entirely, that son could get expert Spanish legal advice, contest the will on the grounds that the law stipulates that half of the inheritance is his, and win his case, thus getting title to half the villa.

So, if you foresee any possible challenge from one of Spain's legitimate inheritors, such as a child or a spouse, you should make other arrangements, such as transferring the title of the property to your chosen heir while you are still alive. You can always maintain the usufruct over the property, which gives you the right to use it as long as you are still living, although the title has formally passed to another person.

If you are quite certain that no possibility exists of successfully contesting it, then go ahead and make your Spanish will as you choose in the confidence that it will be executed as you have written it.

You also need to make a foreign will disposing of any assets you have in other countries. Be sure that any foreign will states clearly that it disposes only of your assets in that country and make sure to say in your Spanish will that it disposes only of your assets in Spain.

There have been unfortunate cases where a person has made one will in Spain stating that all assets are left to one inheritor and another will later made in Germany or Australia, saying the same thing, but leaving "everything" to a different person.

In one particular case, the testator intended to leave all her German assets to family members and her Spanish villa to the friend who had looked after her for years. She made a Spanish will leaving everything to her friend in Spain and then made a German will, dated after the Spanish will, also leaving "everything" to her German family members. These inheritors later had the German will translated and legalised in Spain, and took possession of the Spanish property as well.

They were able to do this because the German will made no

distinction of country and it was dated after the Spanish will, so it took precedence. So, the testator's wishes were not carried out and the faithful friend who had looked after the ill and dying person in Spain did not inherit the villa as she was supposed to.

This story is a good argument for taking legal advice when you make your Spanish will.

### FOREIGN WILL IS VALID IN SPAIN

Legally, it is not absolutely necessary for you to make a Spanish will to dispose of your assets in Spain. A Briton who owns property in Spain can bequeath his Spanish apartment in the same British will he uses to dispose of his property in England, and his will can be probated in Spain. However, there are a number of steps that must take place in order to do this.

If you have lived in Spain for a long time it may be necessary for you to re-create a legal domicile in your home country for purposes of making a will. You may be able to do this by filing an official "letter of intent" with your lawyers. This letter states that, even though you hold a Spanish residence permit now, you really intend to return to your home country in the end. This should be sufficient for establishing a legal domicile in your home country and will allow its laws to apply.

Let us suppose that you are able to establish domicile in your home country and that its laws will apply. Your foreign will (which can be made at your Consulate in Spain as long as the proper formalities are observed) must go through the following process before it can dispose of your Spanish assets:

1.  A certified copy of the grant of probate must be legalised by the Spanish Consul in the testator's home country, and a Spanish translation of this certified copy prepared. A Spanish lawyer must then be empowered to prepare a list of the assets in Spain, see that the Spanish inheritance taxes are paid, and handle the rest of the paperwork involved in distributing the assets.

2.  Two lawyers registered in your home country, or a notary, or a Spanish Consul-General in your home country, must prepare a certificate of law, a *certificado de ley,* which

affirms that the testator had the legal capacity to make a will; that the will is valid; that the Spanish law of obligatory heirs and the dispositions relating to property of spouses do not exist in the law of your country; that the will has been duly proved, and that the trustees named have the correct legal powers to administer the estate.

3. Finally, your will is declared effective to dispose of your assets in Spain, and your Spanish lawyer can carry this out.

It's a complicated, time-consuming and expensive process, and it is clearly better to make a Spanish will disposing of your assets in Spain.

## MAKING A SPANISH WILL

You go to see a Spanish lawyer and explain your wishes to him. In the case of the death of one spouse, for example, you may wish to leave all possible assets directly to the other spouse, without any inheritance to the children. As a foreigner, you should be able to do this.

Even if surviving children inherit their legal portion, it is not usually necessary for the house to be sold and the proceeds divided, for example. The surviving spouse continues to live in the house and administer it for the good of the children still at home. If the house is later sold, the children can then get their legal share of the price.

The lawyer will advise you as to how the will should read in order to carry out your intentions. People sometimes say that they want their Spanish flat sold and the proceeds divided among the children, for example.

Your lawyer will tell you that you cannot do this. You must leave the flat to the children in equal parts. They can then sell it and divide the proceeds, but you cannot order its sale in your will. There may be other provisions on which your lawyer can advise.

The will is made out in two columns, one in Spanish and one in English, or in whatever language the testator prefers. The

251

will is then checked by the *notario* and signed in his presence and that of three witnesses. This is called a *testamento abierto,* an open will, which is the usual form. The notary keeps the original in his files, gives you an authorized copy and sends a notification to the central registry in Madrid, called the *Registro Central de Ultima Voluntad.*

The certification numbers of all Spanish wills are kept on file here to ensure that a legal copy can always be found. If the will is lost or if you do not know whether the deceased person has made a Spanish will or not, you can apply to the central registry to find out if a Spanish will exists under that name. If it does exist, the registry will give you the number and the name of the notary who made it in the first place. You can get a copy of the will from the notary. Having a Spanish will certainly speeds up the legal processes of inheritance.

The notary will charge around €60 for the will and the lawyer's fee could be about the same, a total of €120, although this could go much higher if the will is complicated or involves large sums of money.

Remember that husband and wife must each make separate wills, as they each own property separately.

You can also find out almost exactly how much inheritance tax your Spanish estate will attract. Your lawyer will consult the table of rates and then you will know what to expect.

All too often, the existence of Spanish inheritance tax seems to come as a complete surprise to foreign property owners. This tax is charged even when the inheritance is between spouses, with only a minimum exemption, as explained in the next section.

## SECRET WILLS

Should you wish to keep secret the provisions of your will, you can also execute a *testamento cerrado,* a closed will. It is, of course, important to have a Spanish lawyer advise you to make sure your wishes square with Spanish law. Otherwise, you might find your desires cannot lawfully be carried out. You take this closed will, in an envelope, to the *notario,* who seals the envelope and signs it along with the witnesses. He then files it, just as with the open will.

Other types of wills are also valid. You can make a holographic will, in your own handwriting, but this later has to be authenticated as genuine before a judge, which means more time, trouble and expense. You can even make a verbal will, in the presence of five witnesses. Each of the five witnesses then has to testify to the *notario* that these are truly the wishes of the deceased. The *notario* then prepares a written will and certifies it.

## INHERITANCE TAX

Spain's *Ley de Sucesiones* provides no large exemption from inheritance tax when property is passed to a spouse or to family members. The present law provides a total exemption from taxes only for legacies under €16,000. To be exact, the exemption is €15,956.87. This long number results from the addition of yearly inflation to an original round number, plus the conversion from pesetas into euros. We shall call it simply €16,000.

The €16,000 exemption seems rather small, but it applies to each inheritor, not to the total estate. So, if you have a property worth €120,000, your half equals an estate valued at €60,000, and you leave it equally divided among your spouse and three children, each will receive an inheritance worth €15,000, and the bequest will attract no tax at all.

In addition, an inheritor under the age of 21 can have an exemption of up to €48,000. For each year younger than 21, he deducts €4,000 more, until he arrives at the maximum at the age of 13.

This exemption applies to bequests between parents, children, spouses and brothers and sisters. For uncles, cousins and nephews, the exemption is cut by half to €8,000. For more distant relatives, or those not related at all, there is no exemption.

## 95% REDUCTION IN TAX BASE

Official residents of Spain leaving their principal residence to wife or children, who are also official residents, may be eligible for a 95 per cent reduction in their tax base. (99.9 per cent in Andalusia). There are three conditions. They are:

1. You must have held an official residence permit for at least three years.

2. The home you transmit must be your principal residence and you must have lived in it for at least three years.

3. The inheritor must undertake not to sell the property for 10 years. If they do, they are subject to tax.

This reduction applies up to a maximum of €120,000.

That is, if your inheritance is a property worth €120,000, you can reduce this total by 95 per cent, taking off €114,000. So you pay tax on only €6,000, meaning no tax at all.

But if your family home in Spain has a market value of €360,000, then half of that is €180,000. Your reduction stops at the maximum of €120,000, meaning you must pay Spanish inheritance tax on €60,000, which comes to just over €6,000 in tax.

This reduction is also available for a principal dwelling left to a brother or sister over 65 years of age who has been living with the testator for the previous two years.

The reduction does not apply to any other property, such as a car or a yacht or shares in companies, only to the home itself.

The inheritor, in turn, must keep the property for at least 10 years. If he or she attempts to sell it, there will be tax due on the original inheritance.

This measure forms part of a package of laws designed to help small family businesses rather than retired foreigners. Many small businesses in Spain have failed on the death of the founder because his inheritors were unable to deal with the inheritance tax on the property, such as a shop or a small factory. Now the children can freely inherit, as long as they continue to operate the business for 10 years.

Retired foreign couples can also benefit, as described above, because the family home is included in the law. When one of the couple dies, his or her share of the house or flat will be just about tax free to the surviving partner.

Non-residents cannot take advantage of this reduction.

## SETTING TAX VALUES

Spain has a set system for evaluating assets for purposes of inheritance tax. These are:

**REAL ESTATE:** Property is valued either at market price or at the *valor catastral,* the rated value, or at the value set by Hacienda for purposes of wealth tax, whichever is greater. So, in almost all cases, you will find that the declared sales price on your title deed, or today's market value, will be the value used. That is, if you bought your flat 20 years ago for €60,000, and it is worth €150,000 on the market today, Spain's tax agency will value it at €150,000 for purposes of calculating inheritance tax.

When you make your inheritance tax declaration, if you declare the flat as worth only €120,000, you might get away with it, or you might get a notice from Hacienda that they have valued it at €150,000 and you must pay tax on €30,000 more.

Remember that Hacienda has its own office of valuation and is perfectly aware of the market price of real estate. They will not fine you, but they will charge you the extra tax. They do this frequently.

If you disagree with their valuation, you can request an independent survey, a *tasación*.

**PERSONAL EFFECTS:** The furniture, clothing, personal possessions and so on of the deceased are called the *ajuar.* For inheritance tax purposes they are routinely valued at 3 per cent of the price of the property. If valuable works of art or antique furniture pieces are included, they may be valued separately. In general, add 3 per cent of the property value to your estate.

**AUTOMOBILES:** Most property owners have automobiles, and these are included separately in the estate. Spain's Tax Agency publishes tables each year for the value of used cars. Other items, such as yachts or airplanes, will be valued separately.

**STOCKS AND SHARES:** Stocks and shares in companies or mutual funds or other investments are valued at their price on the day of the person's death.

**LIFE INSURANCE:** If received by children, the total amount is added to the estate, after a reduction of €9,000. If received by surviving spouse, half of the amount is added to the estate, and the other half is taxed as a capital gain in the spouse's yearly income tax. Spouse also has reduction of €9,000.

**BANK ACCOUNTS:** The balance on the day of death is added to the estate.

### Spanish Inheritance Tax Rates Year 2004

Euros - rounding centimos

| Tax Base | Tax | Marginal Percentage |
|---|---|---|
| 0.00 | 0.00 | 7.65 |
| 7,993 | 611 | 8.50 |
| 15,980 | 1,290 | 9.35 |
| 23,968 | 2,037 | 10.20 |
| 31,955 | 2,852 | 11.05 |
| 39,943 | 3,735 | 11.90 |
| 47,930 | 4,685 | 12.75 |
| 55,918 | 5,703 | 13.60 |
| 63,905 | 6,790 | 14.45 |
| 71,893 | 7,944 | 15.30 |
| 79,880 | 9,166 | 16.15 |
| 119,757 | 15,606 | 18.70 |
| 159,634 | 23,063 | 21.25 |
| 239,389 | 40,011 | 25.50 |
| 398,777 | 80,655 | 29.75 |
| 797,555 | 199,291 | 34.00 |

### How to Use the Tax Table

You can calculate your own inheritance tax by using the tables shown here.

First, figure your total value by referring to the section above on valuations.

Then subtract from this amount any debts owed by the deceased. This would include a mortgage still unpaid on the property, for example. You can also deduct the expenses of the last illness and the funeral and burial.

After making any deductions allowed you for the inheritance tax such as your basic exemption of €15,956.87 if the estate is passing to close family, let's suppose that your final taxable inheritance is about €42,000.

Look at the table to find the nearest figure below that amount. In this case it is €39,943. The tax due on that amount is €3,735.

Now you need to consult the marginal percentage list, for the rate charged on the difference between the steps.

In your case you find that you must pay 11.90 per cent of the difference between €39,943 and your inheritance of €42,000.

The difference is €2,057. Multiply this by 11.90 percent and this gives you another €244.78. Add the two together and you have a total tax of €3,980, a little less than 10 per cent of your base.

These numbers were originally nice round numbers like five million in pesetas, but they have been increased according to inflation since the law was originally passed, and even more decimals arose when they were converted directly and exactly into euros.

In cases where the debts of an estate are greater than the assets, which could happen when a small business constitutes the estate, for example, the inheritors can refuse to accept the inheritance, thus being free of their parent's debts.

## SOME SPANISH REGIONS HAVE DIFFERENT TAX SCALES

Madrid, Catalonia and the Valencian Community, using their independence from the central state government, have prepared their own inheritance tax scales.

Also, Madrid and its province has added to its inheritance laws that an unmarried couple who are registered in the registry of common-law couples can take advantage of the lower tax rates applied to married couples. This is not true in the other autonomous regions.

257

## WEALTHY PEOPLE PAY MORE

From this table, it looks as if 34 per cent is the absolute top rate of Spanish inheritance tax. This is true when the estate is passed in direct line of descent or between spouses. But it can be much higher when bequests are made to more distant relatives or to non-relatives. And it can be even higher when the inheritor is already wealthy. Remember that the sliding scale of Spanish inheritance tax is designed to favour the poor and soak the rich.

This scale provides multiplying coefficients for the degree of relationship and also for the amount of existing wealth of the inheritor. To get the amount of tax due from those who are more distant relatives or non-related and those who already have sizeable fortunes, you must multiply the basic tax rates above by the coefficients given in the table below.

| Euros - rounding centimos | | | |
| --- | --- | --- | --- |
| Existing Assets | Spouses Children | Cousins Uncles | Non-Relatives |
| 0 to 402,678 | 1.0000 | 1.5882 | 2.0000 |
| 402,678 to 2,007,380 | 1.0500 | 1.6676 | 2.1000 |
| 2,007,388 to 4,020,770 | 1.1000 | 1.7471 | 2.2000 |
| More than 4,020,770 | 1.2000 | 1.9059 | 2.4000 |

So, if you are fortunate enough to possess assets worth more than four million euros, and you inherit more than €797,555 from someone who is not related to you, the Spanish tax ministry will multiply the 34 per cent by the 2.4 coefficient and will demand a tax from you of 81.6 per cent.

This system penalises inheritance to non-relations because it is designed to protect the family structure as well as the poor. It has caused problems for same-sex couples and for couples who may have lived together for many years in a stable relationship but are not married.

The high rate of inheritance tax and low exemptions in Spain cause many to seek ways round paying it, some of which are legal, some not.

258

## POWER OF ATTORNEY

A note of warning: Many foreigners have been misled by the wording in English of an "Enduring Power of Attorney".

Such a power of attorney does not mean that the power endures beyond the death of the person who grants it. A power of attorney dies with its maker, in Spain and in the UK. The "enduring" simply means that it has no other fixed date of expiry.

People sometimes think that such a power of attorney will allow them to dispose of property, such as a villa in Spain, after the death of the owner, thus avoiding the formalities of a will and inheritance tax.

This is not so. The power of attorney legally expires when the maker of it dies. Some people have used the trick of failing to inform the authorities of the death and then using the power of attorney to sell a property.

If swiftly done, the authorities are not likely to catch you, but it is against the law. Further, if someone had reason to protest such a sale, they could have it annulled as a fraudulent act.

**Family Trust:** Among the perfectly legal ways of avoiding inheritance taxes is the formation of a family corporation or trust, in which the family's wealth passes into the hands of the company, with each family member becoming a director of the company. So when one member of the family dies, it involves only a reorganisation of the board of directors and a transfer of some of the company shares, attracting very little tax.

**Off-shore Company:** For non-Spaniards, the constitution of a Gibraltar-based company or other offshore operation in order to own real property in Spain has been another way to avoid Spanish inheritance taxes. In this case, when the founder of the company dies he leaves his shares in the company to whomever he chooses, in a will made outside of Spain. But as far as Spain is concerned, the same company continues to own the property and no transfer has taken place, hence there is no tax (See chapter on taxes for more information), but be warned that Spain has placed a special tax on properties owned by companies registered in off-shore tax havens. You will need expert legal advice on your individual circumstances and the possible disadvantages of this offshore ownership before you decide.

259

**Four-Year Limit:** Another trick takes advantage of the fact that the statute of limitations on inheritance tax, and all other taxes, runs out after four years. That is, the State cannot collect the tax once four years have elapsed. So the scheme is to "lose" the deceased's will for four years, not declaring the property for inheritance. At the end of four years, the inheritor "discovers" the will and takes possession of the property, free of any inheritance tax.

Be warned, however, that Spanish law requires that an inheritance be declared within six months of the death, and if you are found out, you can be subject to a surcharge of 25 per cent on the tax due, or even higher penalties if the Spanish authorities rule that deliberate fraud is involved.

Also be warned that the six-month period is included in the statute of limitations, so you really have to wait four years and six months for *prescripción*, the Spanish term for statute of limitations.

**Gift:** You can also make a gift of the property to your inheritors while you are still living, perhaps reserving the right to inhabit the flat as long as you live, but remember that the Spanish gift tax is exactly the same as the inheritance tax. The law in fact is called the Law on Inheritance and Gifts.

**"Sell" Property Now:** Or you might "sell" your property to your heir, again reserving the *usufructo* or lifetime right to inhabit it yourself. At property transfer costs of around 10 per cent, this could save your inheritor a sizeable sum when the valuation is more than €50,000 and the inheritor is a non-relative.

You have to go on living for at least five years after you carry out this operation, however, or the State will assume that you did it only to avoid tax and will charge you the full amount.

This particular method has many attractions for same-sex couples where one party owns the property and wishes to leave it to the other, without suffering the very high rate of taxation applied to non-relatives.

Each case needs individual study so it makes sense to consult a Spanish lawyer when making your will.

## GLOSSARY

**Ajuar** – The contents of a home, furnishings and equipment

**Certificado de Ley** – Certificate of Law, usually certifying that the law of another country is applicable.

**Exención** – Exemption

**Herederos Forzosos** – Compulsory heirs

**Pareja de Hecho** – Unmarried couple living together as man and wife

**Poder** – Power of Attorney

**Prescripción** – Time limit on legal action, statue of limitations

**Registro Central de Ultima Voluntad** – Central Registry of Wills

**Tasación** – valuation, of property or other asset

**Testamento** – Will, testament

**Testamento Cerrado** – Secret, closed will

**Ultima Voluntad** – Last will and testament

**Usufructo** – Usufruct, right to enjoy

**Valor Catastral** – Officially rated value of property

# 15    Your Legal Advisers

**W**ho are these advisers we keep telling you to consult? What can the *abogado*, the *gestor*, the *asesor fiscal*, the *notario* and the *administrador de fincas* do for you?

They can do a lot to steer you right and save you time as well as protecting you from a load of paperwork, problems and headaches. Let's examine each of them.

## YOUR *ABOGADO*

*Abogado* means lawyer, solicitor or attorney. Do not be afraid to consult a Spanish lawyer. They are trained professionals whose job is to serve their clients within the law.

Many of them who practice in areas where foreigners settle speak excellent English, among other languages, and are accustomed to dealing with foreign residents in Spain and their special problems.

In towns such as Marbella on the Costa del Sol, foreigners make up more than half the clients of many local lawyers, while in the nearby resort of Fuengirola, more than 40 per cent of all court cases involve foreigners. These Spanish lawyers make their living by serving their foreign clients, and they are prepared to serve you as well.

If you are purchasing property in Spain, starting a business, attempting to get a work permit, investing in a Spanish business or making a Spanish will, you need a Spanish lawyer to advise you.

A lawyer will check the title of the property you wish to buy in order to discover if the seller really holds clear title or if there are unpaid taxes on the property. He will vet your contract to make sure the provisions are the normal ones and do not contain any tricky clauses working to your disadvantage.

In a country where you do not speak the language, do not have any local knowledge and are not familiar with the law, it seems basic common sense to get expert help, for your own protection.

Doing it yourself is often penny-wise and pound-foolish. Yes, you can get a standard form to make a Spanish will and have the *notario* register it for a small fee, but only a lawyer will explain to you whether or not you can legally make such a will. Your terms may not be valid in Spanish law.

In any case, when it is time to probate the will and distribute the estate, a lawyer's services will be necessary and the lawyer who prepared the will in the first place will be familiar with its terms and fully prepared to see they are carried out.

There are dozens of ways a lawyer can help you. If you instruct a lawyer to act for you in your absence, you can be sure that your taxes, fees and other matters will be correctly handled while you are away.

Spanish lawyers work with another professional called a *procurador,* who handles much of the complicated routine of preparation and presentation of documents to the court.

**Lawyer's fees:** these can vary widely in Spain, just as they do in most countries, because they depend on the amount of work involved. Handling a property purchase may cost you as little as €500 or it could run into thousands of euros if the lawyer discovers complications that need sorting out.

One rough estimate for property transactions is one per cent of the amount involved, although many lawyers will try to charge more.

Ask in advance, and try to establish an agreed fee or percentage before you assign your case to a lawyer. Many of them will agree to this and you can avoid unpleasant surprises later.

The *Colegio de Abogados* publishes a list of guidelines, setting minimum recommended fees. The follow are an example:

**Property purchase:** one per cent of the total price is standard.

**Residence and work permit:** €150 for a married couple.

**Disputes over money**: There is a sliding scale. To claim €600,000, a lawyer will charge 10 per cent. For €300,00, the base fee is five per cent.

**Divorce:** where there are no children and no property ast stake and the divorce is by mutual agreement, the charge is a minimum of €1000.

**Preparing a will**: the charge is a minimum €100 and about €60 more for the notary.

---

**BILL OF RIGHTS**

A Bill of Rights for Citizens before the Administration of Justice has been presented to the Spanish Congress.

The bill provides for the *hoja de encargo,* a work order, which lists the services that the lawyer will provide and the fees he will charge.

This work order provision is part of a 41-point programme to make the citizen's contact with the legal system more user-friendly (see section on Courts and Judges on page 332 for more details).

As lawyers are notoriously reluctant to tell clients what their fees will be, we can only hope that this laudable initiative works out in practice. On the lawyer's side, it is difficult for them to calculate in advance just how difficult a case is going to be.

Nevertheless, it is certainly worth mentioning this *Carta de Derechos de los Ciudadanos Ante la Justicia* when you are discussing fees with your lawyer.

265

What can you do if you are convinced your lawyer is not doing the work you are paying him for? What action can you take, for example, if you have waited two years for your title deed and you hear nothing from him?

**How to Complain:** there is a law society in Spain called the *Ilustre Colegio de Abogados*, the Illustrious College of Lawyers, the professional organisation that watches standards and defends the interests of its members.

It has branches in each province and you can complain directly to this body about the activities of one of its member lawyers. As in many countries, the watchdog committee of lawyers is usually quite reluctant to condemn a fellow attorney, but they will hear your complaint and look into it.

The *Colegio* publishes a booklet each year, listing approximate fees for various legal services. Although they are not binding, they are supposed to represent minimum fees. The list is aimed at preventing lawyers from under-cutting one another but, at the same time, it can indicate whether or not your lawyer is over-charging you. If his fees are very much higher than the corresponding fees in the booklet, you could have a good case against him.

You would probably want another lawyer to help you prepare a letter of complaint to the College. They would question your original lawyer and he would have to explain the basis for his fees. If the explanation does not satisfy the College, you could be compensated.

In more serious cases, the College can take stronger action against a member lawyer. A number of Spanish lawyers currently face charges for failure to perform the services for which they were instructed or for using their clients' money for their own purposes or for participating in schemes to cheat their clients.

These lawyers can be fined, disbarred and even imprisoned. It does happen, so do not hesitate to make your complaint if you feel that you have been wronged. Remember that it also helps to have your agreement with your lawyer written and signed. This will help both in negotiating fees and in establishing the facts if you have a complaint.

266

**Free Legal Assistance:** If you are a resident of modest means, you could be entitled to free legal aid in Spain.

Low-income persons have been guaranteed cost-free access to legal defence since the granting of the Spanish Constitution in 1978, but the system was sharply criticised for the limited service provided, for abuse by persons falsely claiming to be poor, and for the fact that the State paid the public defenders too little and too late, which did not encourage them to work hard for their clients.

A new law called *Asistencia Juridica Gratuita*, the Free Legal Assistance law, has been enacted to remedy these defects. It provides easier access to legal help, greatly widens the scope of the help available, and attempts to check the abuse of the system by persons who in fact have sufficient means to pay their own private lawyer.

For the foreigner, the good news is that even a non-resident of Spain may qualify for free legal aid. Resident foreigners of course are entitled.

Persons of incomes less than 2.5 times the official minimum wage are entitled to free legal aid. The Spanish minimum wage is a little more than €6,000 a year.

Furthermore, the *Colegio de Abogados*, the College of Lawyers, has installed its own legal aid offices in the law court building, usually called the *Palacio de Justicia*, in each judicial district in Spain. Those seeking free legal aid can present themselves at these local offices and request the forms to apply for aid.

Applying for legal aid is rather complicated. In an attempt to identify false applicants, the forms require copies of your Spanish income tax declaration or a certificate from Hacienda that you do not pay income tax, a certificate from your town hall listing any properties you own, and even a note from the Traffic Department giving details of any automobiles you own in Spain.

Workers and beneficiaries of the Spanish Social Security system also have the right to free representation before the labour court, so employees who feel they have been mistreated by their Spanish employers can be sure of professional assistance to plead their case.

For the first time, legal aid includes advice and planning before any court action takes place. This means a low-income person who wants to bring a lawsuit against anyone for any reason can get legal advice and help before taking any action. Perhaps a pointed letter from the lawyer will settle the matter out of court, thus saving time and money for the taxpayers as well as the persons involved.

The law also provides free access to the services of court-appointed experts, those professionals who evaluate the costs of a botched plumbing or carpentry job, for example, so the judge can assign a value.

In Spanish such an expert is called a *perito judicial*. Even the threat of calling one can often make the offending supplier back off on his attempts to collect a bill for substandard work.

Even more important, the new legal aid law provides an exemption from the deposits necessary in many legal actions. Often, you must make a deposit of a certain percentage of the amount you are seeking in order for the court to accept your suit. This is to discourage people from making idle lawsuits simply for the nuisance value. Unfortunately it also had the effect of preventing persons of modest means from bringing some justified legal actions. Now, exempted from having to pay a deposit, they can do so.

A false declaration of poverty or the concealment of financial resources can result in an order to repay to the State any expenses incurred on behalf of the person who has requested free legal aid. This is to prevent abuses of the system, which occurred all too frequently under the former law.

## YOUR *GESTORIA*

All countries have bureaucracies and red tape but some people say Spanish red tape is in a class all its own. Not only foreigners in Spain have to deal with *papeleo*, paperchase. Spaniards themselves have the same forms to deal with and are driven just as mad by their own bureaucracy. This situation has given rise to the *gestoría,* a peculiarly Spanish institution licensed by the government.

The *gestor* is the middleman between you and Spanish

bureaucracy. When you are standing in a long line waiting to present the papers for your residence renewal and you see a man with a folder of papers pass directly behind the counter and engage the attention of one of the clerks while you and the rest of the people wait, that is the man from the *gestoría*.

He is doing exactly what you are doing, but he is doing it for half a dozen or so people who have paid him to handle the matter. He receives prompt attention from the clerks not because he pays them bribes but because he saves them work. They know that his forms will be properly filled in and all necessary documents present.

The *gestoría* can save you a lot of time and trouble, usually for a rather small fee. The *gestor* has no official powers, but he must pass an exam and is licensed by the authorities as a professional. He can be held to account if he mishandles your applications or charges for services he does not perform.

The gestor, if he is experienced, can do a great deal more than save you time in the queue. There are gestorías in large cities with 30 or 40 employees, where you find experts on one floor arranging the Social Security payments for a company's employees, while on the next floor someone is processing the papers to renew the tourist licence plates for a foreigner's car, and on the ground floor a messenger is picking up clients' property purchase contracts to take along to the registry office.

They carry out all the operations described in this book, and many more besides. They can advise you on all sorts of transactions.

If you are starting a business, you will definitely need a good *gestoría* to steer you through the complexities of licensing, administration, book-keeping and taxation. There are also small *gestorías* which simply do not have the expertise to handle a lot of the often complex problems involving foreigners, so it is necessary to ask among old hands for a *gestoría* which has given them satisfactory service.

The *gestor*, as a licensed professional, also has a *Colegio*, and if you feel that you have not received satisfactory service, you may lodge a complaint. Ask in advance what the fees are for the service you require. If they seem high to you, try another *gestoría*. The *Colegio* sets fees, but these are minimums, not

269

maximums, unfortunately, as their primary aim is to prevent a price war.

Note of warning: Although a good *gestor* can provide many services, including the arranging of rental contracts and the hiring and paying of employees, we advise you to use the services of a lawyer and a tax consultant as well, in order to make sure that you are fully protected.

Sometimes a busy *gestor* will apply a standard contract in a situation where legal or tax complications can later arise, so do not be lulled into a false sense of security when he says that your contract is the one everyone uses. He is probably right, but check with the lawyer and tax consultant just to be sure.

## YOUR *ASESOR FISCAL*

Literally translated, this is a "fiscal adviser", basically a chartered accountant.

You may not need an accountant during the first stages of your residence in Spain, but when it is time for you to pay Spanish income tax, or at least declare for it, you should certainly consult an *asesor fiscal*. If you have any investments in Spain or are starting a business, you will also need an accountant or financial consultant.

He can save you money and see that you keep on the right side of the ever-changing tax laws as well. Again, you should ask long-time residents to recommend a good *asesor fiscal*.

Otherwise, you might share the frustrating experience of one resident who, out of curiosity, consulted three accountants, two gestorías, and the information office of Hacienda about his income tax, and received six different answers.

As discussed in the section on "You and Your Taxes", the income tax situation in Spain is gradually becoming more strict, and foreigners have the additional complications of taxes paid outside Spain or income arising outside Spain, which means they need expert advice.

In business, you will need to know things such as how much holiday pay your workers should get, what expenses you can deduct, and so on, and will certainly need an accountant's services.

## THE *NOTARIO*

The *notario,* public notary, is a public official, like a judge, and you can not employ him as your agent or instruct him to act for you in the same way you engage a lawyer or accountant, although he can give you useful advice.

His principal mission is to make sure that certain matters are officially noted and registered. These include wills, as discussed in the section on "Making A Will", and various sorts of contracts, such as your purchase contract when you buy property. He will register your foreign money contribution when you buy your property. He also registers the charters of companies, and the official book of minutes of a Community of Property Owners is presented for his stamp, which makes the book an official matter of public record.

You might also need a notarised letter when you notify the tenant of your property that you wish to end the rental when the contract term ends, or to make some other official notification.

The Notary receives fees from you for these services, which are fixed by law.

They currently run about €75 for a will and about €300 for a property sales contract under €60,000.

For most foreign property purchasers, their big moment comes when they sign their contract at the notary's office. The notary or your lawyer then passes the contract to the Property Registry for inscription.

The original of your property contract, the *escritura,* stays in the notary's office, where you can always request an authorised copy. He also keeps the original copies of Spanish wills made before him.

In the past, Spanish notaries have not hesitated to register sales contracts that obviously under-declared the real amount of the purchase price, nor did they involve themselves with payment of taxes.

Now, however, they are required to warn the parties to contracts that if they undervalue the purchase by more than €12,000 or 20 per cent, they will be subject to fines if Hacienda discovers this.

They must also verify that five per cent of the purchase price is withheld and paid to Hacienda when property is sold by a non-resident, as a guarantee against the 35 per cent capital gains tax.

## HOW TO CHOOSE A LEGAL ADVISER

Probably the best way to find out who the good legal advisers are in your area is to ask all the long-time foreign residents and Spaniards you know, especially those in business, for recommendations.

If you are so new to the area you do not yet know anyone, you can walk straight into the nearest bar or hairdresser and ask them to recommend a lawyer or a tax consultant. Anybody in business will have an opinion, whether they are foreign or Spanish.

Visit three establishments and you will have a list of advisers that people can recommend and another list of advisers to stay away from. You will also have a fund of useful information about how things really work in Spain, because every foreign resident has a story and loves to tell it.

The consulates of all nations maintain lists of lawyers, tax consultants, doctors and other professionals who speak the language of their nation. These lists are not necessarily professionals whom the consulate is recommending. They are simply noted as speaking your language.

## THE *ADMINISTRADOR DE FINCAS*

This licensed professional is a property administrator.

He can handle all of the matters that come up with your property, such as seeing that taxes are paid, managing rentals and making sure that books are properly kept and taxes correctly paid. He is licensed to serve as a paid administrator for property owners' communities.

Although there is no legal requirement that a community administrator be a licenced professional, it is often a good idea to employ an *administrador de fincas* because he will see that the community's affairs are handled professionally.

"Finca" in this case does not mean a little house in the countryside. It refers to all property in general.

He can advise you about any aspect of owning and purchasing property. Like the other professional groups, there is a *Colegio* that oversees standards for these property consultants, and you can formally complain to this College if you feel your administrator has not given you reasonable service.

## GLOSSARY

**Abogado** – lawyer, attorney, solicitor

**Administrador de Fincas** – licensed property administrator and manager

**Asesor Fiscal** – tax consultant and accountant

**Asistencia Juridica Gratuita** – free legal aid

**Colegio** – official College of professionals

**Gestoría** – licensed administrative office

**Notario** – Public Notary

**Perito Judicial** – court-appointed technical expert

**Procurador** – legal expert who works with lawyer

# 16   You and the Spanish authorities

In your home country you are probably familiar with the various official authorities all of us come in contact with: the town hall, regional or national government, the police, the courts and judges, and so on. Spain is organised in very much the same way as most European countries.

## YOUR TOWN HALL

Your town hall, or *ayuntamiento,* is important to you in many ways.

It is here you pay your annual motor vehicle circulation tax and annual property tax, apply for a building permit, discover how much your *plus valía* tax will be before you buy or sell property, register as an inhabitant of the town in order to exercise your right to vote in municipal elections, and so on.

All you have to do is find the right window or *ventanilla*.

If your town is located in an area with a large foreign population you will probably find someone in your town hall who speaks English.

Towns with many foreign residents, such as Mijas and Fuengirola on the Costa del Sol, maintain special departments to assist the foreigners.

If you are fortunate enough to live in a town with a foreign residents' department, this will be your starting place for most queries.

The mayor is called the *alcalde* and the members of the town council are called *concejales*. You may make any complaints you have to these officials. There are *concejales* delegated as responsible for each area of municipal services, such as rubbish collection, building permits and so on. Ask for the appropriate one, and he or she will give you a hearing.

As foreign residents make up a large part of both the population and the income of many towns, officials generally try to keep you happy.

They are now aware that European Union citizens resident in Spain have the right to vote in local elections and even to be elected to the municipal government (see next page).

If your Town Hall does not have a foreigners' department or anyone who speaks your language well, you should get some Spanish assistance and present your complaint or request in writing. This will be stamped as *recibido,* received, when you present it.

Spanish regulations on local administration declare that all cases presented in this way must be acted upon, either positively or negatively, in a reasonable period of time.

This "reasonable period" of time can seem quite long but complaints about things such as burning rubbish or noisy bars are read and registered, and when enough of them pile up, usually something eventually gets done.

## Register to Vote

If you are a European Union citizen, you are entitled not only to vote in the municipal elections in the town where you are registered but to be elected to office as well. This right applies even if you do not hold a Spanish residence permit.

Local Spanish politicians have recruited foreign candidates in towns along the Costa Blanca and the Costa del Sol for the municipal elections. A few foreigners were even elected as town councillors.

First, however, you must be registered as residing in your town and then you must make sure your name is on the list of voters.

Go into your Town Hall with your passport or your residence permit or some evidence that you live in the municipality, such as a rental contract or a property deed, and inscribe yourself in the *padron,* the list of local residents, and receive a *certificado de empadronamiento*, a registry certificate for this municipality.

Town halls are generally happy to inscribe anyone residing within their limits because their slice of the national or regional tax pie are bigger when they can demonstrate a larger population. However, they will not register just anyone who walks in.

The principal requirement is that you spend more than six months residing in the municipality. This rule applies to both Spaniards and foreigners. Persons are prohibited from being *empadronado* in two municipalities at the same time. This requirement applies to Spaniards and to foreigners.

If you are from the UK, for example, but you register as an inhabitant of a town in Spain, you will be required to vote for your European Union representative in Spain, not in the UK.

Once you are *empadronado,* you can then request that your name appear on the *censo electoral,* the voter registration list, and you will be ready to vote for your local European parliamentary representative and candidates standing for mayor and town councillor in the next municipal elections. Or even stand for office yourself.

277

## PROVINCIAL, REGIONAL AND NATIONAL AUTHORITIES

In modern Spain where regional autonomy has become the order of the day, you may find, as Spaniards also do, some confusion above the town hall level. Many responsibilities formerly handled by the central government in Madrid have been passed down to the regional governments such as the *Junta de Andalucía* or the *Generalitat Valenciana.*

### Provincial Authorities

Each of Spain's 50 provincial authorities has its own legislature, called the *Diputacion Provincial,* which is responsible for various areas, such as consumer complaints and some secondary roads. Through their tourism departments they promote the local attractions and they organise cultural events. They oversee projects that affect various municipalities, such as a province-wide sewage system, for example, or an urban development plan cutting across town boundaries.

### Regional Authorities

These regional governments set standards for property development and building. They usually operate the health care system and have the power to make changes in a number of national taxes. This means that a resident in Marbella gets health care from the Andalusian Health Service, not the national health service, and that inheritance taxes may differ from the Valencian region to Madrid. You apply to your regional government for hunting and fishing licences. Both the Basques and the Catalans have their own special statutes granting them various degrees of autonomy, including the teaching of their own languages in the public schools and their own regional police forces. The governments of the autonomous regions also fight with the central government in Madrid over things such as their share of the national taxes.

278

## National Authorities

The central government in Madrid has gradually been devolving powers to the autonomous regions. This includes the assignment of a share of the national taxes to each region to meet their expenses.

The Madrid government's chief representative in each province is called the *Sub-Delegado del Gobierno*. He is in charge of residence permits, among other matters, because immigration is a national policy.

Sometimes there are areas where municipal, provincial and regional authorities conflict and overlap. You may find that you are dealing with the national government when you could easily think it's the provincial one.

When you apply for a work permit, for example, you deal with the *Delegación Provincial* of the *Ministerio de Trabajo*. This is the office of the Labour ministry located in your province, but it is not a provincial organ.

And so it goes, with various state organisms in charge of different areas. Some will be important to you and others will not.

## POLICE FORCES

There are three kinds of police, and sometimes four, operating in the same areas, which can be confusing for a foreigner.

There are municipal police, national police and the *Guardia Civil*. Some autonomous regions, such as the Basque Country and Catalonia, have their own regional police as well.

You will most likely come into contact with the municipal police when a young municipal policewoman slaps a 30-euro parking ticket on your illegally parked car, with the national police when you present your application for a residence permit at your local *comisaría*, or police station of the *Policía Nacional*, and with the *Guardia Civil* when you drive too fast on the highway and are pulled over by a motor-cycle policeman in a green uniform.

279

## Municipal Police

First, there are the municipal police of your town, called *Policia Local*. They are there to see you obey the local laws. They direct traffic, help schoolchildren and old folk across the road, see that bars close on time and do not make too much noise, assist inhabitants who have a problem with a neighbour, and so on.

The local police have a device that measures the decibel-level of the noise coming from a bar and they can fine the proprietor if the noise is above permitted levels. They have even been seen in the streets applying this meter to the motors of those ear-splitting 50-cc motorbikes that infuriate Spaniards and foreigners alike.

People often say the police do nothing about the noisy bikes, but in fact they confiscate hundreds of them every year and oblige the offending owners to fit proper silencers.

If you have a problem with a neighbour or a noisy bar, you can always go along to your local police station and make a complaint or *denuncia* (see box). Whatever your contact with your local police, as a general rule you will find them polite and helpful.

---

**FACT:** *23 per cent of all prisoners in Spanish gaols are foreigners.*

---

## National Police

Then there are the national police, who are more thoroughly trained, and are in charge of dealing with most crime. There are national police stations in towns of any size. Here you find the *extranjeros* or foreigners department where you apply for a residence card. The national police are charged with the documentation and control of foreigners in Spain, including the wave of illegal immigrants pouring in from Africa. The national Police have specialised units dealing with matters such as organised crime rings, drug smuggling and money laundering.

## Guardia Civil

Finally, there is the Guardia Civil. This body was originally organised to provide police protection in country areas, and they have little to do with large cities or even big towns. If you live in a village, though, there will be a Guardia Civil station instead of a national police unit, and you report crimes to them.

Your principal contact with them will most likely be through their mission of patrolling the highways. They assist motorists in difficulty. On the other hand, they might be around a curve with modern radar equipment that times your speed, and identifies your licence number. You won't even know you have been clocked until you get the *multa*, or fine, in the mail.

You can choose to protest it or pay it, at the *Jefatura de Trafico*. the provincial highway department You can usually pay a speeding fine by *giro postal,* a post office money order, which will save you a trip. If you pay within 10 days, you get a 30 per cent discount for most offences.

You might also have contact with the Guardia Civil when they mount a checkpoint along the highway to apply random breatherlyser tests.

The Guardia Civil have specialised units at borders and at sea where they pursue drug-smugglers and boatloads of illegal immigrants. They have bomb de-activation experts and anti-terrorist specialists, and they also have teams of high-tech computer experts who try to keep tabs on sophisticated computer crimes.

## Reporting a Theft

You need to contact the police when your home is burgled, your car is stolen car or your purse is snatched on the street.

In large towns, you report thefts to the national police rather than to the municipal police. In small villages or in the country, you will report to the Guardia Civil post. Procedures for reporting theft are much the same in Spain as in any country.

You may have to wait with others for the chance to make your report. A police clerk records the details. The sad reality in all countries is that most stolen items are never seen again.

Nevertheless, the Spanish police recover thousands of stolen items every year. These items can be viewed at the police station.

Remember that you must make this report and obtain an official copy of it if you are going to make an insurance claim.

---

**REPORT BY PHONE:** *Call police on 902-102112 and report a theft or loss. This report will be sent to your local police station where you must later sign it to obtain a copy.*

---

In tourist-area towns, you may find the report forms available in four or five languages. In some cities there will be interpreters on the spot.

**If You Are Arrested**

If you are arrested by the Spanish police, you have the same basic rights you have in any modern democracy: the right to remain silent; the right to hear the charges against you; the right to legal counsel; the right to contact a lawyer.

You can be held for three days before being taken before a judge, but the judge must be informed of your arrest within 24 hours. In practice, the police hold very few suspects for 72 hours without bringing them before the judge to be formally charged or set free.

### What Is a *Denuncia*?

Sooner or later, you will hear the Spanish word *denuncia*.

Because it sounds so much like the English verb "to denounce" it is often thought by foreigners to have some special Spanish legal significance. It sounds threatening to them.

In Spanish legal terms, the word *denunciar* means only "to report, to declare". When your wallet is stolen, you go to the police post and make a *denuncia*, a report. So, when someone threatens to have you denounced, it only means he's going to have you reported, as one might report a neighbour's noisy television set or a wall being built which will cut off your protected view.

Reporting an infraction to the police is not the same as bringing charges in court. If your neighbour's barking dog is disturbing you throughout the night, you might call the police and they might or might not pay him a visit. In most cases, the matter ends here.

But if you go in person to the *juzgado de guardia,* the duty court, to present a formal charge of disturbing the peace, this is more serious.

You must sign the charges and be prepared to back up your case. The judge will order the offending dog owner to appear, along with you yourself, to hear the case.

## COURTS AND JUDGES

With a little luck, you won't have anything to do with courts and judges in Spain. Taking a case through a court can be frustrating and time consuming. The mills of justice tend to grind exceedingly slowly. Spanish courts have been reprimanded and fined by the European Union for the slowness of their proceedings.

The Spanish courts do function, however, and lawsuits are settled and judgements awarded.

If you intend to sue someone in Spain, you consult a lawyer, who explains either that you have no case in law for this or that reason, or who says that, yes, you have an excellent chance of getting the damages you seek. Your lawyer then prepares the papers and the process is set into motion.

### Juez de Paz

It may be that a neighbour in your village has begun to build a wall on your property or that your landlord has denied you access to the roof terrace when your contract clearly states that you are entitled to it. The *juez de paz,* the Justice of the Peace, is often the first level court in small disputes of this type.

At this level, neither party need be represented by counsel. Often enough, just the fact that you have gone to the Justice of the Peace and cited your neighbour to a hearing will be sufficient to solve the problem peaceably.

These Justice of the Peace courts exist only in small towns where there is no higher court locally available. They are empowered to settle only very minor matters.

### Juzgado de Primera Instancia

The next step up in the court scheme is the *Juzgado de Primera Instancia,* the Court of First Instance. Here you can bring suit to recover unpaid debts and deal with more serious matters, such as divorce or a breach of contract. A lawsuit is called a *demanda* and to sue is *demandar.* Now you need a lawyer.

In the First Instance Court you might sue a business client who has not paid his debts to you for goods and services. If your case is sound and the amount of the debts not too great, you may get a ruling in your favour within six months – or you might wait three years – depending on the caseload.

Here also you can sue the contractor whose work has not met the standards specified in the contract or a repairman whose bill seems too high.

**Perito Judicial:** In many cases of this type, your lawyer may ask for the appointment of a *perito judicial,* a court-appointed expert on plumbing, electrical installations, or whatever is the subject of the dispute. This expert will evaluate the quality of the work and the price paid. Again, in situations of overcharging a client, very often the mere threat of this *perito judicial* will be enough to cause settlement of the case.

### Audiencia Provincial & Tribunal Supremo

Legal action usually begins in the Court of First Instance. Any case, however, can lead to a series of appeals and counter appeals to higher courts, such as the *Audiencia Provincial,* with its four separate branches or *salas* for civil, criminal, administrative or labour cases, right on up to the *Tribunal Supremo,* the highest court of all.

If questions about basic constitutional rights are involved, the case will go to the *Tribunal Constitucional,* the Constitutional Court.

284

A case might even begin in one of these higher courts when serious criminal activity is involved or where large sums of money are disputed in civil matters.

So, there is a functioning legal system in Spain, which you can make work for you by obtaining skilled legal counsel. Just as in most countries, some Spanish courts function quickly and effectively, but most are slow and overloaded. Nevertheless, there is legal recourse for you and the Spanish State is spending millions of euros to expand and modernise the court system.

## Lawsuit without a Lawyer

Spain's new Law of Civil Judgement, which went into effect in January of 2001, has made it much easier for businesses and services to pursue their cases against debtors who just won't pay up.

The law allows you to make your claim without a lawyer or procurator, filling in a simple form at your nearest court, for debts up to €30,000. The words to remember are *proceso monitorio*. This is the equivalent of small claims court in the UK.

The creditor presents himself at the court with some evidence of the debt, such as an unpaid bill or a work order, preferably with the signature or stamp of the debtor, though this is not strictly necessary. The creditor must have the address of the debtor for official notification, and he must bring his case in the court district where the debtor resides.

The two principles of the new system are immediate action and rapid verbal hearings.

Once you have presented your case, the judge should order a hearing within a short time, citing both parties to appear. At the hearing the two sides give their arguments in the presence of the judge, and the process is recorded on videotape. Yes, you will be filmed.

If the debtor does not appear, of if the judge decides he has not presented a valid reason for not paying the debt, he will order the debtor to pay up within 20 days. If the debtor does not pay, the judge will order his assets seized by the court in an amount sufficient to cover the debt.

These assets will be seized even if the debtor appeals to a higher court. It is now easier for courts to act against assets such as bank accounts, as well, which can speed up the seizure process.

Yes, all this sounds very well for creditors, but does it work in practice?

Most Spanish courts are simply unprepared to put the new law into effect. Not enough courtrooms have the required videotape and recording equipment, and there are not enough judges to handle all of the verbal hearings.

Furthermore, although the process can be started very simply for debts up to €30,000, if the debtor chooses to contest the case and the amount is more than €9,000, lawyers and procurators will then be required, meaning extra expense for the creditor.

Nevertheless, the new *proceso monitorio* should be a useful tool for small businesses and self-employed persons. It also enables Communities of Property Owners to proceed immediately and effectively against owners who do not pay their Community fees.

## CLIENT BILL OF RIGHTS

### Bill of Rights before the Law

Spain's major political parties have, unusually, worked together to produce a 41-point "Bill of Rights for Citizens before the Administration of Justice"or the *Carta de los Derechos de los Ciudadanos ante la Justicia.*

The listing of rights is part of a programme to make the Spanish administration of justice more user-friendly and we can only hope that it will be put effectively into practice.

Here are some of the major points:

**Information:** Citizens have the right to be informed by the courts of the stages of any proceedings, and the probable length of time they will take.

**Direct contact:** Citizens have the right to direct contact with the judges or court secretaries involved in their cases.

**Compensation:** Citizens' claims for compensation from the State for judicial errors shall have preferential treatment.

**Lawyer´s estimate:** Citizens may require a cost estimate from their lawyers, so they know about how much a legal proceeding will cost them.

Legal experts fear that the plan is unrealisable without greatly raising the present budget, but they also praise any attempt to improve the presently poor relations between citizens and the administration of justice.

## YOUR CONSULATE

Consulates generally carry out routine paperwork with your home country's government, such as the renewal of your passport. They usually have lists of English-speaking doctors, lawyers and so on.

They sometimes help persons in distress, who have lost their passports and money, for example.

What your consulate *cannot* do is solve your personal problems in your new country. If you are accused of a crime and put into gaol, your consular representative may visit you, but he is not in charge of handling your defence.

If you have a dispute with your Spanish neighbour, this is not the consulate's line of work. They do, however, try to be helpful and often go far beyond the call of duty in emergencies.

## YOU AND THE SPANISH CONSTITUTION

Since King Juan Carlos I signed it into law on December 27, 1978, Spain has had a Constitution similar to that of any modern European state.

It guarantees the basic liberties of free speech and belief, equality before the law, freedom of religion, the right to due process of law for anyone accused of crimes, and abolishes the death penalty. It states that human freedoms will be protected by the law as set out in the Universal Declaration of Human Rights.

It declares that a person has a right to privacy and that his

287

home may not be entered or searched without a warrant unless a serious crime is suspected. It establishes the right to a proper legal defence by a lawyer, and so on. All the normal rights and obligations of a modern democratic state.

In Article 13, it declares that foreigners in Spain shall also enjoy all the rights established in the Constitution. Article 13 first opened the door for the possibility of foreigners to vote in municipal elections where they reside in Spain.

Many foreigners voted in the 1999 municipal elections and a few were even elected as town councillors.

If you are a European Union citizen, even if you do not hold a residence permit in Spain and you wish to exercise your right to vote in Spain, make sure that you are *empadronado,* registered at your town hall and then be sure to check that you are on the *censo electoral,* the voter registration list, when the next municipal elections come around.

## SPAIN'S LAW FOR FOREIGNERS

Foreigners in Spain can be forgiven if sometimes they are not quite sure where they stand under the law. Or even what law they stand under.

In January of 2000 the Spanish Congress passed a sweeping law called the *"Ley de derechos y libertades de los extranjeros en Espana",* the "Law for the Rights and Freedoms of Foreigners in Spain".

The new law replaced the Foreigners Law passed in 1985 and greatly liberalised the requirements for obtaining work and residence permits for non-European Union citizens. EU citizens already enjoy almost all of the rights of Spaniards themselves.

Together with the new Foreigners Law came a complete programme designed to help the thousands of illegal immigrants, largely from North African countries, to legalise their situation in Spain, obtaining permits and access to Spanish health care and other services.

Then the Congress, fearing the wave of illegal immigrants pouring in from Africa, turned around and made the law stiffer again, in January of 2001.

Now, under charges of inhumanity, they are discussing further changes to liberalise the law again.

Nevertheless, in its basic outlines the law opens the door for even non-EU citizens living in Spain to obtain the vote in future municipal elections and strengthens the rights of foreign workers in the country.

The Foreigners Law deals with many of the things discussed in this book, including entry formalities, resident status, work permits and penalties for foreigners living or working in Spain illegally.

It mentions what criteria will be used in granting a work permit, listing circumstances that will work in favour of the applicant, such as having been born in Spain, or being the spouse or child of a foreigner who already holds a work permit.

Another important section lists the circumstances under which a foreigner can be expelled from Spain, which include working without a permit, or having been convicted of a serious crime, either in Spain or abroad. The foreigner can appeal the decision. If he doesn't, he can be given 72 hours to leave Spain, and he will not be able to return for at least three years.

It also establishes a new system of "permanent" and "temporary" work and residence permits, especially designed to ease the situation of the immigrant workers, but which can also be applied to other non-EU citizens as well, such as Canadians and Australians.

## GLOSSARY

**Alcalde** – mayor

**Ayuntamiento** – Town Hall

**Censo Electoral** – voter list

**Certificado de Empadronamiento** – certificate of residence in the municipality

**Comisaria** – police station

**Concejal** – municipal councillor

**Demanda** – lawsuit

**Demandar** – To sue

**Denuncia** – report to authorities of an infraction

**Diputación** – provincial legislature

**Juez** – judge

**Juicio** – trial, hearing

**Juzgado** – court

**Ley** – law

**Multa** – fine

**Oficina Municipal de Información al Consumidor** – municipal consumer information office, receives complaints

**Perito Judicial** – court-appointed technical expert

**Plus Valía** – municipal capital gains tax

**Proceso Monitorio** – procedure to recover debt without lawyer involved

**Querella** – criminal charge

**Reclamación** – complaint

**Votar** – to vote

# 17    How to Complain

**S**ometimes people will put up with mistreatment because they are confused and ignorant of how to go about protesting in their new country. But even though consumer protection in Spain still lags behind other countries, you can usually get a hearing when you have a complaint.

## TOWN HALL

Town halls maintain offices where you make a *reclamacion,* complaint, in writing if your complaint has to do with municipal services such as poor rubbish collection or cuts in the water supply.

The Law of Local Administrations requires the town hall to accept your complaint and register it as received for consideration. They are supposed to respond within a relatively short period of time, whether or not their answer is positive or negative, but in practice we find that many complaints are slow to produce results.

You may follow up by asking for the appropriate *concejal,* or council member. Each councillor is assigned a particular area of responsibility, such as rubbish collection or street maintenance, and he or she will probably give you an appointment so that you can discuss your problem in person with him or her. If you don't speak Spanish, take an interpreter with you.

## OMIC

Most towns maintain consumer information and complaint offices called *Oficina Municipal de Informacion al Consumidor* that can inform you about prices, quality requirements for merchandise, and also process complaints.

These offices are sometimes located at the Municipal Market and sometimes they are in the town hall itself.

The OMIC offices are usually very helpful and make an effort to see that action is taken. The offices themselves have no legal power to compel the return of an item or punish offenders, but they see that the proper authorities are informed.

We recommend the OMIC as the place to start almost every sort of complaint. Even if the problem does not come under their competence, they will help you to find the most effective method of dealing with it.

The OMIC is not limited to basic consumer problems such as defective goods or abusive prices. They can also process complaints relating to timeshare, rentals, and even property purchases.

## HOJA DE RECLAMACIÓN

Many foreigners first become acquainted with the *hoja de reclamación* (see page 371 for form) in a restaurant or bar, where it is usually prominently displayed. You should ask for it if you feel you have been overcharged or received bad service.

In fact, all businesses are required by law to keep this official complaint sheet and are obliged to produce it when a customer asks for it.

The *hoja de reclamación* comes in three copies. The establishment keeps one copy and the customer takes the other two, one to keep and the other to present at the local OMIC office. If the establishment does not provide the sheet, it can be fined.

Each province has a consumer affairs department. If you want to make sure your complaint is heard, you can follow up your *hoja de reclamacion* by telephoning this office to check on whether they have examined the sheet from the offending establishment.

The offending establishment must respond to a client's complaint within 10 days. If it does not, the client can take his case to the OMIC, and the business can face fines of up to six thousand Euros.

You can also make a complaint to the tourist office which most towns maintain. Although these offices are primarily there to give information, they will direct you to the appropriate place for making your particular complaint known.

If you have a serious complaint concerning weights and measures, you can direct this to the *Jefatura Provincial de Comercio Interior,* the Provincial Department of Internal Commerce, in your province.

This office is charged with seeing that weights are honest, that prices are within certain margins on controlled items, and that merchandise is up to standard. Although they probably will not oblige a market stall to replace the kilo of rotten oranges they sold you, these offices maintain a staff of inspectors who will visit an offending establishment. If they find any violations, the shopkeeper will be warned or fined.

## OMBUDSMAN

If your complaint to the Town Hall, as mentioned above, fails to bring the desired result, or if you feel that you have been unjustly treated by any government agency, you may have recourse to the *Defensor del Pueblo,* the regional or national ombudsman. You must have exhausted all normal administrative channels before he will accept your case, but this Defender of the People is the last resort when you are convinced that justice has not been done.

**EUROPEAN CONSUMER DIRECTIVE COMES TO SPAIN**

When you buy any kind of appliance you will be pleased to find that a new European Consumer Directive obliging manufacturers to extend guarantees to two years has now been put into practice in Spain. (Remember you must fill in your guarantee form and have it stamped to assure this).

## CONSUMER ORGANISATIONS

There are a number of national consumer organisations as well as others that operate in the various provinces or autonomous regions. These organisations generally require that you become a member and pay their yearly fees, which are not high, in order to benefit from their services.

One of the largest and most effective of the national organisations, with a good record of assistance to consumers, is the OCU, the *Organizacion de Consumidores y Usuarios.*

Their head office is in Madrid and their telephone number is 91-300 00 45. Or send them a fax at 91 388 73 72. They offer an advice service weekdays from 10am to 1pm on 91 388 74 24. Their Barcelona office also offers consumer advice on 93 218 06 11 from 10am to 12 noon.

The OCU publishes a magazine called *Compra Maestra,* which analyses different products, and another called *Dinero y Derechos,* which concentrates on legal and financial matters. Both of these publications are excellent sources of consumer information.

There are more consumer organisations to be found in the telephone book of your area. These locally-based consumer associations may be particularly effective in different areas.

Other areas concerned with consumer rights and protection include:

## Banks

Every Spanish bank has its own central *Defensor del Cliente,* the Defender of the Customer, who will hear your complaint when you do not get satisfaction from the branch office. If you are still unsatisfied, you have recourse to the complaint department of the Bank of Spain. **Ausbanc**, the association of bank customers, is a consumer defence group that will advise you if you are a paid-up member. They also carry out campaigns against banking practices they consider abusive, such as high commissions and mortgage contracts that round off interest rates upwards. You can find your local Ausbanc affiliate by contacting their website at www.ausbanc.es.

## Doctors

If you have a complaint against the treatment given you by a private doctor, you can present this to the *Colegio de Medicos,* the College of Physicians, which is the professional body overseeing doctors. If you feel that you have a case for malpractice, you can bring a civil suit against the doctor for damages and suffering. These cases are now appearing with more frequency in Spain, and courts have made large awards. There is also an association for the Defence of the Patient that has branches in major cities.

## Lawyers

As mentioned in the section on lawyers (see page 263), the body that controls professional standards and fees is called the *Colegio de Abogados.* Your best bet is probably to consult another lawyer and explain your case to him. He will help you put your complaint in proper form. You can also go directly to the *Colegio* office in your province if you feel you have been over-charged or improperly treated.

## Real Estate Agents

In some European countries, the responsibilities of real estate agents are very carefully regulated. Unfortunately, in practical terms, this is not the case in Spain. Anyone may mediate in property transactions and "buyer beware" is the only advice we can give. There are professional bodies for registered agents such as the API, the *Agente de la Propiedad Inmobiliaria,* which enforces standards. However, many property agencies are not registered and the law does not require this.

### Tax consultants

If your Spanish *asesor fiscal,* tax consultant, has given you bad advice that has cost you money, your only remedy is to bring a civil lawsuit against him. Although many tax consultants have advanced training and are members of the various associations that exist, there is no professional oversight body, and anyone at all can hang out his shingle and call himself a tax consultant.

## GLOSSARY

**OMIC** – *Oficina Municipal de Información al Consumidor*

**Hoja de Reclamación** – complaint sheet

**Jefatura Provincial de Comercio Interior** – Provincial Department of Internal Commerce

**OCU** – a national consumer organisation

**Defensor del Pueblo** – ombudsman

**Defensor del Cliente** – a bank´s consumer protection department

**Colegio de Medicos** – College of Physicians

**Colegio de Abogados** – College of Lawyers

**Concejal** – Municipal Councillor

**API** – official body of real estate agents

# 18    You and Your Community

**W**hen you buy  a property in Spain - as more than one million foreigners already have - you automatically become a member of a community of property owners, whether you like it or not.  Whether the property is your retirement home or a holiday flat, whether it is an apartment, a townhouse or a detached villa on an urbanisation, you will find your own interests affected by the community and the decisions of your neighbours. You will pay your community fees every year, and you will meet with your neighbours at the Annual General Meeting to argue about whether to paint the outside of the building or whether to fire the gardener.

If your building or urbanisation is new, you may even take part in the original organisation of the community, with all its problems of drafting the statutes, electing a president, fixing the amount of community fees, planning the budget and defining the relation of the property promoter and his still unsold properties to the rest of the community.

Only those who buy an individual house in a town street or a farmhouse on a large tract of rural land will not have to deal with belonging to a Spanish *Comunidad de Propietarios*.  A well-run community can add thouands of euros of value to an otherwise unremarkable house, and a poorly-run community can cut thousands off the value of even a very nice apartment.

Before you buy any Spanish property, find out as much as you can about the operations of the community. See the list of questions to ask in the Capsule Guide that follows.

Over the years problems arising from community life have produced hundreds of letters to my magazine column and many, many telephone calls to my radio programme. People want to know if the annual general meeting can be held in English, how to fire an administrator who is not properly serving the interests of all the owners, how to form a legal community on an unregistered urbanisation, how to collect community fees from non-payers, and hundreds of other matters.

This and the following two chapters aim to answer these questions as well as:

- To help you understand your rights and obligations as a member of the community of property owners.

- To show you how to participate effectively in community life, both in and out of the Annual General Meeting.

- To make suggestions for dealing with problems that most frequently arise.

- To provide a ready reference to the complete English translation of Spain's Law of Horizontal Property, the law that regulates communities of property owners.

Beware, however. If the law itself were perfectly clear to the normal citizen, we would not need lawyers to help us interpret it. This is just as true of Spanish law as it is of any other country's law.

So we have provided explanatory comments for each article of the law, telling how the rules work out in practice.

Keep in mind also that the English translation of the law is only informative. The real law is the one in Spanish.

Remember also that this book can only guide you in a general way. If there are serious disputes within your community that involve legal action, do not hesitate to obtain the services of a Spanish lawyer skilled in community matters. Often, a group of members can share the expenses. The courts of law are not an appropriate arena for the do-it-yourselfer.

298

## COMMUNITY OF PROPERTY OWNERS

The community of property owners - *comunidad de propietarios* - is the Spanish system for regulating the joint ownership of common property. In an apartment building this means the entranceway, the staircases, the lift, the roof space, the grounds and any other shared spaces used by all the owners. On an urbanisation it will include the roads, gardens, communal pools, lighting system, drains and other services.

This type of ownership is often called "condominium", for co-ownership. The community sets out the manner in which all the co-owners manage their joint affairs for the best administration of the shared property. The co-owners must decide how much money they want to pay for the maintenance and management of their building, and how this money will be spent.

The law that regulates this system is called the Law of Horizontal Property - *la ley de propiedad horizontal.* This law, originally passed in 1960 and amended in April 1999, is actually more vertical than horizontal because it applies mainly to apartment buildings, although it also covers townhouse developments of attached units.

Communities of owners on urbanisations of detached villas do not come under the Horizontal Law, although provisions of the new 1999 law make it easier for them to use the Horizontal Law's protection.

Urbanisations are regulated by other laws included in several sections of the Land Law, the *Ley del Suelo.* These communities may be of several sorts, but the most effective are called *entidad urbanistica colaboradora de gestión y conservación.* This mouthful translates as "collaborating urbanistic entity of management and maintenance," and is often shortened to EUC.

Estates of detached villas require a different body of law because they present different problems. The roads, drains and lighting installations of the urbanisation may serve the public as well as the residents, thus having a quasi-public aspect that requires collaboration between the urbanisation owners and the town hall authorities. This interaction between the town and the estate demands extra regulation not needed in the case of apartment buildings.

299

But in both cases the idea of the law is the same: to provide a framework in which the community becomes a legal force. It can go to court, enforce the payment of community fees, make contracts. It can also be sued itself. Many problems have arisen in communities of detached villas because they were not originally formed according to the correct laws.

*SEE: Law of Horizontal Property, Articles 1 through 5, pp. 311-316, Article 24, pp. 351-353, and Legal Communities for Urbanisations, p. 355.*

## BEFORE YOU BUY

When you buy property in Spain, you become a member of the community of property owners. You should know five things about this community before you sign any purchase contract. Ask these five questions:

### 1.How much will I have to pay each year in community charges?

Whether you buy an apartment, a townhouse or a detached villa, the property will have a participation share assigned to it, the *cuota*, which determines the amount of the yearly fees for community expenses. This can vary from as little as €50 a month in a modest apartment building up to €400 a month and even more on a luxurious urbanisation with many services to maintain.

These fees can be expected to rise with the general cost of living. The community members may have unexpected expenses, such as repairing the lift or the roof, or they may vote improvements which will add to the costs.

Keep in mind that community fees only cover the operating and maintenance of the building or estate. In addition, you will have to pay your individual annual real estate taxes and your water and electricity bills.

Ask your seller for his last paid-up community fee receipt. He is obligated by law to justify this or to declare the amount of the debt. If this is not possible, you can find out your property's share by asking the promoter of the building or the president of the community.

## 2. Are the community fees paid up to date?

The new Horizontal Law requires the President of the Community to produce a certificate stating that the property's fees are paid up, or listing the amount of the debt owed. The seller of the property should arrange for this. In any case, the buyer can be held liable only for the Community fees of this year and last year.

The law makes the seller responsible for unpaid community fees and for concealing any hidden debt that may attach to the property.

## 3. Can I see the community statutes?

Of course you can, and you can learn many things from them about life in your new community. Remember that the regulations of the statutes will be binding on you as a member of the community. If they prohibit dogs, you will not be able to keep Rover, for example.

Many sales contracts contain a clause in which the buyer states that he accepts the statutes of the community, understands them and agrees to abide by them. Even when there is not such a reference, the buyer is legally bound when he becomes the owner of the property. He cannot refuse to join a community that legally exists.

Ask your seller, the president of the community, or the real estate promoter of a new building for a copy of the statutes. If they are not available, it may mean problems ahead for you, which brings us to the next question.

## 4. Does the community legally exist?

Sometimes a community of property owners does not have a proper legal existence, even when required by law. This can occur in a new building or urbanisation when sales are not yet completed and the community has not yet been constituted and its statutes registered with the Property Registry, in the case of apartment buildings, or the Registry of Conservation Entities, in the case of an urbanisation. Yes, a properly constituted

301

community is registered in the Property Registry. After all, it owns property, such as the garden spaces or the roads.

This legal vacuum can also occur when an established urbanisation either is illegal and unregistered or when the owners have formed their association under laws not properly designed for communities of property owners. Unless these associations of owners are registered and the new buyers agree in their contracts to abide by the statutes, their rules may not be legally enforceable. This doesn't mean you don´t have to pay your community charges. Spanish courts have often ruled that such associations have a *de facto* existence and a right to collect the fees for the common good.

Ask to see the legal registration of the community in one of the registries listed above.

If the community does not yet exist or is not properly registered, you will sooner or later have problems to sort out, either in the formation of the community or in making it a legal body. In either case, lawyers will be involved and there will be fees to pay.

### 5. Is the community in debt?

If the community has had to borrow money in order to pay for unexpected repairs on the building, you will assume your share of this debt when you become a member. Inform yourself in advance.

You can find out this and many other things by looking at the official minutes of the last Annual General Meeting of the community, along with the accounts.Your seller should have a copy of the minutes and the accounts. If he has not, you can obtain them from the president of the community or from the promoter of the real estate where you are purchasing.

A reading of the minutes will give you an idea of the sort of problems and expenses that arise in this particular community. It will contain a record of the voting as well, so that you can see if one individual has voted the proxies of many others, as often happens in communities where many of the owners are absent from their properties much of the time.

If the minutes show that the principal business of the last

meeting was how to deal with the persistent water problems or with the backlog of unpaid fees, you will know you have trouble ahead.

These official minutes will be in Spanish, but it will be well worth your time to have at least a rough translation made. The administrator or president of the community is obliged by law to keep these records at the disposal of the members.

*SEE: For proper registration of community, Law of Horizontal Property, Articles 5 and 6, pp. 313-316, Article 24, 26 and Urban Regulations of the Land Law, Articles 25 and 26, pp. 360-361.*

## YOUR RIGHTS AND OBLIGATIONS

As a member of the community of property owners, you have the right to attend the annual general meeting, and any other meetings of the community, along with the right to be properly informed in advance of the dates and the order of business of any meeting called. If you are not correctly informed, you can protest and even have the results of the meeting annulled by a court.

At the meeting you have the right to voice your opinion, the right to vote, and to present motions for the vote of the other members. You have the right to be elected and to hold office in the community. You may be the president, the vice-president or the secretary. You may be charged with administrating the affairs of the community.

You have the right to see all of the documentation and records of the community. The administrator or other officers are legally bound to keep these records and accounts at the disposal of the members. If they refuse to show them to you, you can obtain a court order to see the documents.

You have the right to hold and to vote proxies issued by other members who are absent from the meeting. This is common practice in communities where the foreign owners are absent much of the time. Most communities in fact have a standard Proxy Form on which an absent member can delegate his vote to another member.

If you feel that a decision voted by the majority of the community is illegal or contrary to the statutes, you, acting alone, can ask the local court to rule on the matter. If you feel that the decision is legal but seriously prejudicial to your own interests and you can unite 25 per cent of the owners and shares, you can petition the court to have the decision annulled, or you can oblige the president to call an Extraordinary General Meeting. You will need skilled legal counsel for either of these actions.

You are obligated to pay the *cuotas* - community fees that have been properly voted by the members at the Annual General Meeting. If you do not pay, the community can claim the debt in court and even have your property sold at auction.

You are obligated to abide by the statutes of the community. If these statutes require all owners to paint their properties white and forbid owners to keep dogs, then you must paint your property white and you may not keep a dog. If you violate the statutes, the community members can vote to ask the court to issue an injunction that will forbid you from entering your property for a period of up to two years. This seldom occurs but the threat is there and it has been carried out in a few isolated cases.

Both the Law of Horizontal Property and the statutes of most communities make provision for such obligations as maintaining your property in good condition so that it does not cause damage to the other owners, and permitting workmen to enter your property when it is necessary for repairs on the building.

*SEE: Law of Horizontal Property, Articles 9 and 10, pp. 319-324. For violation of statutes, see Article 18, pp. 341-342.*

## THE PRESIDENT

The only community officer required by law is the president. He must be elected from among the members of the community, and he can carry out all the administrative work if no other officers are elected or appointed.

The president acts as the legal representative of the community in action. He signs contracts and cheques and can bring lawsuits in the name of the community when he is authorized by the vote of the general meeting. He himself can be sued by the community if the members feel his actions have prejudiced their interests. If the community is sued, perhaps by someone who fell through a badly-maintained balustrade, the president, acting through a lawyer, will be their representative in court. The president gives orders to the administrator.

The president will prepare the notices of general meetings, along with the order of business. He will see that the notices are sent out well in advance. He will oversee the preparation of the accounts of expenditures and income and he will prepare the budget for the coming year. He makes sure that the minutes of the meeting are carefully kept and notarized. He presides over the meeting and informs the absent members in writing of the decisions taken. If they do not register any protest within 30 days, their agreement to the decisions is assumed.

The president, when acting as the sole officer of the community, will oversee the management of the common elements of the property, will hear the complaints of the community members, and has full responsibility for the operation of the community, subject only to the approval of the annual general meeting.

The president is so important that the law says the community must never be without one. The usual term of office is one year, although the statutes may specify other time periods, but if the community does not act to elect a new president when the time is up, the old one continues in office until a new president is elected.

Many small communities where the president is the only officer find difficulty in persuading one of the members to take on this time-consuming responsibility. In many buildings, the flat owners take it in turn each year to be the president. Under the revised 1999 law, the president can even be paid for his services.

*SEE: For duties of the president, Law of Horizontal Property, Article 13, pp. 326-331.*

## THE ADMINISTRATOR

Because so many details demand the attention of the person who runs a community, most communities choose to name a professional administrator for this job. The administrator is contracted to manage the services of the community and is paid a regular fee for this service.

Although many communities choose to employ a licenced *Adminstrador de Fincas,* or professional property administrator, or a licenced tax consultant or accountant, the community administrator need not hold any official title.

Many people think that the professional administrator is an elected officer of the community. This is not so. He is a hired professional, usually contracted for a period of one year. The community may vote to renew his contract, vary his payment, or name a new administrator at the annual general meeting. The president may terminate the services of the administrator at any time if he feels that the administrator is not carrying out the duties specified in his contract. This decision must be submitted to the general meeting for approval, but this can take place after the action.

Relations between communities and their professional administrators have caused many problems. The administrator's contract must be very carefully drafted to make sure that both parties know their rights and duties.

The administrator's duties are the normal ones of seeing to the proper management of the common elements of the community. Unless otherwise specified in the statutes of a particular community, the horizontal law says that the administrator shall prepare the budget and present it to the meeting, maintain the building, inform the owners of his activities and carry out any other function conferred by the general meeting.

Many administrators carry out the work of the community effectively and rapidly, doing their best to keep all of the owners satisfied and well informed. They charge a reasonable fee for their services and they present the community members with clear accounts each year at the general meeting. These administrators are treasures.

In other cases, members complain that the administrators do not carry out the work for which they are responsible, that they arrange community affairs to suit themselves rather than the members, and that their accounts are vague and confusing, which leads the members to worry about where the money has gone. These administrators should be replaced.

Replacing the administrator, like electing the president, is an important step and will require the majority vote of the community members. This brings us to the Annual General Meeting.

*SEE: For duties of the Administrator, Law of Horizontal Property, Article 20, pp. 344-346.*

## ANNUAL GENERAL MEETING

The Annual General Meeting is the maximum authority of the community of property owners, who are required by law to meet at least once each year to elect a president, discuss issues affecting the community, to examine and approve the accounts of expenditures of the previous year and to decide upon the budget - and the fees each member will pay— for the coming year.

The book of minutes, the *libro de actas,* which records details of the meeting and voting, is an official legal document that can be used in Spanish court proceedings. It must be stamped as authentic by a notary or a judge. This book establishes the right of the community president in court to bring a lawsuit against a community member who has not paid his fees, the *cuotas*. It records the names of members who voted in favour of a measure, either in person or by proxy, and the names of those who voted against each measure.

This becomes important when a minority of community member wish to bring a legal protest against the decision of the majority, claiming that their interests have been seriously damaged, even though the majority vote was otherwise quite in order. In a court case, the dissenting minority must bring action against the majority. So the minutes book, as a legal document, establishes the names of those who voted on either side. The book is evidence in court, and decisions made by the community are serious matters.

Before you attend your first meeting, you should try to meet the president and the administrator of your community, as well as other members, to get an idea of the problems facing the members. If you already have a motion that you want passed by community vote, you can begin to assemble the proxy votes of members who support your position and who will be absent from the meeting. This proxy can be a simple written authorization that enables you to cast the vote of the absentee.

You must be notified at least eight days in advance of the meeting's date, time and place. You should also receive a written agenda, the order of business to be transacted, though this is not strictly necessary. The members can bring up any new business they wish at the meeting. It need not be listed on the agenda. At the meeting, you will register your attendance, and any proxies you will vote, with the secretary or keeper of the minutes book.

The president will preside over the meeting. The first item will be the reading and voting to approve the minutes of the previous meeting. If the minutes do not meet with your approval, either because they are false or incomplete, you can vote against accepting them. Your protest will be registered in the book and can serve as evidence in court if you wish to make a claim.

The accounts of the previous year's income and expenditures will then be presented for the members' approval. You should have received your copy of these accounts before the meeting. Sometimes they are perfectly clear and other times they are quite incomprehensible. Ask the president, administrator or treasurer to explain any points not clear to you.

Then discussion will start on proposed plans and expenses for the coming year. Many issues can arise. Perhaps one group wishes to paint the building or to install a swimming pool, but others protest that this will raise the fees too high.

Tempers can run high at community meetings. They often degenerate into multilingual shouting matches when not properly managed. At one meeting a woman became enraged when she felt she was not getting her fair chance to speak and she threw an ash-tray at the table of the presiding officers. A heavy ash-tray.

Even in the best of circumstances, meetings tend to be longwinded, as different members insist on discussing minor details. One community voted unanimously to limit each member's speaking time to five minutes, and to limit each member to two speeches.

When it is time to vote, you will vote according to your *cuota,* or community share. This *cuota,* based on the size of your property, determines both your share of community fees and the weight of your vote. Usually, the majority of members is also the majority of the *cuotas*, but sometimes a few members with large properties can dominate the workings of a community. This can happen on an urbanisation where the developer still controls the votes of the unsold parcels of land and runs the community to suit himself.

The votes of the members will be recorded in the minutes book and action will be taken accordingly. A new president will be elected by majority vote and the building will be painted or not, according to the majority decision. There is always the possibility of protest, remember, when a minority of members feel they have been pushed around by the majority.

If a decision requires a unanimous vote, such as a change in the statutes or a construction project that will alter the participation shares of the community members, this unanimity can be achieved by informing any absent members of the decision. If they do not respond negatively within one month the motion is considered as passed unanimously.

One recent amendment to the horizontal law provides that the installation of ramps and other facilities for the handicapped requires only a three-fifths majority, even when such an alteration of the building would normally need a unanimous vote. This does not exactly give the handicapped a free rein, but it does improve their negotiating position. The new law came from a court case in which one person in a building had blocked the installation of ramps. This was perfectly legal although not very nice, and the Spanish Congress voted, in July 1990, to amend the law.

Finally, the meeting will be adjourned, with some members pleased and others not pleased at all. This is truly democracy in action, with all its advantages and disadvantages. When people are unhappy with their community, they always refer to it as "they." The community is never "they." It is always "we".

*SEE: For proxy votes, Law of Horizontal Property, Article 15, pp. 333-336. For annual general meeting, Article 14, pp. 331-333. For minutes book, see Article 19, pp. 342-344.*

# 19     The Law of Horizontal Property In English

New text of Law 49/1960 of July 21, as amended by Law 8/1999 of April 6, published in the Official State Bulletin April 8, 1999

## CHAPTER I: GENERAL DISPOSITIONS

### Article 1

The purpose of the present Law is the regulation of the special form of property ownership set out in Article 396 of the Civil Code, called horizontal property.

For the purposes of this Law, any part of a building which may be subject to independent use by virtue of an entrance either to the public thoroughfare or to a common area of the building itself shall be considered as "premises".

### Article 2

This Law shall apply to:

  a) Communities of Owners constituted under the provisions of Article 5.

  b) Communities which fulfil the requirements established in Article 396 but which have not filed their charter or constitution as horizontal property. These communities shall be governed, in any case, by the dispositions of this Law in matters regarding the legal framework of ownership of the property, of its individual parts and of its common elements, as well as matters referring to the reciprocal rights and obligations of the community members.

  c) Private real estate complexes (urbanisations or estates), in the terms established in this Law.

**What it means**

The big news in the 1999 law is that urbanisations, or private housing estates, can be governed by the Horizontal Law, even if they have never registered their Statutes or constituted themselves legally as communities. If they meet the terms of Article 396 of the Civil Code, which basically means that the community shares some common elements, they can obtain the full force of the law in compelling the payment of debts and enforcing their rules.

Formerly, the only way for such non-registered urbanisations to obtain full legal status was through the complicated process of creating a Collaborating Urbanistic Entity. This still is necessary in some cases but the 1999 law permits many urbanisations to function as real communities.

## CHAPTER II: REGARDING THE SYSTEM OF OWNERSHIP BY FLATS OR BUSINESS PREMISES.

**Article 3**

In the system of ownership set forth in Article 396 of the Civil Code, the owner of each flat or business premises shall have:

a) The unique and exclusive ownership rights over an adequately delimited area subject to independent usage, along with the architectural features and all types of installations, apparent or not, which may be included within its boundaries and which serve the owner exclusively, as well as any ancillary property expressly mentioned in the property deed, even when they are located outside the delimited area.

b) Co-ownership, with the other owners of flats and premises, of the remaining common areas, appurtenances and services.

To each flat or commercial premises there will be assigned a share of participation (cuota) relative to the total value of the property, expressed as a percentage of it. Said share (cuota) will serve as a basis to determine participation in the expenses and earnings of the community. The improvements or deterioration of each flat or premises will not alter the assigned share, which can only be changed by unanimous agreement.

Each owner may freely dispose of his property right, but he may not separate the elements composIng it and any transmission of the property right shall not affect the obligations arising from this system of property ownership.

## What it means

The provisions of Article 3 are quite clear, setting out the terms of separate individual ownership of flats and the joint ownership of the common elements of the building. In paragraph A, the reference to "ancillary properties" means such things as garages or storage space in the basement that go with each apartment.

The final section of paragraph B establishes the principle that an owner may not subdivide his property. Later - in Article 8 - we shall see that he can indeed divide his property into smaller units, but this requires the consent of the community, as it will affect the participation shares.

## Article 4

The action of division shall not proceed to terminate the situation regulated by this Law. It can only be affected by each co-owner in regard to one flat or premises, is limited to that property, and providing that the joint ownership has not been established intentionally for the common service or use of all the owners.

## What it means

Article 4 makes it clear that any further action of subdivision of the property will not affect the scheme of Horizontal Property regulating the building in general. The last line means that a gardener, for example, who is given a flat in the building for his use, may not subdivide it. This action of division usually occurs when a property is inherited by several owners.

## Article 5

The charter of constitution of the condominium (ownership by

313

flats or premises) will describe, besides the property as a whole, each one of those units to which a correlative number is assigned. The description of the overall property must express the details required by the mortgage legislation and the services and installations belonging to it. The description of each flat or premises will express its area, boundaries, the floor on which it is located, and any ancillary properties such as garage, attic or basement.

This same charter shall determine the share of participation that pertains to each flat or premises, to be set by the sole owner of the building at the beginning of its sale by flats, by the agreement of all existing owners, by arbitration, or by court order. For this determination, the useful surface area of each flat or premises relative to the total area of the building, its exterior or interior emplacement, its situation, and the use it can reasonably be assumed to make of the common services and installations shall be taken as a basis.

The charter may also contain regulations for the establishment and exercise of this property right and other dispositions not prohibited by law relating to the use and purpose of the building, its various flats or premises, installations and services, expenses, administration and management, insurance, maintenance and repairs, forming private statutes which shall not prejudice third parties if they have not been registered in the Registry of Property.

In any modification of the property title and apart from what is disposed regarding the validity of community decisions, the same requirements shall be applied as for the charter of constitution.

**What it means**

In Article 5 we find several important points about the constitution of the community of owners. In the first paragraph the method of describing the property is set out. In the second paragraph, we find that each owner's *cuota*, or participation share, is fixed when the community is legally constituted and registered. Afterwards it can only be changed by unanimous vote of all members.

This paragraph also notes that the use each property makes of the common services shall be taken into account when setting the *cuotas*. This provision allows variation between flats and commercial premises, for example. Sometimes commercial premises pay a *cuota* per square metre higher than that of flats, on the grounds that the people they attract make extra use of common elements. In one case, the promoter of the building (who can set the *cuotas* when the flats are first sold) provided in the statutes of the community that the commercial premises would pay no *cuotas* at all until they were sold. This is because the flats always sell first and the commercial premises sometimes remain vacant for a year, or even more. By this means the promoter avoided paying any *cuotas* on his unsold business premises, and the community of owners had a lower income than they otherwise would expect.

This provision in the statutes - written by the promoter - is perfectly legal, even if unfair to the other new flat buyers, and is only one of the little tricks available to the promoter when he constitutes the community. It is always wise to read the statutes of the building or urbanisation where you are going to purchase.

In the case of the community cited above, the flat owners were preparing to vote against the promoter's rule in the statutes, charging that their interests were prejudiced by it.

Article 5 continues to note that the private statutes of the community will not be binding unless they are registered in the Registry of Property as part of the registration of the building itself.

It is perfectly possible for a community to exist without private statutes, which means that it will be regulated only by the terms set out here in the Horizontal Property Law. These regulations are sufficient for the orderly government of the community, but most buildings also require some special statutes to suit their individual circumstances.

## Article 6

In order to regulate the details of their co-existence and the proper usage of the services and common elements and within the limits established by the Law and the statutes, the body of proprietors shall be able to make internal rules binding on all owners unless they are modified in the manner set forth for making decisions regarding administration.

## What it means

Article 6 is clear in itself. It allows the members of the community to make internal rules by majority vote. This would include matters such as the banning of pets or a requirement to make all awnings the same colour. This is the Horizontal Law for flats. In most urbanisations, such internal rules may only be enforceable when the new purchasers have specifically agreed to accept the statutes in their purchase contract.

However, as we shall see, the new 1999 law allows urbanisations to register their communities under the terms of the Horizontal Law, making their rules binding on the members.

## Article 7

1. The owner of each flat or business premises may modify the architectural features, installations and services of the flat, so long as it does not diminish or alter the safety of the building, its general structure, its form or its exterior condition nor prejudice the rights of another owner, reporting such alterations beforehand to the representative of the community. In the rest of the building he may not make any alteration whatsoever and if he observes the need for any urgent repairs, he should communicate this to the administrator without delay.

2. The owner and the occupant of the flat or business premises are forbidden to carry on in the flat or in the rest of the building any activities which are not permitted in the statutes, which damage the property, or which violate laws regulating activities that are a nuisance, unhealthy, noxious, dangerous, or illegal.

The President of the community, either on his own initiative, or at the request of any of the owners or occupants, shall require the immediate ceasing of any of the activities prohibited in this section, under warning of appropriate legal action.

If the offender persists in his conduct, the President, upon authorisation by the General Assembly, duly convened for this purpose, can seek a court injunction against him, which, where not expressly provided in this section, shall proceed according to the "Cognisance Hearing" regulations.

Once the action is brought, along with the accreditation of formal notification to the offender and the certification of the resolution voted by the General Assembly, the court, as a precautionary measure, may order the immediate ceasing of the prohibited activity, warning that non-compliance will constitute contempt of court. The court may likewise order as many such immediate measures as deemed necessary to ensure the effectiveness of the cease and desist order. The action must be brought against the owner of the property or, in such case, against the occupant.

If the sentence is in favour of the plaintiff, the court may order, as well as the final ending of the prohibited activity and the awarding of damages involved, the deprival of the defendant's right to use the flat or premises for a period not to exceed three years, depending on the seriousness of the violation and the damages caused to the community. If the offender is not the owner, the sentence can terminate all the offender's rights over the flat or premises as well as order his immediate eviction.

**What it means**

Paragraph 2 of Article 7 sets forth the manner in which the Community can protect itself from truly unsocial elements in its midst.

If one of the owners or his tenants is brewing poisons in his kitchen, with nasty fumes in the air vents, or if they insist on making loud noises all night long, or if they scatter garbage through the halls, the Community can go to court against them and obtain an injunction order to cease the offending activity.

The Community can also seek cash damages for the problems and suffering involved.

317

If the offender does not obey the order, he can be considered as in contempt of court, and ordered to leave the property for up to three years.

If he is a tenant, he can be evicted immediately, as well as losing any contractual rights he has over the property.

Included in the list of banned activities are those forbidden by the Statutes. Thus, dogs may be prohibited, for example, and owners must abide by this.

If an owner ignores the statutory prohibition, the community, by majority vote, may take legal action against him. Article 7 also limits the owner's right to alter his property to interior elements only, and only when it does not threaten the structural soundness of the building or alter its appearance. One problem that arises here is the closing-in of the terraces. Because the enclosure of the terrace with glass panels alters the exterior form of the building and would change the pattern of participation shares because of the greater enclosed area, it is strictly prohibited by this article. So, when an owner goes to the community president and asks for permission to glass in his terrace, this must be denied. As you may notice, however, about 75 per cent of all the terraces in Spain have been glassed in. You guessed it. None of these owners asked anyone's permission. They just went ahead and did it. If neither the community nor the Town Hall presents any complaint, the terrace remains enclosed. The possibility of protest does exist, however.

## Article 8

Flats or commercial premises and their ancillary elements can be the object of physical division to form other, smaller independent units and made larger by the incorporation of adjoining units of the same building, or made smaller by the separation of some part.

In such cases, besides the consent of the affected property owners, there will be required the approval of the Annual General Meeting of the owners, to which pertains the determination of the new participation shares (*cuotas*) for the modified flats subject to the dispositions of Article 5, without altering the participation shares of the remaining properties.

## What it means

We saw in Article 3 that the right of an owner to divide his property in smaller units is limited, but it can be done. It requires, however, the approval of the Annual General Meeting.

## Article 9

The obligations of each owner shall be:

a) To respect the general installations of the community and any other common elements, whether for general or private use by any of the owners, whether or not they are included in his unit, making appropriate use of them and avoiding any damage or deterioration at all times.

b) To maintain his own flat and private installations in a good state of order in conditions that do not prejudice the community or the other owners, making good any damages caused by his lack of care or that of any persons for whom he is responsible.

c) To permit in his flat or premises the repairs required for the service of the building and to permit in his flat the necessary rights of passage required for the creation of common services of general interest, voted according to the terms of Article 17, having the right to be indemnified by the community for any damage and prejudice.

d) To allow entry into his flat for the purposes stated in the three preceding paragraphs.

e) To contribute, according to the participation share (*cuota*) determined in his property title or according to any system especially established, to the general expenses for the proper upkeep of the building, its services, taxes, charges and responsibilities that are not subject to individual allocation.

Amounts due to the community deriving from the obligation to contribute to the payment of the general expenses which correspond to the fees assessed for the period up to date of the current year and for the previous year shall be deemed preferential debts under the terms of Article 1923 of the Civil Code and take preference for their settlement over those listed in paragraphs 3, 4, and 5 of that law without prejudicing the preference in favour of salary charges in the Workers' Law.

Any person acquiring a dwelling unit or commercial premises in the system of horizontal property, even with a title inscribed in the Property Registry, is held responsible,with the acquired property as guaranty, for the amounts owed by previous owners to the community for the payment of general expenses up to the limit of fees charged for the period to date of the year in which the purchase took place and for the immediately preceding year. The property itself is legally encumbered for the fulfilment of this obligation.

In the public contract or deed of sale by which the property is transferred in any way, the seller must declare that he is up to date with payment for general expenses of the community, or he must list what he owes. The seller must present certification of the state of his balance with the community, coinciding with this declaration, without which no public title can be authorised, unless the buyer should expressly waive the seller from this obligation. This certification shall be issued in a maximun of seven days from the request by the person acting as Secretary of the Community, with the authorisation of the President. In the case of fault or negligence, they shall be held liable for the accuracy of the information and for damages caused by delay in its issue.

f) To contribute, according to their respective participation shares (*cuotas*), to the reserve fund which shall exist in the community for the maintenance and repair of the property.

The reserve fund, which is held by the community to all effects, shall be supplied with an amount that in no case shall be less than five per cent of the last ordinary budget.

The community may use the reserve fund to take out an insurance policy covering damages to the property or to undertake a permanent maintenance contract for the building and its general installations.

g) To observe due care in the use of the property and in their relations with the other owners and to be responsible to them for any infractions committed or damages caused.

h) To notify the person acting as Community Secretary, by any means which allows evidence of service, of their domicile in Spain for the purpose of receiving citations and notifications of any sort related to the Community. In the absence of this notification, the flat or premises in the Community shall be considered the domicile for receiving communications from the Community, and delivery to its occupant shall constitute full legal notification.

Should notification to the owner prove impossible at the place indicated in the previous paragraph, it shall be deemed to have taken place if the notice is posted on the notice board of the community, or in a visible place set aside for this purpose, indicating the date and the reasons for which this form of notification has been employed, signed by the person acting as Community Secretary and endorsed by the President. Notice served in this way shall produce full legal effect in three days.

i) To notify the person acting as Secretary of the Community, by any means providing certification of delivery, of any change in ownership of the unit.

Any owner who fails to comply with this obligation will be held liable to the Community jointly with the new owner for debts incurred after the transfer, without prejudicing his right to claim repayment from the new owner.

1. These terms shall not apply when any of the governing bodies of the community established in Article 13 have been notified of the change of owners by any other means or by definite

actions of the new owner or when the transfer is publicly known.

2. For the application of the preceding regulations, expenses will be deemed as general when they are not imputable to one or several flats, nor shall the non-usage of a service bring exemption from the fulfilment of the corresponding obligations, subject to the terms of Article 11.2 of this Law.

## What it means

The first paragraphs of this Article set out owners' obligations clearly enough.

Paragraph E tells us that the new buyer in a community is held responsible only for the community fees of this year and the year before, with the property itself acting as the final guaranty for payment.

This paragraph also tells us that the seller is obliged to present certification of payment up to date or the amount of his debt at the time of signing the contract, which means at the Spanish notary's office. The President of the Community must vouch for this certification.

Further, without the certification of payment or debt, the Notary will not stamp the contract of sale, unless the buyer specifically waives the requirement.

Paragraph F provides for the establishment of a reserve fund in all communities, which must be at least five per cent of the normal operating budget, and sets out the obligation of each owner to contribute to this fund. The fund can be used for an insurance policy or a maintenance contract, thus protecting the installations.

Paragraph H requires every member to notify the Community of the address in Spain where he wishes to receive any legal notices. One way to do this is to use the Burofax system of the Spanish postal service. They will certify both the content of the message and its delivery. Lacking an address, the Community can notify the owner at the property itself, and, if for some reason this cannot be done, simply posting the notice on the notice board will take full legal effect within three days.

This is a big change from previous practice, which made the notification so complicated that Communities just gave up trying.

This procedure used to be so difficult and time-consuming that it was hardly worthwhile in most cases. The community had to prove that the defaulter had received in a certified manner each of the unpaid bills, and that he had been informed of the debt and had acknowledged receipt, and every stage of the process was complex.

The last paragraph of this article settles another common dispute. Sometimes an owner will declare that, because he does not use the swimming pool, which he voted against in the meeting, he will not pay this portion of his community charges. This line says he is obliged to pay, abiding by the majority decision.

Even so, in many communities, the members will vote to exempt non-users from the payment for a particular amenity.

## Article 10

1. The Community is obligated to carry out work necessary for the proper upkeep and maintenance of the building and its services to ensure adequate structural, waterproof, habitability and safety conditions.

2. Any owners who unjustifiably oppose or delay the execution of orders issued by public authorities shall be held responsible individually for any administrative fines that are charged as a result.

3. Disagreements concerning the nature of works to be carried out shall be resolved by the General Assembly of Owners. The parties may also apply for arbitration or for a technical report in the terms established by law.

4. The payment of expenses arising from maintenance work referred to in this article shall attach to the flat or premises in the same terms and conditions set out in Article 9 for general expenses.

## Article 11

1. No owner can demand new installations, services or

improvements not required for the adequate maintenance and habitation of the building, in accordance with its nature and characteristics.

2. When decisions are lawfully made to carry out improvements not required in accordance with the terms of the preceding paragraph and the proportionate cost of installation exceeds the amount of three ordinary monthly payments for common expenses, a dissenter shall not be obligated, nor shall his fee be altered, even in the case that he cannot be deprived of the improvement or innovation.

If the dissenter wishes at any time to take advantage of the improvement he must pay his share of the expenses of installation and maintenance, brought up to date by application of the legal interest rate.

3. Innovations that render any part of the building unserviceable for the use and enjoyment of an individual owner shall require his express consent.

4. Special assessments for improvements made or to be made in the community shall be charged to the owner of the property at the time when such payments fall due.

**What it means**

Article 11 requires some careful interpretation and amplification. There is more in it than it seems to say.

The first paragraph seems clear enough. No single owner or minority group can demand unnecessary improvements. The definition of "necessary" is here related to the building's category or standard of luxury. Central air-conditioning may be "necessary" in a luxury building. A swimming pool or satellite TV will not be necessary in a modest block of flats, and no single owner can demand it. Majority rules.

It's what this paragraph doesn't say that is more important. It implies that one single owner can demand "necessary" improvements, with legal right on his side. That is, there exists in law a principle that the property must be properly maintained.

If the majority of owners refuses to repair the broken lift, fix the broken windows or doors, one single owner can demand of the court that the community be obliged to carry out this normal maintenance. He can cite this article, along with Article 16, to back up his case.

He will find additional support if the building has become a health or safety hazard, as the community's decision to let it fall into ruin will then run contrary to law.

Of course, honest dispute is also possible about what constitutes "necessary" and people can spend hours arguing this in the community meeting.

In the second paragraph of Article 10, we find another sore point relating to "necessary" improvements. If the Annual General Meeting votes to carry out some improvement that is clearly not required for adequate maintenance, and the cost of this improvement exceeds the amount of three months community *cuotas*, a dissenter can legally refuse to pay for it. This could be a new swimming pool, for example.

Even though the next two lines make reference to his eventual payment should he wish to make use of the improvement, Spanish courts have ruled that the dissenter cannot be deprived of the use of the improvement even though he does not pay for it.

Paragraph 3 gives the individual owner the power to block any change in the building which would affect his use and enjoyment of the property. This would include the building of a wall in front of his window, for example.

Paragraph 4 settles an area where confusion may arise.

The new owner of the property might refuse to make the next payment on a new swimming pool that was voted before he bought his flat. He can't do that. He assumes all the Community expenses and projects when he becomes a member.

The same principle applies if the Community has previously voted to make special assessments in order to pay off a debt that existed before our new buyer came in. He must pay his share as he is the owner when the payment comes due.

He cannot charge the debt to the previous owner, even if the debt was incurred in the previous owner's time and has nothing to do with the new owner.

## Article 12

The construction of new floors and any other change in the supporting structure or walls of the building or in the common elements affect the charter of constitution and must be submitted to the procedures established for modifications of it. The resolution that is adopted shall determine the nature of the modification, the alterations it produces in the description of the property and the flats or premises, the variation of the participation shares (cuotas) and the owner or owners of the new premises or flats.

## What it means

Article 12 is clear enough. When it says that any major modification of the structure must be submitted to the same procedure as for changes in the community's charter, it means by unanimous vote. The resolution so passed must be specific and completely detailed.

## Article 13

1. The governing bodies of the community shall be the following:

   a) The General Assembly of owners.

   b) The President and, when applicable, the Vice-Presidents

   c) The Secretary

   d) The Administrator

   The Statutes or a majority vote by the General Assembly may establish other governing bodies for the Community but these may not detract from the functions and responsibilities with regard to third parties which this Law confers on those mentioned above.

2. The President shall be chosen from among the owners in the Community by election or by turns in rotation or by drawing lots. Acceptance shall be compulsory, although

the designated owner may request the Court to relieve him of the office, within one month of taking office, citing his reasons for it. The Court, following the procedure established in Article 17.3, will rule on the matter, designating in the same ruling which of the owners will substitute for the President in the office, until a new President is chosen in a time set by the Judge.

Likewise, the Court may be approached when it has proved impossible for the Assembly to choose a President for some reason.

3. The President legally represents the Community both in and out of court and in all matters affecting it.

4. The existence of Vice-Presidents is voluntary. They shall be chosen by the same procedure established for the designation of the President.

   The Vice-President or Vice-Presidents in the order prescribed, shall replace the President in cases of absence, vacancy or incapacity and assist him in carrying out his duties according to the terms established by the General Assembly.

5. The functions of secretary and administrator shall be carried out by the President of the Community, except when the Statutes or the General Assembly, by majority vote, provide that such office be held separately from the presidency.

6. The posts of Secretary and Administrator may be vested in the same person or separately chosen.

   The posts of administrator or secretary-administrator may be held by any owner or by individuals with sufficient professional qualifications or legally licensed to carry out such functions. The post can also go to a company or other corporate entity in the terms set out by law.

7. Unless otherwise provided by Community Statutes, the term of office of all governing bodies will be for one year.

The persons designated to can be removed from their offices before the expiry of their terms by a resolution of the General Assembly, convoked for an extraordinary meeting.

8. When the number of owners in the community is no more than four, they can govern themselves by the administrative system of Article 398 of the Civil Code, if their Statutes expressly establish this.

## What it means

Article 13 states that the president must be a member of the community. A simple majority vote in the Annual General Meeting suffices to elect him, and a simple majority vote can put him out, along with any other officer of the community.

There is nothing in the rule book that says the president must speak Spanish, or be Spanish, or even an official full-time resident of Spain. It would be difficult for an absentee president to serve his community well, of course, but the only requirement is that the president be a member of the community.

By law, the president is the only officer that a community must elect. He can combine in himself the duties of the secretary, treasurer and administrator, and in many smaller communities this is the case. In larger blocks - sometimes numbering more than 100 members— communities may elect a vice-president to stand in for the president when he is absent, a secretary to keep the official minutes book of the meetings, a treasurer to take charge of the funds, and appoint a professional administrator to handle the maintenance of the property. The professional administrator, paid for his services, may not in principle be a member of the community as this would be an obvious conflict of interests.

The community can see that the President's expenses are covered and they can even pay him a wage if they choose.

The responsibilities of the president include:

Convening the Annual General Meeting, giving reasonable advance notice, along with the order of business. Any owner who was not properly notified of the meeting can later protest and have the results of the meeting annulled by a judge.

Presiding over the general meeting, seeing that the order of business is followed and making sure that each person gets a fair hearing. This can be a very arduous task.

Representing the community in its relations with the individual members. That is, if you have a complaint about water dripping from the terrace of your upstairs neighbour, you take this complaint to the president.

Representing the community to all third parties, which would include the company contracted to paint the building. It is the president who signs the contract in the name of the community.

Carrying out any legal action for which he has been authorized by the majority vote of the owners assembled in the general meeting.

It is a serious matter to be president of a legally-registered community of property owners. The president cannot simply resign his office, for example, if things do not go well. He officially holds the post until a new president is elected. This is because the community can never be without a legal representative. So, if the president wants out, he must convene an extraordinary general meeting for the election of his successor or petition the Court to relieve him.

Further, if the community members feel that the president, through negligence or error, has seriously damaged their interests, they can bring suit against him for monetary damages.

Normally the president is elected for one year, unless the community statutes specify a longer term of office. At the end of this year, his mandate will continue unless the general meeting votes to replace him. So it is perfectly possible for a president to continue in office year after year without any new elections.

If any member of the community wants to contest this continuance, he can either ask for an election notice to be included in the agenda of the meeting, or he can call for elections in the meeting itself. Remember that the Annual General Meeting is the supreme authority of the community. It can, by majority vote, elect a new president whenever it desires to do so. The normal procedure would be to convoke an extraordinary general meeting for this purpose. Remember also, that whenever 25 per cent of the members agree, they can call for such an extraordinary general meeting.

This unpaid job of president is often so unrewarding that, in some buildings, rather than actually hold elections, the community members agree to take the post in turns, with a different member taking up the task each year. When your turn comes, you are unanimously "elected" and this is shown in the Minutes Book.

If the community chooses to contract a paid professional administrator, the president can hire and fire this administrator, subject always to the specific contract made, giving account later to the community.

Sometimes community presidents act in a high-handed manner, spending the funds incorrectly and favouring one group of owners over another. This might happen when one member controls many votes. Far more often the president is a civic-minded spirit who is willing to take his turn at handling the problems which arise in any community, only to discover that his co-owners find fault with every decision he makes and are utterly ungrateful for his efforts to help the common good. So he is vastly relieved when his term of office ends and he absolutely refuses to be elected again.

If the community chooses to name a secretary, his function will be the normal work of a secretary in any organization: to send or deliver the notices of meetings; to take the minutes of the meeting and see that they are recorded in the official *libro de actas* , or minutes book, which is stamped by the Notary; to keep the records, correspondence and documents of the community and to show these to any member who wishes to inspect them, and to send out notification of the decisions taken in the annual general meeting to any absent members. This is obligatory. Members who were absent from any meeting must be reliably informed of any decisions taken at that meeting. They then have 30 days starting from the date they received the notification, in which to make a protest ff they are opposed to the decision. If they do not make a written protest, they are considered as accepting any action taken by the meeting. If the meeting has adopted a measure needed unanimous approval, the non-reply of the absentees is included as approval, thus making the vote "unanimous".

Although the law of horizontal property does not require a vice-president or a treasurer, the community statutes can provide for the election of these officers, or the members may vote at the annual general meeting to create the offices and elect members to carry them out.

The treasurer would prepare the proposed budget of expenses for the forthcoming year for the approval of the meeting; would collect and keep the funds of the community; would be responsible for the accounts, and make payments and prepare the yearly accounting for the members' approval. He might also order an independent auditing of the accounts, specially if the community is a large one with important sums of money coming in and going out.

An important point to note about a possible vice-president in a community is that this office must be specifically mentioned, with its powers, in the statutes or in the official minutes book of the community. If not, the vice-president will not be empowered to use the faculties of the president in his absence. He will not be able to sign cheques, represent the community or take legal action.

Article 13 closes with a mention of Article 398 of the Civil Code, which provides a much simpler legal framework for organizing the affairs of communities with four or fewer members.

## Article 14

The functions of the Annual General Meeting are:

   a)   To appoint and to remove the persons who hold the official posts mentioned in the preceding article and to settle any complaints that the property owners may bring against their actions.

   b)   To approve the budget of foreseeable expenses and income and the pertinent accounts.

c) To approve bids and the carrying out of all repair work on the property, whether ordinary or extraordinary, and to be informed of any urgent measures taken by the Administrator in accordance with the terms of Article 20, paragraph c.

d) To approve or change the statutes and to make bylaws for internal management.

e) To be informed and to decide on the other matters of general interest to the community, taking any necessary or advisable measures for the best common service.

## What it means

Article 14 states the basic functions of the Annual General Meeting. The general meeting, ordinary or extraordinary, is the supreme authority of the community. Its decisions, either by majority vote or unanimous vote when necessary, are binding on all officers and members of the community.

Majority vote will elect the officers and also put them out if necessary. If the members are unhappy with the president, for example, they themselves can convoke an extraordinary general meeting, and vote him out. If they have contracted a professional administrator for one year, they can vote at the meeting not to renew his contract.

The meeting will hear the budget of expenses prepared for the coming year. They must approve the expenses or the officials will not be empowered to spend the money. It is here that the fighting often starts. Does the community need a full-time gardener? Should they paint the building or let it go another year? Each point of view will have its backers. They present their opposing arguments, a vote is called, and majority rules. If a dissenter feels his own private interests are seriously damaged by a decision of the majority, he has the power to protest before a court.

The community must also approve the accounts presented for the preceding year. Here again there are often many protests, as some presidents and even some professional administrators often fail to keep adequate records. This is sometimes due to concealment of payments to the administrator but more often results from careless bookkeeping. Many larger communities are beginning to require an independent audit of the accounts as a regular yearly practice.

The third item of the functions of the annual general meeting is probably the one that causes most fireworks: the execution of extraordinary works and the necessary funding. In every community there is someone who wants a swimming pool, or a new lighting system, or satellite television. And in every community there is someone who does not want these things and says he will refuse to pay for them.

Remember that a dissenter can refuse to pay - legally - if the improvement is not 'necessary" and if his share of it comes to more than three month's *cuota*.

The annual general meeting has the power to change the statutes - but only by unanimous vote - and to make internal regulations. These would include things like the prohibition of pets in the building, or the denial of permission to hang out laundry on the roof terrace.

Of course the members must have information in order to decide matters of general interest to the community, as noted in the final section. This means that the administrator and president must present complete information to the meeting. It is their legal obligation to allow community members to examine the community's accounts and documents.

Paragraph C makes special mention of the Assembly's right to be informed by the Administrator of any urgent measures he has taken. Administrators sometimes treat communities as their own property and fail to keep the members well informed of their actions.

## Article 15

1. Attendance at the general meeting of owners shall be in person or by legal or voluntary representation, a written authorisation signed by the owner being sufficient to accredit this representation.

If a flat belongs jointly to several owners, these shall name one representative to attend and to vote in the meetings.

If the flat is held in usufruct, the attendance and the vote belong to the original owner who, except for his manifestation to the contrary, shall be held to be represented by the holder of the usufruct, this representation requiring to be specifically expressed when the vote is on the matters referred to in the First paragraph of Article 17 or on extraordinary works or improvements.

2.  Owners who at the time of the Assembly are not current in the payment of all their debts owed to the Community, and who have not legally challenged these debts or deposited the amount of them in court shall be allowed to take part in discussion but shall not have the right to vote. The minutes of the meeting will show the names of the owners deprived of their voting rights and neither the person nor the participation share shall be computed when calculating the majorities required by this Law.

**What it means**

The first paragraph of Article 15 makes provision for the representation of a community member by proxy if he cannot attend in person.

A simple "written authorization" is sufficient to establish this proxy legally. There is no specific form required. All it need say is that you authorize such-and-such a person to vote in your name at the meeting of the community on such-and-such a day, and it should include the phrase, "any postponement of that meeting," because very often the community does not have a full quorum when the meeting is first called and so it will be held on the 'second convocation," usually specified as half an hour later.

But this sort of open proxy can be dangerous if you do not fully trust the person exercising it. He can vote against your best interests if he chooses. You can also make a specific and detailed proxy, which authorizes its holder to cast your vote only in certain ways. That is, the proxy can declare that its holder must vote "yes" on items three and five of the meeting agenda and can vote "no" on items one and four, and that he must abstain from voting on the other issues. The secretary of the meeting will ask to see the proxy forms when he registers each member's attendance at the meeting, so he will know this.

Most communities have proxy forms already printed and available from the secretary, but they are the open sort, so you must make your own if you want to be specific. There is no provision for absentee voting by post.

Proxies have caused many problems in communities. Foreign owners absent from Spain tend to give their proxy to some influential person in the community. This person is often the developer of the building, who still has unsold units, and so is a member of the community. He votes the shares of the unsold flats still in his name, along with the proxies he has been given, and can often control the operations of the community in this way. Or it may be the president who keeps himself in office with these proxies. In one case, it was the representative of a rental agency that owned some flats in a building and managed others. With the proxies the agency controlled, they ran the building to suit the renters and to the disadvantage of the permanent residents. So there are many tricks available with proxies.

Article 15 also refers to flats held in usufruct. This means that the owner has granted the right to occupy the flat to another person, as sometimes happens when the property is held in the name of a son or daughter. The son or daughter, by a legal document, grants to the parent the lifetime right - usufruct - to inhabit the property. This is sometimes done in order to skip over one generation of inheritance taxes. When the parent dies, the son or daughter simply takes possession of the property which has always been his. The holder of this usufruct is considered the owner's representative at the community meeting for all normal matters. If, however, the community is voting to change its statutes or to authorize extraordinary works, then the holder of the usufruct will need a specific written authorization from the owner of record.

Paragraph 2 of the article contains the real change in the new law. For the first time, community debtors are both deprived of the right to vote and are listed for all to see. Unless these debtors have impugned the court decision against them and deposited the funds, they cannot vote.

## Article 16

1. The general meeting of proprietors will be held at least once a year to approve the budgets and accounts and at any other time the president considers it advisable or when one quarter of the owners request it, or any number of owners who represent at least 25 per cent of the participation shares.

2. The president shall convoke the meeting and, in the absence of this, the promoters of the meeting, giving notice of the agenda of business, the time, day and place of the meeting for the first call, and, when applicable, the second call. Notification shall be given in the form set out in Article 9. The notice of meeting shall contain a list of the owners who are not current in the payment of debts to the Community and will warn of the loss of the right to vote under the conditions expressed in Article 15.2

Any owner can request the General Meeting to examine and resolve on any matter of interest to the Community.

For this purpose he should present to the President in writing the clearly specified points he wishes dealt with. The President shall include them in the agenda of the following General Meeting.

If the majority of owners, representing at the same time the majority of participation shares (*cuotas*) are not present at the time of the first call, the meeting shall be convened again on second call, without the need for a quorum.

The meeting shall be held on the second call at the time, date and place indicated in the first notification. It can be held on the same day, as long as at least half an hour has passed since the first call.

Failing this, it shall be convened again, according to the forms established in this Article, within eight days following the meeting not held. In such case, notification must be made at least three days before the meeting.

336

3. Notification of the ordinary Annual General Meeting will be given at least six days beforehand and, for extraordinary meetings with as much advance notice as possible so that it can come to the attention of all the parties involved. The general meeting can lawfully take place even without the convocation of the president, providing that all of the proprietors agree and decide this.

**What it means**

Article 15 states that, by law, a general meeting must be held at least once a year. The only item of business legally required is the approval by the members of the accounts and budget. It is not strictly necessary to hold elections for a new president because the old one will continue in office until he is replaced by majority vote.

But the expenses must be approved by a legally registered vote of the community members. It is perfectly possible for them to decide that they will not pay out any money for the next year. This means, of course, that the electric company will cut off the lights and the building's insurance policy will lapse. But no money can be spent without the majority vote of the members.

This annual general meeting is the ordinary meeting. Other meetings, known as extraordinary meetings, may also take place. The president may call such a meeting at any time, giving adequate notice. This question of what constitutes "adequate" notification is a little tricky, especially when three quarters of the members of the community are residing in another country at any particular moment, but any president will try to give sufficient notice because he knows that a member who feels he has not been correctly warned of the meeting can protest and a court may rule the results of the meeting void.

An extraordinary meeting can also be called whenever one quarter of the members of the community, or people who represent one-quarter of the participation shares, request it. The president is then obligated to convene the meeting. In the case of the president's absence or incapacitation, the promoters of the meeting may also convoke it.

The law mentions one-quarter of the participation shares, or *cuotas*, because in many cases one or two owners may control a much larger share of the building than the owner of a single flat. One such example would be a large department store that holds more than one-quarter of the *cuotas* all on its own. Another would be the developer himself, who controls and votes all the shares of the unsold flats. This situation, in which one owner holds great voting power, has caused problems in more than one community.

It is common practice for the second calling of the meeting to appear on the original notification, usually set for a half hour after the first calling.

This means that, if a majority of members or *cuotas* is not present - and often it isn't - the meeting can still take place, no matter how few owners or shares are present. Their decisions will be perfectly valid if not protested by the other owners within 30 days after they are notified of the actions.

## Article 17

Decisions of the general meeting shall be subject to the following rules:

1. Unanimity shall only be required for the validity of those resolutions that involve approval or modification of rules contained in the charter of constitution of the property or in the Community Statutes.

   The establishment or elimination of the life, janitor, reception desk, security services or other common services of general interest, even when they involve modification of the charter of constitution or the Community Statutes, shall require the vote in favour of three fifths of the total number of owners, who at the same time represent three fifths of the cuotas, or participation shares. The leasing out of common elements which have no specific use assigned them in the building shall also require the favourable vote of three fifths of the total number of owners who, at the same time represent three fifths of the participation shares, as well as the consent of the owner directly affected, should there be one.

Work executed or new common services established to eliminate structural barriers which hinder the access or mobility of handicapped persons, even when this involves the modification of the charter of constitution or the Community Statutes, shall require the favourable vote of a simple majority of the owners, who at the same time represent the majority of the *cuotas*.

For effects established in the preceding paragraph, the votes of correctly notified owners absent from the meeting shall be computed as favourable when, having been informed of the decision taken by those present, in accordance with the procedure set out in Article 9, they did not express dissent to the person acting as Community Secretary within 30 days, by any certified means of delivery.

Decisions validly taken according to the dispositions of this rule are binding on all owners.

2.  The installation of common facilities providing access to telecommunication services regulated in Royal Decree-Law 1/1998 of February 27, or the adaptation of existing systems, as well as the installation of solar energy systems, whether common or private, and facilities necessary for obtaining new collective energy sources, may be agreed, at the request of any one owner, by one third of the members of the community representing one third of the *cuotas*.

The Community shall not charge the cost of the installation or adaptation of the above-mentioned facilities, nor the costs arising from its conservation and maintenance, to those owners who did not expressly vote in the meeting in favour of the decision. Nevertheless, if they later request access to the telecommunication system or to the energy supplies and this requires the use of the new facilities or the adaptations carried out on the pre-existing systems, this can be granted, providing that they pay the amount that would have corresponded to them, correctly brought up to date by applying the corresponding legal interest.

339

Without prejudice to the above-mentioned expenses of upkeep and maintenance, the new facilities shall have the status, to all effects established by this Law, of common elements.

3.  For the validity of all other resolutions, the favourable vote of the majority of the owners that at the same time represents the majority of the *cuotas* shall suffice.

On the second calling of the meeting decisions voted by the majority of those present, provided that they represent more than half the participation shares present, shall be valid.

When a majority cannot be achieved by the procedures established in the foregoing paragraphs, the Court, at the petition of one of the parties within a month of the date of the second meeting, and hearing any dissenters, who must be duly notified, will rule in equity within 20 days of the petition, and will rule on the assignment of legal costs as well.

**What it means**

Under the previous Law of Horizontal Property, a unanimous vote was required for any modification of the building, which led to necessary and useful action being blocked by one or two dissenters.

The new law sets out very carefully the sort of actions that now require only a three-fifths majority.

It also notes that your vote will be counted as favourable if you were absent from the meeting and did not protest within 30 days of being informed, and you will then be bound by the decision of those present at the meeting.

Sometimes a very small number of owners really make the decisions for the Community.

If you are baffled by references in this Article to access to telecommunications, don't worry. They mean communal television aerials, which require only a one-third vote in order to bind all of the owners. The same goes for work to install any renewable energy source.

All other Community votes require only a simple majority, including the election of the President.

And if you are puzzled by the requirement that this majority must be a majority of the number of owners present as well as a majority of the amounts of When there is a conflict, when, for example, one owner controls many shares because he owns ten apartments in the building or for some other reason, Spanish courts have usually ruled in favour of the number of owners rather than the amount of *cuotas* when deciding a contested vote.

## Article 18

1. Decisions voted by the Annual General Meeting may be challenged in court, following the provisions of the general procedural law, in the following situations:

   a) When such decisions are contrary to the law or to the Community Statutes.

   b) When they are seriously damaging to the interests of the community itself and benefit one or several owners.

   c) When they cause serious harm to an owner who has no legal obligation to suffer this harm, or when the decisions have been made by abusing the law.

2. Owners who expressly registered a dissenting vote in the meeting, those who were absent for any reason, and those who were incorrectly deprived of their right to vote are legally entitled to impugn these decisions. To challenge a resolution of the Meeting, an owner must be current in his payment of debts owed to the Community or he must deposit the amount of the debt with the Court beforehand. This rule shall not apply when challenging a decision regarding the establishment or alteration of the participation shares referred to in Article 9.

3. The action lapses three months after the decision taken by the general meeting unless the decision is contrary to law or to the Community Statutes, in which case the period

is one year. For those owners who were absent this period is counted from the date of notification of the decision according to the procedure set out in Article 9.

4. Impugning a decision of the general meeting does not suspend its being put into force unless the Court orders so, as a precautionary measure, at the petition of the plaintiff and having heard the community of owners.

**What it means**

Article 18 means that even one owner can challenge a community decision in court, if it seriously harms the interests of one of the members, or if it seems to benefit a few people to the detriment of the community as a whole, or if it is contrary to law or the Statutes of the Community.

Dissenters, be warned that you must have your vote against the measure reflected in the official minutes book if you want to impugn the decision.

Absentees have three months in most cases, and they had better have their fees paid up.

**Article 19**

1. Decisions of the general meeting shall be recorded in a book of minutes stamped and validated by the Property Registrar in the form set out by law.

2. The minutes of each meeting must express at least the following circumstances:

   a) The date and place of the meeting

   b) The name of the caller of the meeting, or the names of the owners who promoted it.

   c) Whether it was ordinary or extraordinary and whether it was held on first or second call.

   d) List of all those attending and their respective offices, as well as those owners represented by proxy, with the cuotas of each one.

e) The agenda for the meeting.

f) Decisions taken, showing, where it is relevant for the validity of the decision, the names of those owners who voted in favour and those who voted against them, as well as the participation shares they respectively represent.

3.  The minutes book should close with the signatures of the president and the secretary at the end of the meeting or within ten days after. At the signing of the minutes book, the resolutions of the meeting shall be in force, unless the law disposes otherwise.

    The minutes shall be sent to the absent owners, following the procedure set out in Article 9.

    Errors or defects in the minutes are rectifiable, provided that the book unmistakeably indicates the date and place of the meeting, the owners in attendance, either present or represented by proxy, the decisions taken, with notation of the votes for and against, as well as the participation shares represented and that the book has been signed by the president and secretary. Said rectification should be made before the following general assembly, which must ratify the corrections.

4.  The Secretary will keep the minutes books of the general meeting. He will likewise retain, during a period of five years, the convocations, communications, powers of attorney and other documents relating to the meetings.

## What it means

The official minutes book described here must be kept in Spanish because it is a legal document, registering the acts of the community. This *libro de actas* must be stamped by the Registrar of Property and its contents can be cited in court.

The book must record the names of the members and proxies present at the meeting; tell who presided; when and where the meeting was held; give the agenda for the meeting; mention the main points of view discussed in the debate; list the resolutions taken and record the voting results.

If any member or group wishes to contest a resolution of the community, either in person or by certified post, this also should be recorded.

This minutes book establishes the powers of the president and any other officer to act for the community, and justifies the actions by its recording of the community's votes.

The annual general meeting usually begins with the reading of the minutes of the previous meeting, which must be approved by the members. If any member has a protest against the book, it must be registered officially in the book itself. It sometimes happens that the official record does not agree with one person's version of what actually happened, so it is necessary to be attentive.

## Article 20

It is the function of the administrator:

a) To ensure the proper management of the house, its installations and services and, to this effect, provide the owners with timely information and warnings.

b) To prepare the budget of anticipated expenses sufficiently in advance and submit it to the general meeting, proposing the necessary measures to cover the expenses.

c) To attend to the conservation and maintenance of the building, arranging for the ordinary repairs and taking urgent measures regarding extraordinary repairs, giving an immediate report to the general meeting or, as the case may be, to the property owners.

d) To carry out resolutions taken regarding works and to make any payments and receive any monies as properly disposed.

e) To act, when the case arises, as secretary of the general meeting and to keep custody, at the disposition of the owners, of the documentation of the community.

f) Any other functions conferred by the general meeting.

## What does it mean

Contrary to popular belief, the administrator, when he is a paid professional, is not an elected officer of the community. He is contracted for his services, usually for one year, and the community may choose not to renew his contract at its termination, and to employ another paid professional administrator.

Of course, a community member, the president or another, may carry out the many duties of administrating the building, but he may not be paid for it.

Article 20 lists the functions of the administrator. He must run the building properly and keep the owners informed about it. If there is no treasurer, the administrator prepares the budget for the coming year, attends to repairs in the building, makes payments and receives money, acts as secretary and keeps the community records safe and at the disposition of the members, and any other functions voted to him by the community.

Because the administrator may be a volunteer member of the community, the law sets no requirement for carrying out this mission. The administrator needs no professional title or special qualifications. He does not have to be Spanish or even to speak Spanish.

Nevertheless, many of the paid professional administrators hold titles as lawyers, *gestors* or, best of all, as an *administrador de fincas*, a professional property management expert.

Most administrators try to give good service to the community, charge reasonable fees, and put up with many petty complaints from the members. But others are not so honest, and more than one community has had bad experiences with administrators who seem to feel that the community works for them, rather than the other way around.

Sometimes promoters, in order to maintain their influence in the community, even have the names of administrators written into the original community statutes when they register the building. They are counting on the fact that any change in the statutes requires a unanimous vote, which is very difficult to achieve, so the members could not put out the administrator. Their legal position here is quite shaky, though, as the law also says that the annual general meeting has the power to change the president and the administrator.

In any case, if the community feels that the administrator is not presenting proper accounts, or his fees are too high, or he has purchased supplies from his cousin when he could have got them more cheaply from another source, they can vote him out.

The administrator, whether professional or volunteer, can also be sued in court for damages caused by his misconduct or negligence in office.

## Article 21

1. The obligations referred to in paragraphs e) and f) of Article 9 must be fulfilled by the owner of the flat or premises in the time and form determined by the General Meeting. If not, the President or the Administrator, if so disposed by the General Meeting, can seek legal redress by the procedure established in this Article.

2. Use of this procedure will require the prior notification of the decision of the General Meeting approving the claim of the debt with the Community by the person acting as Secretary, with the endorsement of the President, providing that this decision has been notified to the owners affected in the form set out in Article 9.

3. Territorial jurisdiction shall correspond exclusively to the Court of the place where the property is located. Representation by a lawyer or procurator shall not be compulsory, subject to the dispositions of paragraph 10. of this Article.

4. Proceedings begin with a simple claim form, accompanied by the certification referred to in Number 2. of this Article. In case the previous owner of the property is liable jointly for the debt, without affecting his right to claim repayment

from the present owner, action should be brought against him jointly with the present owner. In any case, the action must be brought against the registered owner.

5. Once the claim has been presented and accepted for procedure, the judge shall summon the defendant and order him to pay the plaintiff with 20 days and accredit this to the Court, or to appear before the court and present his allegations justifying that he does not owe, either in whole or in part, the amount claimed. The summons should be served at the domicile in Spain previously designated by the debtor, or in its absence, at the flat itself, with the admonition that, if he neither pays nor appears to declare his reasons for refusal to pay, the court will rule against him in the manner set out in the following Number.

6. If the defendant does not appear before the Court and does not oppose the claim, the Judge shall issue a writ of execution that shall proceed according to the provisions for court rulings, for the amount owed plus interest and foreseeable costs and for prior extra-judicial costs for the notifications of the debt if the services of a Notary were used.

   The plaintiff in this procedure and the debtor acted against shall not be able to respectively claim the amount or seek the refund of monies paid out in a subsequent ordinary civil action.

   From the time the writ is issued, the debt will draw interest at the legal interest rate plus two per cent.

7. If the debtor pays upon demand, as soon as he accredits this to the court he will be given the document registering the debt and the case will be dropped.

   Nevertheless, the legal costs cited in Number 10 of this Article and the expenses set out in the preceding Number will be for his account.

8. If the debtor opposes the claim, giving reasons for refusal to pay, in whole or in part, the Judge, after transmitting

the opposition plea to the plaintiff, shall follow the procedure for oral hearings from the time of the summons. However, once opposition is declared, the plaintiff may seek a lien or attachment on assets of the debtor of sufficient value to cover the amount claimed, interest, and costs.

The Judge will dispose such lien in any case without the necessity of the creditor posting bond. The debtor can avoid the lien by presenting a bank guarantee for the amount set in the preventive lien.

9. If the debtor appears on time in court and opposes the payment only in part, alleging overcharging, his plea will be admitted only when he accredits having either paid or placed at the disposition of the plaintiff, before the claim was made, the amount he recognizes as his debt. If the opposition is based on overcharging, the lien can only be sought for the amount not paid by the debtor.

10. The court's ruling will have the force of "final judgment"

Costs will be charged to the party whose claim is totally rejected. If the claim is partially granted, each party will pay its own individual costs and half of the common costs. The order to pay costs will include legal fees to lawyer and procurator of the winning side, if they have used these professional services in their claim or opposition.

11. Community fees which fall due while the case is in process can be added to the amount without having to recommence the proceedings, considering them as common to the debt and affected by the procedural stages which went before. This faculty shall extend through the execution of the writ.

This addition during the process of community fees falling due after the presentation of the claim shall require prior accreditation by a new certification of the community decision approving the claim, issued according to the provisions of Number 2.

12. No appeal against the ruling will be admitted to court unless the defendant accredits having settled the debt or deposited the amount of the judgment with the court before he brings the appeal.

If the ruling orders the payment of certain sums for late payment or for unpaid fees due, the appeal will be annulled if the appellant ceases to pay or to deposit with the court on time the payments of the same class which continue to come due during the procedure.

## What it means

This article sets out the real changes in the new 1999 law. It is a law with some teeth in it.

The community can now certify the debt and go immediately into court for a lien against the debtor's property. If the debtor does not pay up, the court will order some of his assets seized to pay the debt. If the debtor chooses to fight the bill, he himself must put up either his assets or a bank guarantee for the amount. Formerly, the community was required to make a deposit with the court when they sought to collect the back fees. No longer.

Furthermore, any community debts that accumulate during the procedure are simply added into the original debt. No complications.

Furthermore, if the debtor fights to drag out the case, he will be liable for the community's legal costs if he loses.

This new tool for collecting Community debts has proven so effective that, in less than a year, more than 40 per cent of all outstanding Community fees in Spain have been collected, most of them on the threat of going to court.

## Article 22

1. The Community of Property Owners will be liable with all its assets and credits for any debt to third parties. In addition, the creditor can act against each individual owner who took part in the process for his proportional share of the unpaid amount, after serving a demand for payment on such owners.

2.  Any owner can oppose the claim by justifying that he is fully current in the payment of all debts due to the community at the time the demand referred to above was made.

    If the debtor immediately pays the demand, he will be charged the proportional part of the costs involved.

## What it means

It happens with a certain frequency that Communities of Property Owners cannot pay their debts to suppliers or service providers simply because their members have not paid their annual Community fees.

This Article gives Community creditors a handle on direct action. They can proceed against the members themselves as individuals. Those members who are fully paid up cannot be made to pay.

## Article 23

The legal structure of horizontal property (condominium) is terminated:

1.  By the destruction of the building, unless there is agreement to the contrary.

    Such destruction shall be deemed to exist when the cost of rebuilding exceeds fifty per cent of the value of the property at the time the event occurs, unless the amount in excess of the aforesaid cost is covered by insurance.

    Second.  By conversion into ordinary ownership or joint ownership.

## What it means

Clearly, the horizontal property scheme must be terminated when the building is destroyed. The second paragraph refers to the sale of the building to one owner or several joint owners. Yes, the community can even vote - unanimously, of course - to sell itself and divide the cash among the owners

## CHAPTER III: REGARDING PRIVATE REAL ESTATE COMPLEXES

### Article 24

1. The special scheme of property ownership set out in Article 396 of the Civil Code shall be applicable to those private real estate complexes THAT meet the following requirements:

   a) Being made up of two or more buildings or independent plots whose principal use is dwellings or commercial premises.

   b) The owners of these buildings or properties or of the units into which they are divided horizontally, with an inherent nature for this right, participate in an indivisible co-ownership of other real estate elements, such as roads, installations or services.

2. Private real estate complexes referred to in the previous Number may:

   a) Constitute themselves as one only Community of Owners by means of any of the procedures established in the second paragraph of Article 5. In this case they will be subject to the dispositions of this Law, which will be fully applied to them.

   b) Constitute themselves as a grouping of Communities of Owners. To this effect, the Charter of Constitution of the new grouped Community must be granted by the only and single owner of the complex or by the Presidents of all the Communities to compose it, previously authorised by majority vote of their respective general meetings. The Charter of Constitution will contain the description of the real estate complex in its setting and descriptions of the elements, roads, installations and common services. Likewise, it will fix the participation shares (cuotas) of each of the component Communities, which will be jointly liable for the obligation to contribute to the general expenses of the group macro-community. This title of charter and the Statutes of the Community can be inscribed in the Property Registry.

3. The grouping of Communities referred to above shall, to all effects, enjoy the same legal situation as Communities of Owners and will be governed by the dispositions of this Law, with the following special provisions:

   a) The general assembly of owners, unless otherwise agreed, will be composed of the Presidents of the communities forming the group, who will represent the individual owners of each Community .

   b) The making of decisions for which the Law requires qualified majorities will require, in all cases, the prior vote of the majority required in each of the individual Communities that compose the grouping.

   c) Except by agreement of the general meeting otherwise, the dispositions of Article 9 of this Law regarding the reserve fund shall not apply to the group community.

   The jurisdiction of the governing organs of the group community cover only the real estate elements, roads, installations and common services. In no case shall their decisions prejudice the faculties corresponding to the governing bodies of the Communities of Owners which make up the grouping of Communities.

4. The dispositions of this Law, with the same special provisions, shall be applicable to those private real estate complexes which do not adopt any of the legal forms indicated in Number 2 as a complement to agreements made by the co-owners among themselves.

**What it means**

This is the big one. For the first time, the Horizontal Law takes account of urbanisations of detached houses, or groupings of townhouses, flats and detached villas.

The full protection of the new Horizontal Law is now available for these urbanisations, with very little effort on their part. They can vote for it, write themselves a set of Statutes, and go straight to the Property Registry.

Until now, urbanisations had to form themselves as Collaborating Urbanistic Entities, a complex process which often proved extremely expensive for the owners and involved long and tortuous negotiations with the Town Hall.

Sometimes the formation of an EUC will be the only possibility for an urbanisation, but many of them will now find their way smoothed to legality, and the capacity to enforce debt collection.

## ADDITIONAL DISPOSITION

1.  Without prejudice to any dispositions which, using the powers conferred on them, the Regional Governments may make, the constitution of the reserve fund regulated in Article 9.1.f) shall comply with the following rules:

    a) The fund must be created when the General Meeting approves the ordinary yearly budget, corresponding to the year immediately following the putting into effect of this Law.

    New Communities shall create the fund when they approve their first ordinary budget.

    b) When constituted, the fund shall be endowed with no less than 2.5 per cent of the ordinary budget of the Community. To this effect, the owners must make in advance the necessary contributions proportionally to their participation shares.

    c) When the ordinary budget for the financial year following that in which the fund was established is passed, the amount of the reserve fund should reach the minimum quantity established in Article 9.

2.  The amount of the reserve fund at no time during the budget period shall be less than the minimum legally established.

Amounts drawn from the reserve fund during the budget period in order to pay the expenses on maintenance and repairs of the property permitted by the present law shall be computed as an integral part of the fund for purposes of calculating its minimum amount.

At the beginning of the following financial year there shall be made the contributions necessary to cover the amounts drawn from the reserve fund in accordance with the terms of the preceding paragraph.

# 20 Communities of detached villas

$\text{T}$hose who live in urbanisations of detached villas have a more complicated set of problems than those living in flats. Before 1978 it was very difficult for them to form any sort of community with the legal power to enforce its statutes and compel payment of fees.

The inhabitants of these housing estates, or urbanisations, a rather new invention in Spain at that time, had to find ways of financing their roads, lighting, security, gardens, etc, as well as establishing the basic services of water, electric power and rubbish collection.

Even when they can now come under the protection of the Horizontal Law, they still have these basic problems not related to the pure legality of their existence.

In addition, the urbanisations often had complex relations with the Town Hall of their municipality. If the road passing through the estate continues on to other properties and is used by the general public, who pays for its maintenance? Can the inhabitants cut this road and seal off the community, or are they obliged to permit the public to use it? Will the Town Hall rubbish collectors enter the estate, or must all rubbish be placed at a central point for collection? A thousand questions arise.

What is basically important for the formation of a community is Royal Decree 3288/1978 of August 25, which sets forth the regulations for urban administration based on the existing *Ley del Suelo*, the Land Law. Even the 1978 regulations are complex and confusing, but they can provide a framework for setting up an effective community.

These regulations establish the figure of the *Entidad Urbanistica Colaboradora de Gestión y Conservación,* the Collaborating Urbanistic Entity of Maintenance and Management. A real mouthful to describe the quasi-public functions of the urbanisation of detached villas. This is often shortened today to EUC.

YOU AND THE LAW IN SPAIN

In a perfect world, you would find that your dream villa was located on an urbanisation where all roads, lighting and services were carefully provided by a benevolent and foresighted municipal administration, just as they are in many countries. But you are more likely to encounter a situation where the developer is no longer maintaining the roads and services, where the Town Hall refuses to help because all the requirements in the original building permission were not fulfilled by the developers, and the owners are unable to establish an effective community.

You need to start with Article 25 of the 1978 regulations. If you are lucky, your situation will come under Section 3 of this law which provides for the forming of collaborating entities which group all owners in a certain zone, whether they want to join or not. Without the power to compel all owners to belong to the entity, it would be meaningless.

Then you can study Article 67, which provides that the Town Hall will take charge of maintaining and providing all normal services once these have been ceded to the Town Hall. That is, the association of owners or the developer will transfer the roads, sewage, lighting and perhaps some common green zone to the Town Hall.

The catch here is that the Town Hall may very well refuse to accept this transfer until the roads and other services have been put into good condition. Guess who must pay for this. Right. Either the developer, or the owners as a group. Some parts of the regulations can even oblige the urbanisation to pay all costs for establishing connections to the nearest town roads, sewers and lighting systems.

The great advantage of the collaborating entity is that the urbanisation then becomes a normal part of the municipality for the provision of basic services, and, if one of the members refuses to pay his share of community fees, the Town Hall itself may act against him with the threat to seize his property or bank account to satisfy the unpaid debt. This procedure is much more effective and rapid than going through the courts.

So you begin to see that the collaborating entity must work closely with the municipal authorities because the urbanisation is not separated from the rest of the world the way an apartment building is.

In fact, the authorisation of the Town Hall is required for the formation of this entity.

All these negotiations between the owners and the municipal authorities will require the counsel and representation of a Spanish lawyer or property administrator who is knowledgeable in this area. In one recent case on the Costa del Sol, the backers of a very large estate worked closely with the existing owners and the Town Hall. First the existing owners voted unanimously to form an association. Then the developers, acting on the requirements of the Town Hall, put all the services in good order. Costs were shared by the owners and the developer. Then the backers had to pay the Town Hall a fine of €120,000 for not fulfilling all their original obligations. (The Town Hall first wanted €480,000, but were argued into the lower figure.) Finally, the Town Hall accepted the transfer of the roads and other services, and authorized the formation of a collaborating urban entity. This was properly registered in the registry of such entities, which exists at the provincial urban office, giving it a legal personality.

Any new purchaser in this zone must now become a member of the entity by virtue of his purchase. This is clearly stated in each sales contract. Both the developer and the present owners have bound themselves to include such a clause in any sales deed. Even if they didn't, the legal personality of the entity requires it.

Now the members only have to squabble among themselves about how much to pay for the security patrol, whether they want an extra tennis court and how to act against the owner with the barking dogs. Of course they also have to fight with their new partners in the Town Hall about the size of their assessment for the sewage repairs, compared to the urbanisation just down the road. The problems will never end, but at least they have a dear and coherent system for dealing with them.

These particular members are now up in arms because they feel they are being charged twice for municipal services. That is because they pay their annual real estate taxes to the Town

357

Hall, the IBI, just like other owners. But they also pay their annual fees to the EUC, which, they argue, covers basically the same services, so they are being forced to pay twice. The argument is still going on.

Things can be much worse in a situation where the owners cannot agree at the beginning and where the developer is not willing to help. But if the whole thing seems like too much trouble, remember that a well-run community can add thousands of euros to your property's value and a poorly-maintained urbanisation can cut thousands off your price.

The following section contains an English translation of Spanish regulations affecting the formation of conservation entities. It is not complete because many different bodies of law can come into play, but it gives a good idea of the legislation.

## LAW FOR DETACHED VILLAS

Land Law Regulations III: Regulations of Urban Administration
Title 1: General dispositions
CHAPTER 1 (Section 6)
SUBJECTS AND MEANS OF ADMINISTRATION

### Article 21

1. Affected parties may participate in urban administration through the creation of Collaborating Urban Entities.

2. Collaborating Urban Entities are:

   a) Compensation Boards.

   b) Administrative Associations of owners in the co-operation system.

   c) Entities of Conservation.

3. Collaborating Urban Entities will be governed by their Statutes and by the dispositions of this section, without prejudice to the application of the specific precepts contained in Chapters 11 and III of Title V of these Regulations for Compensation Boards and Administrative

Associations of owners in the co-operation system, nor to the provisions established in Chapter 1-V of Title III for the conservation of the works of urbanisation.

## What it means

These regulations establish a legal basis for private citizens to participate in public administration. Keep in mind that streets, lighting, main drains, sewage systems and electric conduits passing through the land of the urbanisation to the next property will be of public nature. It is not like a building of flats, in which the services are simply connected and do not pass on to other properties.

This article of the regulations allows private persons to share administration of these services with the municipal authorities through the formation of one of three types of collaborating urban entities.

The first mentioned, the compensation board, is created when land is being re-zoned or subdivided and where several owners may be involved. The situation can get complicated. Imagine an area which includes a large working farm, a small factory with lots of land around it, a dozen homes built on large rural plots, and maybe a developer who has bought a big tract which he wants to urbanize. The nearby town is expanding and a new road is being put in. The entire zone will be declared building land.

The compensation board is the legal structure created for the purpose of sorting out all the problems that will arise and for seeing that each participant is fairly treated. The Town Hall is represented, too, as it will be expropriating land from some of the owners for the road and other services. The members of the board will squabble and negotiate until they agree on each party's share of the rights and obligations. This is one form of urban entity.

The compensation board operates principally as a forum to ensure the equitable distribution of problems and profits in such a re-zoning situation. But what happens after the subdivision is complete?

One scheme set up in law is the second structure mentioned in this article: the administrative association of owners in the co-operation system. Here the owners co-operate with each other and with the Town Hall to organize smooth functioning of the services in the area they share. This is much like the conservation entity, but its legal underpinnings are different, involving several different ownerships.

Both the compensation board and the administrative association are designed to serve in the early stages of a transformation in the ownership pattern of land. Either of them can be changed into a conservation entity, the legal framework for the ongoing maintenance of an established urbanisation.

## Article 25

1.  The constitution of the Compensation Boards and of the Administrative Associations of owners in the co-operation system shall be adapted to the provisions of the regulations contained in the respective schemes of action.

2.  Entities of conservation of the works of urbanisation may be constituted as a result of the transformation of some pre-existing Entity of those set out in the previous number or, specifically for these purposes, without previously having constituted any Entity for the execution of the works of urbanisation.

3.  The constitution of a conservation Entity will be obligatory whenever the duty of conservation of the works of urbanisation falls upon the owners included in a determined zone or unit of action by virtue of the dispositions of the town urban Plan or the bases of the urban action programme or if it results expressly from legal dispositions. In such cases membership in the conservation entity will be obligatory for all owners included in its territorial range.

## What it means

The big news comes here in the last sentence of paragraph 3, which provides that membership in the conservation entity shall

360

be obligatory for all owners in the zone, and that the formation of the conservation entity shall be obligatory when provided by law, meaning that it may be set out in the town urban development plan, or in a Plan of Urbanistic Action, a development plan for a restricted area, or it may simply be a regulation passed by the Town Council. Any legal disposition will suffice.

In practice this means some urbanisations will find that the law requires them to form a conservation entity and that all must be members, and other urbanisations will find it is not legally necessary for them to do so.

## Article 26

1. Collaborating urbanistic Entities shall have an administrative character and shall be dependent in this order on the acting urbanistic Administration.

2. The legal personality of collaborating urbanistic Entities shall be understood as acquired from the moment of their inscription in the corresponding Registry.

## What it means

The first paragraph of this article grants to these entities powers to act legally, and notes that this power depends on the entity's relation to the public administration involved, which would usually be the municipality, though it could also be the province or a special authority ruling some particular piece of terrain.

The second paragraph reminds us that there exists a special Registry for these entities and they cannot act with legal force, to compel payment of debts, for example, until the entity is properly registered.

## Article 27

1. The constitution of collaborating urban entities, as well as their Statutes, must be approved by the acting urban Administration.

2. The document approving this constitution shall be entered in the Registry of Collaborating Urban Entities which is kept by the respective Provincial Urban Commissions, where likewise shall be kept an example of the statutes of the entity authorized by the competent official.

3. The appointments and dismissals of the persons charged with governing and administrating the entity shall also be inscribed in said Registry.

4. Modification of the statutes shall require the approval of the acting urban Administration. The respective resolutions, with the content of the modification, in such case, must be entered in the Registry.

## What it means

This article points up the importance of the cooperation required of the local Town Hall or other urban administration body which has competence over the zone. These official bodies must approve the formation of the entity and its statutes.

The names of its officers, and any changes in its rules, must be registered in the Registry. Any major changes of the statutes will require approval from the municipal authorities.

## Article 28

The transfer of title that determines membership in any of the types of collaborating urbanistic entities shall carry with it the termination of the rights and obligations of the transferring party and the acquirer shall be understood as incorporated into the Entity from the time of transfer.

## What it means

This of course applies only when the Entity is legally constituted and registered. If the owner's community is not an Entity, but only a civil association, then each new buyer's contract must contain a clause stating that he joins the community and agrees to abide by its statutes.

## Article 29

Resolutions of collaborating urbanistic Entities shall be adopted by simple majority of participation shares, unless a special quorum is established in the Statutes or other regulations for certain cases. Such resolutions can be impugned in appeal to the acting urbanistic Administration.

### What it means

Each urban entity can make its own statutes with provisions on where unanimous vote may be required. If they do not, this article of the regulations will apply and a simple majority decision will be sufficient to take action. Any owner who feels his interests have been prejudiced can appeal the vote to the Town Hall or other official administration acting in the case.

*Articles 30 through 57 are of a highly technical nature and do not bear directly on the formation of communities.*

## Article 58

The owners of properties affected by an urbanistic action programme shall be obliged to pay the costs of urbanisation specified in the following articles in proportion to the area of their respective properties, or, as the case may be, to the area figuring in the documents referred to in Article 53 of these regulations.

### What it means

This means that owners shall be assessed payment participation shares according to the size of their properties. Big properties pay more, small properties pay less. The Article 53 referred to relates to various forms of documenting property ownership, such as the *Registro de la Propiedad*, and others.

## Article 59

1. The cost of works of urbanisation which are charged to the account of the owners of a determined zone or unit of action shall include the following:

a) Street works, including works of levelling, compacting and paving of roadways, construction and kerbing of pavements and channelling which must be constructed in the subsurface of the public way for services.

b) Sanitation works, which include general and partial collectors, connections, sewers and culverts for rain waters and purification installations, in the proportion that they affect the action unit or zone.

c) Water supply, in which is included works of obtaining the water, when such are necessary, the distribution to homes of potable water, of irrigation water and of fluid for fire fighting.

d) Supply of electrical current, including its conduction and distribution and public lighting.

e) Gardening and tree planting in parks, gardens and public ways.

2.  Private parties involved in works of urbanisation in a zone or urban action unit may be reimbursed for the expenses of installation of the networks of supply of water and electricity, charged to the concession-holding companies, to the extent that, according to the regulation of such services, these expenses must not be charged to the users. The costs of installation shall be accredited by certification issued by the acting administration.

**What it means**

Have they left anything out? The owners on an urbanisation can find themselves liable for any of the expenses mentioned here. If the developer has failed to carry out all requirements set by the Town Hall, either in the urban plan itself or other subsidiary legislation, the owners can be stuck for it in most cases. It pays to check up first.

## Article 60

Any indemnities owed to the owners and renters of buildings or constructions of any sort which must be knocked down for the correct execution of the plan, as well as indemnity payments arising from the destruction of plantings, works or installations incompatible with the plan being carried out shall likewise be charged to the account of the property owners in the proportions set out in Article 58.

## What it means

Yes, they left something out. Owners are also liable for any payments made to persons suffering loss from the execution of the urbanisation plan.

## Article 61

Also for the account of the owners of land included in the zone or relevant action unit shall be the cost of preparing and processing the Plan of plots and the projects of urbanisation and the total cost of expenses of subdivision or compensation.

## What it means

This expense would fall on the owners of land that is in the process of being subdivided, and will produce profits for them when they sell. It is not likely to affect purchasers on an already-established urbanisation; but be alert because legal expenses can also be charged to the owners.

## Article 62

If agreement exists between the Administration and the affected owners, the payment of all or part of the expenses noted in the three previous articles can be made by the owners ceding to the Administration, for no consideration and free of all charges, buildable land in the amount deemed sufficient for the compensation of such expenses, whose value shall be determined in the agreement itself.

**What it means**

That's good of the administration. If you can't pay, they will accept your valuable land instead. In fact, this situation normally arises when the town itself is re-zoning land. The new building permissions mean large profits for the existing owners so it is expected they pay for it, either in cash or by the transfer of part of the land to the Town Hall.

**Article 63**

Owners of non-programmed developable land which is the object of a Programme of urbanistic action, besides paying the costs of urbanisation set out in the previous articles and satisfying any supplementary charges which the programme may impose on them, must pay for the complete execution or the supplement necessary for the exterior works of infrastructure on which the urbanistic action is based, such as road networks connecting with population centres, installation or amplification of the channels of services of water supply, drains and sewage, purification stations, supply of electricity and any other services necessary for the land subject to the urbanistic action programme to be duly connected through these general systems with the structure of the Municipality in which the programme is carried out.

**What it means**

Owners of land that is improved or made more valuable by any action of the Town Hall can find themselves liable even for these expenses.

Article 64 does not bear directly on communities.

**Article 65**

Incompliance by the owners of the land with the obligations and charges established in these Regulations will give rise to:

a) The collection of the urbanisation costs by executive order under threat of embargo and legal seizure of the property.

b) Expropriation by the Administration of the lands affected by compliance with the charges, the Administration itself, or the Compensation Board, as the case may be, being beneficiaries of the expropriation.

## What it means

This article is what makes the conservation entity such an effective form for communities of owners of detached villas in an urbanisation. The executive order to seize property of nonpayers is a far easier and swifter process than going to court against them, which can take many months, and even years.

Article 66 does not bear directly on communities.

## CHAPTER IV: MAINTENANCE OF THE URBANISATION

### Article 67

The conservation of the works of urbanisation and the maintenance of the equipment and installations of the public services will be the charge of the acting administration, once the transfer of these services has been made.

## What it means

Yes, this is the dream paradise in which the Town Hall provides and maintains all the basic services of the urbanisation. This article obliges them to do so. The catch is that they have to accept the transfer of these services from the private developer or urbanisation first. And they will not accept - and have not done so in many cases - these services until everything is properly installed and functioning. Sometimes this works quite well and the community, the services and the Town Hall co-operate in harmony happily ever after, with the occasional non-payer of fees being forced to produce the money by the threat of executive order. Far more often, the Town Hall finds many deficiencies in the installations and services and will not take over their administration and maintenance until the owners' community has put them right, at great expense. Be warned.

**Article 68**

1. Regardless of the dispositions of the preceding article, the owners of the land included in the zone or action unit will be subject to the aforesaid obligation when it is imposed on them by the Urban Zoning Plan, or by the bases of a programme of urban action or results expressly from legal dispositions.

2. In the case of the preceding number, the owners must form themselves into an Entity of Conservation.

**What it means**

Even though it is clear from both principle and law that the owners will be obliged to maintain the installations, this article exists to remind us of that fact. Even when no specific provision is made for this, that last phrase of Article 68 paragraph 1 - "results expressly from legal dispositions" - gives the Town Hall the power to pass a resolution requiring the owners to maintain their roads in good repair, and the community will be bound by law.

**Article 69**

1. The participation of the owners in the obligation of conservation and maintenance of the works of urbanisation, equipment and installations of the public services, when this is not the charge of the acting administration, shall be determined as a function of the participation share set for them by the Compensation Board, in the subdivision plan, or, as the case may be, in the share specified in the Entity of Conservation.

2. If systems of horizontal property have been constituted over the properties, the contribution of the owners to said obligation of conservation and maintenance shall be determined by the participation share [cuota) with relation to the total value of the property which is assigned in each community.

**What it means**

This article determines the way in which each owner's share of the payment is calculated, and provides also for calculating the shares of apartment dwellers who already have horizontal property systems operating in their buildings located on the parent urbanisation.

**Article 70**

1. Whosoever shall be the subject to whom corresponds the obligation of maintenance referred to in the preceding articles, the Town Hall or the acting administration, in its condition as owner of the lands of public domain, works, equipment and installations of obligatory cession, may require by executive order under threat of embargo the payment of the shares owed, whether acting on its own initiative or at the instance of the collaborating urbanistic Entity.

2. The amount of the payment share will be delivered by the Town Hall or acting administration to the Entity charged with the conservation, when this obligation does not pertain to the Administration.

**What it means**

Paragraph 1 here repeats the power of the Town Hall to carry out an executive order of garnishment or embargo in order to compel payment of participation share fees. It notes that the Town Hall may do this either on its own initiative or when requested by the conservation entity.

Paragraph 2 makes it clear that the Town Hall is to deliver this money to the conservation entity, unless the Town Hall itself is charged with the maintenance of the services. This means the Town Hall can collect the money and provide the services, or collect part of the money and provide part of the services.

Because the Town Hall itself is often a member of the entity, because of its own installations on the 10 per cent of the land that the promoter must transfer to the Town, this gives rise to a situation where the Town Hall may have to collect debts from itself.

## "LEGALITY" OF COMMUNITIES

A final note here on the "legality" of communities. Throughout this text we refer to the inscription of the community in the Property Registry or Registry of Conservation Entities. We point out that the Statutes must be registered in order to be fully legal, and we insist on every point of the law being observed.

This is all well and good. In the real world, however, we find groups of houses built in the property boom that do not really make up an urbanisation, where the owners have simply agreed to organize and pay for some basic services among themselves. We find urbanisations that were never registered as such, where no community Statutes exist, but the owners hold annual meetings and pay dues. We find other urbanisations, where the Community has formal Statutes and regulations, but these are not registered.

Are all these other forms of communities "legal"?

Well, in one sense they are not legal because they are not registered. But if you, as an owner in one of these situations, think you can get away with not paying your fees, perhaps you should think again.

Spanish courts have ruled on a number of occasions that these communities, although not registered, have acquired a legal personality simply by existing through the years, that they function for the benefit of the owners and society in general, and so they can in fact compel the payment of fees and bring a case against a non-payer, even seizing his property and having it sold at auction.

# JUNTA DE ANDALUCIA

Consejería de Salud y Servicios Sociales
Dirección General de Consumo

# HOJA DE RECLAMACION
## COMPLAINTS SHEET

**1.- LUGAR DEL HECHO** - *PLACE OF OCCURRENCE*

EN — *TOWN*      PROVINCIA — *PROVINCE*      FECHA — *DATE*

**2.- IDENTIFICACION DEL RECLAMANTE** - *DETAILS OF COMPLAINANT*

1ª APELLIDO — *SURNAME*      2ª APELLIDO      NOMBRE — *FIRST NAME*

SEXO — *SEX*      EDAD — *AGE*      PROFESION — *PROFESSION*

D.N.I. — *PASSPORT Nº*      DOMICILIO C/ — *ADDRESS ST.*

MUNICIPIO — *TOWN*      PROVINCIA — *PROVINCE*      COD. POST. — *POSTAL CODE*

NACIONALIDAD — *NATIONALITY*      TEL. — *TEL.*

0
1
2
3
4
5
6

**3.- IDENTIFICACION DEL RECLAMADO** - *DETAILS OF PERSON UNDER COMPLAINT*

NOMBRE O RAZON SOCIAL — *NAME OR COMPANY*

C.I.F. O D.N.I. — *FISCAL Nº*      ACTIVIDAD — *ACTIVITY*

DOMICILIO — *ADDRESS ST.*      MUNICIPIO — *TOWN*

PROVINCIA — *PROVINCE*      COD. POST. — *POSTAL CODE*      TEL. — *TEL.*

7
8
9
10

**4.- HECHOS RECLAMADOS** - *DETAILS OF COMPLAINT*

11

DOCUMENTOS QUE SE ACOMPAÑAN - *DOCUMENTS INCLUDED*
FACTURAS, ENTRADAS, MUESTRAS, ETC. - *TICKETS, BILLS, SAMPLES, ETC.*

**5.- FIRMAS** - *SIGNATURES*

CONSUMIDOR: — *CONSUMER*      RECLAMADO: — *PERSON UNDER COMPLAINT*

CONFORME CON LO EXPUESTO - *IN AGREEMENT WITH THE ABOVE*

SERIE A      CONTROL

1271501

EJEMPLAR PARA LA ADMINISTRACION
COPY TO ADMINISTRATION

## FORM 211

This is the form used for declaring your deposit of five per cent paid to Spain's Tax Agency when you purchase property from a non-resident.

**Datos del Adquirente:** Here you enter name, address and details of the buyer, including his NIE, his tax identification number in Spain, even though Form says NIF. If you have Hacienda stickers, *etiquetas,* you can use these instead.

**Devengo:** Date of the sale.

**Datos del Transmitente:** Enter details of the non-resident seller. Where it says: "Clave Pais", a separate sheet gives you a three-digit number code for every country.

**Representante:** If you have a fiscal representative in Spain (not required if you own only one property) you enter his details here.

**Descripción del Inmueble:** Description of the property, including the address, whether or not it is being transmitted through a private document or a public document signed before a Notary, and, if so, the Notary and his registration number of the contract. Finally, enter the Catastral Reference number.

**Liquidación:** The liquidation is the calculation of the amount. Here you enter the declared price of the sale and calculate five per cent of it.

**Adquirente:** Buyer signs, with date.

**Ingreso:** Enter your form of payment, whether in cash or by certified cheque made out to "Tesoro Publico".

Modelo **211**
Impuesto sobre la Renta de no Residentes
DECLARACIÓN/DOCUMENTO DE INGRESO

Agencia Tributaria

211000008507 6

## FORM 212

This is the form on which the non-resident declares his capital gain or loss when he sells his Spanish property. On this form the non-resident seller either applies for a refund, if the deposit of 5 per cent is greater than the tax, or makes an extra payment, if the deposit is less than the tax due.

**Contribuyente:** List your name and address and fiscal number, or, if you have them, affix one of your tax labels here. F/J is "F" for a person and "J" for a company. If spouses declare together, give percentage of ownership. "Codigo Extranjero" is for your tax number in your home country.

**Conyuge:** Fiscal number and name and percentage of ownership of the spouse.

**Representante:** If you have a Fiscal Representative in Spain, enter his details here.

**Adquirente:** List details of the buyer.

**Descripción:** Description of the property. Give the name of the Notary before whom the contract was signed and list his Protocol Number for the document.

**Liquidación:** Liquidation is the calculation of the tax on your capital gain. First, you must list the number of the Form 211 on which your buyer made his payment of the five per cent deposit. Then you enter in Box 1 the net price you received for the property, after you have deducted all your expenses involved in the sale. In Box 2 you enter your original cost of acquiring the property, adding in all your expenses at the time, such as taxes and legal fees. You apply the inflation correction factor at this point. See the text for examples of calculations. In Box 3 you enter the difference. If you bought your property before Dec. 31, 1994, you now apply the 11.11 per cent per year factor, as described in the text, in order to get your tax base, entered in Box 4. The second table is for any additions you have made to the property. Box 4 will then be your taxable base, entered again in Box 9. Your tax rate will be 35 per cent as a non-resident.

Enter total tax in Box 11. Subtract 5 per cent, shown in Box 13, and you have the "Cuota Diferencial", the amount you must either pay or claim back on the second sheet of Form 212 (Not shown).

Agencia Tributaria

Delegación de
Administración de _____ Código _____

MINISTERIO
DE ECONOMÍA
Y HACIENDA

**Impuesto sobre la Renta de no Residentes.**
No residentes sin establecimiento permanente

Modelo
**212**
DECLARACIÓN
DE RENTAS DERIVADAS
DE TRANSMISIONES
DE BIENES INMUEBLES

**Contribuyente**

Espacio reservado para la etiqueta identificativa

212000009816 0

**Devengo**
Fecha de transmisión...........

N.I.F.    F/J    APELLIDOS Y NOMBRE (por este orden) o RAZÓN SOCIAL    Cuota particip. %

Código extranjero    Dirección a efectos de notificación

Código Postal    Municipio    Provincia/País    Código País

**Cónyuge**
N.I.F.    APELLIDOS Y NOMBRE    Cuota particip. Código País %

**Representante**
N.I.F.    F/J    APELLIDOS Y NOMBRE (por este orden) o RAZÓN SOCIAL

Calle/Plaza/Avda.    Número    Esc.    Piso    Prta.    Teléfono

Código Postal    Municipio    Provincia

**Adquirente**
N.I.F.    F/J    APELLIDOS Y NOMBRE (por este orden) o RAZÓN SOCIAL

Calle/Plaza/Avda.    Número    Esc.    Piso    Prta.

Código Postal    Municipio    Provincia/País    Código País

**Descripción del inmueble**
Calle/Plaza/Avda.    Número    Esc.    Piso    Prta.

Código Postal    Municipio    Provincia

Doc. público Doc. privado    Notario o fedatario    Nº de protocolo

Referencia catastral

**Liquidación**
Número de justificante del modelo 211 adjunto

|  | Adquisición | Mejora o 2ª adquisición |
|---|---|---|
| Valor de transmisión | 1 | 5 |
| Valor de adquisición (actualizado) | 2 | 6 |
| Diferencia | 3 | 7 |
| Ganancia | 4 | 8 |

Fecha de adquisición

Fecha de mejora o 2ª adquisición

Base imponible
Tipo gravamen ............ 10 %    Cuota íntegra ............ 9 / 11
Deducción por donativos    12
Retención ............ 13
Cuota diferencial ([11] - [12] - [13]) = 14

**Fecha y firma**
Fecha:    Firma:    Firma:

**Ejemplar para la Administración**

## FORM 213

This is the form on which you either declare and pay your annual tax of 3 per cent on the *valor catastral,* or rated value, of your Spanish property owned by a non-resident company, or on which you cite your non-resident company's exemption from the tax.

**Entidad Sujeta:** Either paste in your Tax Agency label, or fill in the details of the non-resident company. "Codigo Extranjero" is the tax number, if it has one, in the country of registration.

**Devengo:** Enter year for which tax is being paid.

**Representante:** If the company has a fiscal representative in Spain, enter his details here.

**Exenciones:** Companies which are exempt from the tax check the appropriate box here. If your company is not located in a tax haven, and it pays its taxes in a "normal" country, check Box 1, and so on. Only those non-resident companies located in tax havens must pay.

**Liquidación:** Your "Base Imponible" is the *valor catastral* of the property. Tax rate is 3 per cent of that value. If you have owned the property less than a full year, you will have a proportional reduction. Otherwise you pay the full tax. When a company has several owners, some of whom are entitled to exemption and others not, there is a reduction as well.

## NOTE:

**FORM 213** has two other sheets, one of them for listing all properties owned by the company, and another for entering the details of persons owning the company when exemption is requested because the company pays its taxes in a normal jurisdiction and discloses the names of its real owners.

MINISTERIO DE ECONOMÍA Y HACIENDA

Agencia Tributaria

Delegación de

Administración de

Código

**Impuesto sobre la Renta de no Residentes**

Gravamen Especial sobre Bienes Inmuebles de Entidades no Residentes

DECLARACIÓN-LIQUIDACIÓN/ DOCUMENTO DE INGRESO

Modelo

**213**

GRAVAMEN ESPECIAL SOBRE BIENES INMUEBLES DE ENTIDADES NO RESIDENTES

213000001935 0

**Entidad sujeta al gravamen**

Espacio reservado para la etiqueta identificativa
(Si no dispone de etiquetas, haga constar a continuación sus datos identificativos, así como los de su domicilio fiscal)

**Devengo**

Ejercicio ..........................

N.I.F. | Razón social de la entidad

Calle/Plaza/Avda. | Número | Esc. | Piso | Prta. | Teléfono

Código Postal | Municipio | Provincia

Domicilio de la entidad en el país de residencia | Código extranjero

Residencia fiscal: país | Código país | Nacionalidad

**Representante**

N.I.F. | Apellidos y Nombre o Razón social

Calle/Plaza/Avda. | Número | Esc. | Piso | Prta. | Teléfono

Código Postal | Municipio | Provincia | Fecha otorgamiento poder

**Exenciones**

Entidades exentas (artículo 32.5 de la Ley 41/1998, del Impuesto sobre la Renta de no Residentes):

1) Entidades con derecho a la aplicación de un Convenio para evitar la doble imposición que contenga cláusula de intercambio de información, en los términos y con los requisitos del artículo 32.5.b) de la Ley 41/1998.

2) Entidades que desarrollan en España, de modo continuado o habitual, explotaciones económicas diferenciables de la simple tenencia o arrendamiento de los inmuebles en los términos del artículo 7.2 del Reglamento del Impuesto sobre la Renta de no Residentes. Epígrafe del Impuesto sobre Actividades Económicas . . . . . . . . . . . . .

3) Sociedades que coticen en mercados secundarios de valores oficialmente reconocidos.

4) Entidades sin ánimo de lucro de carácter benéfico o cultural, en los términos del artículo 32.5.e) de la Ley 41/1998.

**Liquidación**

**Base imponible** ........................................................ 01

**Cuota (3% de 01 )** ........................................................ 02

**Porcentaje de reducción** ............ 03 %

**Reducción en la cuota** ........................................................ 04

**Cuota a ingresar 02 - 04** ........................................................ 05

**Negativas**

CUOTA CERO

**Declarante**

Fecha:

Firma:

**Ingreso**

**TESORO PÚBLICO.** Cuenta restringida de Caja de la Delegación o Administración de la A.E.A.T.

Forma de pago: Dinero de curso legal | Cheque conformado y nominativo a favor del Tesoro Público

**Importe:** I

Este documento no será válido sin la certificación mecánica o, en su defecto, firma autorizada

**Ejemplar para la Administración**

**FORM 214**

This form is used by non-resident property owners to declare their Spanish capital assets tax, the *patrimonio*, also called wealth tax, and their non-resident property owner's imputed income tax, on the same one-page form. Residents are not subject to this tax on their principal dwelling.

**Contribuyente:** Stick on your Tax Agency printed label, or fill in the form with your name and address. Put your NIE where it says NIF.

**Devengo:** Enter the year.

**Liquidación Patrimonio:** For *patrimonio* tax, you enter the real declared price of the property in Box 1. Enter any debts against it, such as mortgages, in Box 2. The difference is your taxable base, Box 3. The percentages of the tax are given in a table on the back of the form and also in this book.

**Liquidación Renta:** To get Box 5, you apply to the *valor catastral* of the property either 2 per cent, or 1.1 per cent if your property has been sharply valued upward since 1994. Box 5 is your imaginary income. To this you apply 25 per cent, the non-resident income tax, to get Box 6, the amount of the tax.

**Total:** Add your two taxes together.

**Vivienda:** Enter details of the property, including the catastral reference number.

**Representante:** If you have a fiscal representative, list him here.

**Declarante:** Sign your name, with the date.

**Ingreso:** Enter your form of payment, cash or certified cheque.

**MINISTERIO DE ECONOMIA Y HACIENDA**

**Agencia Tributaria**

Delegación de ___

Administración de ___   Código ___

**Impuesto sobre el Patrimonio y sobre la Renta de no Residentes**

No residentes sin establecimiento permanente

DECLARACION-LIQUIDACION / DOCUMENTO DE INGRESO

Modelo **214**

DECLARACIÓN SIMPLIFICADA DE NO RESIDENTES

### Contribuyente

Espacio reservado para la etiqueta identificativa

214000030296 4

### Devengo

Ejercicio.... ___   Período ..... | 0 | A |

| N.I.F. | APELLIDOS Y NOMBRE | Código extranjero |
|---|---|---|

Dirección a efectos de notificaciones: nombre de la vía pública    Número   Esc.   Piso   Prta.   Teléfono

Código Postal   Municipio    Provincia/País

### Liquidación. Impuesto sobre el Patrimonio

| | |
|---|---|
| Valor ............................................................. | 01 |
| Deudas ......................................................... | 02 |
| Base imponible y liquidable ........................ | 03 |

Hasta ___

Resto ___   al % ___

Suma ___

Cuota íntegra. Impuesto Patrimonio ............................ | 04 |

### Liquidación. Impuesto sobre la Renta de no Residentes

| | |
|---|---|
| Base imponible........................................... | 05 |
| Tipo de gravamen ............................ % | |
| Cuota íntegra. Impuesto sobre la Renta de no Residentes ......... | 06 |

### Total

Total a ingresar ( | 04 | + | 06 | ) ........................................ | 07 |

### Vivienda

Calle/Plaza/Avda.    Número   Esc.   Piso   Prta.

Código Postal   Municipio    Provincia

Referencia catastral

### Representante

| N.I.F. | APELLIDOS Y NOMBRE (por este orden) o RAZON SOCIAL |
|---|---|

Calle/Plaza/Avda.    Número   Esc.   Piso   Prta.   Teléfono

Código Postal   Municipio    Provincia

### Declarante

Fecha:

Firma:

### Ingreso

TESORO PÚBLICO. Cuenta restringida de Caja de la Delegación o Administración de la A.E.A.T.

Forma de pago: ☐ Dinero de curso legal   ☐ Cheque conformado y nominativo a favor del Tesoro Público

Importe: | I | ___ |

M 214 0 0   Precio del juego: 60 Ptas./0,36 euros

Ejemplar para la Administración

# Index

# More books on Spain from Santana

**Finca – Renovating an Old Farmhouse in Spain** *by Alec and Erna Fry.* Many of us dream about renovating and old farmhouse in Spain for holidays or as a permanent home. But few of us ever do it. Englishman Alec Fry and his Norwegian-born wife Erna took the plunge and made their dream come true. In this practical and generously illustrated guide they share their experience and take you step by step through every stage of the renovation. "It was hard work," they admit, "but it was also fun and so well worth it."

**Madrid Escapes** *by Peter Stone.* The fertile and varied countryside surrounding Spain's capital Madrid is rich in stunning scenery and wildlife – and dotted all over its 8000 square kilometres of forests, lakes and mountain ranges are many charming and historic pueblos. This well-illustrated guide describes the author's favourite 20 villages. Each of them offers something different and is worth the trip and, if you haven't got a car, all of them can be easily reached by an excellent public transport system of trains and buses.

**Inland Trips from the Costa Blanca** *by Derek Workman.* This 328-page guide – generously illustrated with colour photographs and detailed route maps – takes you on 20 car trips from the Costa Blanca into a region of stunning scenery and timeless pueblos, where you can step back into the past and enter grand old mansions and palaces, witness bizarre fiestas rooted in pagan times, shop for local arts and crafts and feast on hearty fare in country restaurants.

**Back Roads of Southern Spain** by David Baird. A full-coloured guide for those who want to get off the beaten track and visit places where no tourists think to venture, while 25 easy-to-follow routes make sure you don't get lost. Besides the detailed route descriptions there is practical information on what to see, where to eat and where to stay overnight. Driving hints, basic vocabulary and fiesta dates are also included.

**Small Hotels and Inns of Andalusia** by Guy Hunter-Watts. The first guide in English to charming places to stay in southern Spain. More than 100 great places are listed. The guide gives detailed information on rooms, prices and meals, easy-to-follow instructions and maps for finding your hotel, indepth descriptions and colour photographs of each hotel. An essential travelling companion for anyone planning a memorable night away or a longer trip in Andalucía.

**Birdwatching on Spain's Southern Coast** by John R. Butler. A guide to watching birds at 39 major and 35 subsidiary sites on the Costa del Sol, Costa de Almería, Costa del la Luz, Doñana and some inland sites, with detailed maps of all the sites, a calendar giving the best times of the day and year to visit, a complete list of birds personally identified by the author at each site, and information on wheelchair accesibility.

**Cooking in Spain** by Janet Mendel.The definitive guide to cooking in Spain – with more than 400 great recipes, complete information on regional specialities, a culinary history, advice on how to buy the best at the market, an English-Spanish glossary with more than 500 culinary terms, and handy conversion guide. "A brilliant guide to traditional Spanish cooking" is how *Taste* magazine of London described it.

**TAPAS...And more great dishes from Spain** by Janet Mendel.This striking cookbook is a celebration of the sunny flavours of Spain – above all olive oil, garlic, fresh fruits and vegetables – in an attractive presentation of more than 50 classic recipes for tapas and other great dishes from Spain´s premier cookbook author, all of them fully illustrated with stunning colour photographs by the award-winning food photographer John James Wood.

**The Tio Pepe Guide to the Seafood of Spain and Portugal** by Alan Davidson. Seafood is one of the many pleasures of the Iberian Peninsula There is a rich harvest to enjoy. The choice is so wide, it can be confusing. This guide, with its descriptions and drawings of 270 species of the region, will turn you into an expert, whether shopping for fish at the market or scanning a restaurant menu.

**Nord Riley's Spain** by Nord Riley. During the eighties, English-speaking foreigners in Spain had one advantage over expats living in other countries. They had Nord Riley, the man who made them laugh at situations they found themselves in all the time. Some things have change since then, but the insights and humour are timeless and today´s readers will feel very much at home in Nord Riley´s Spain.

**The Story of Spain** by Mark Williams.The dramatic history of Spain from the caves of Altamira to our present day. A story of kings and poets, saints and conquistadors, emperors and revolutionaries. The story of Torquemada, Cervantes, Saint Therea, Picasso, and Franco. The author has drawn on years of rigorous research to re-create the drama, excitement and pathos of crucial events in the history of the western world.

**The Spanish Attraction** By Simon Grayson. A fascinating account, illustrated by 80 black and white photographs, of the powerful impact the British have made on Spain from the industrialists, entrepreneurs and sherry barons of the 19th century up to the 1960's when the beginnings of modern tourism wrought a social, moral and commercial revolution on the Spanish Costas.

**Andalusian Landscapes** by Tim Gartside.A stunning selection of 60 colour photographs by a top photographer that celebrates the astonishing collage of colours and textures in the Andalusian landscape and captures the charm of remote villages and lonely farmhouses, fields ablaze with sunflowers and meadows full of poppies, the play of light on olive groves and the sun on the high sierras.

**Wildflowers of Southern Spain** by Betty Molesworth Allen. An invaluable guide to help you enjoy a region with a rich variety of wildflowers in widely diverse habitats, some of the species growing nowhere else. The author, an award-winning botanist, describes more than 200 common plants, each illustrated in full colour with a simple text for easy identification, and provides a handy glossary and index of plant names in English and Latin.

**Walking in Andalucía** by Guy Hunter-Watts. A guide to 34 walks in six of Andalusia´s natural parks. All of the full and half-day walks, many of them virtually unknown, start from beautiful villages. The book also includes easy-to-follow detailed route notes with times, distances and gradings, full colour maps and photographs for each walk, and advice on what to pack, when to walk and the best places to stay and eat in each are

**Gardening in Spain** *by Marcelle Pitt.*Your most valuable tool for successful gardening in Spain, this easy-to-follow, step-by-step guide tells you how to plan your garden, what to plant, when and how to plant it, and how to make the most of your flowers, trees, shrubs and herbs. Includes average rainfall and temperatures in the various regions of Spain, a comprehensive English-Spanish and Spanish-English vocabulary and index of plants.

**Caring for Your Pet in Spain** by Erny and Peter Harrison. Conditions for keeping animals in Spain differ from those in colder climates. Unfamiliar diseases exist to the surprise and consternation of foreign residents. The authors, who own boarding kennels and a cattery in southern Spain, wrote this practical guide to help pet owners avoid the pitfalls and create an environment in which their pets can live a happier and healthier life in Spain.

Santana Books,
Apartado 422,
29640 Fuengirola (Málaga).
Phone 952 485 838.
Fax 952 485 367.
Email: sales @santanabooks.com
www.santanabooks.com


UK Representatives
Aldington Books Ltd.,
Unit 3(b) Frith Business Centre,
Frith Road, Aldington,
Ashford, Kent TN25 7HJ.
Tel: 01233 720 123. Fax: 01233 721 272
E-mail: sales@aldingtonbooks.co.uk
www.aldingtonbooks.co.uk